The Fleet Street Sewer Rat

First published in Great Britain in 2005
by Artnik
341b Queenstown Road
London SW8 4LH
UK

© Artnik 2005

ISBN 1 903906 15 6

Design: Mark Lloyd
Edited: John McVicar

Printed and bound in India by Quadra

The Fleet Street
Sewer Rat

Mark Watts

ARTNIK

FOREWORD

John McVicar

The first time I met Benjamin Pell was in July 1998 in Soho's Groucho Club, then a druggies' den of iniquity where – despite the fact that he doesn't even use SSRIs never mind cocaine to regulate his serotonin levels – Pell looked quite at home. Not that his clothes matched his unfazed demeanour: shiny navy trousers, scruffy leathershoes worn down to a pronated list that would sink a ship, a grubby nylon shirt that was doing a fine job at not just cooking but breeding the BO. Groucho louche Pell is not. Then there was the spittle shower that sprayed my notepad every time he talked. And can Pell talk...the word speed is like a Gatling on an old newsdesk typewriter.

My editor at *Punch* magazine, James Steen, had inflicted this on me. He had decided that he wanted a cover on the Hendon hacker who was causing havoc with Elton John, All Saints and sundry other celebs, and it was my job to stand up the rumour that Pell was a computer geek supremo.

In fact, Pell didn't even own a computer, which I didn't really want to find out even though all the clues popped up when I asked him about what programmes and cracks he was using. He knew nothing about computers but the hacker story was too good to knock down. I filed accordingly and 'computer hacker who hits the stars' went on the cover. Luckily – it certainly wasn't good journalism – one of Pell's friends convinced me that he was just a binman. I had time to correct the copy inside the magazine but it was too late for the cover. If he thinks I need a dose of cringe, James Steen still reminds me of my howler.

While I was on the case for the *Punch* cover, I actually did Pell a big favour – in return he had deliberately set me up. I confronted him with his treachery. 'But I told you I used other methods to get information, and the bins is one method.' True...by only by Pell's characteristically Talmudic (il)logic. It was a throwaway remark. In fact, he'd suckered me. But I was easy meat: I went looking for a hacker and he let me find one.

Pell moved swiftly to sweeten my bitterness: he began feeding me newsworthy documents, which like a good guttersnipe I bought and used in my articles. Yet, like many of the journalists to whom Pell sold his stolen intellectual property (and they named in *The Fleet Street Sewer Rat*), our relationship was no simple exchange. With Pell nothing is simple; he thrives on complexity.

The cash nexus is always a binding link in any relationship with Pell, but above that he is always looking to ensnarl whomever it is into his web. He becomes generous, friendly and helpful, he interests himself in your problems and assists you with solving them...he inveigles you into becoming dependent on him. Meanwhile, he is logging your weaknesses, vulnerabilities, vices, secrets...for when he turns on you...as he does everyone with whom he fakes a friendship.

Once a 'friend' does not do what Pell regards as proper repayment for all the help he has given them, then he becomes a viper: poisonous, vindictive, malignant and, most of all, righteous. Invariably 'proper payment' is not doing what he thinks should be done to ensure that the world recognises and celebrates his uniqueness, intelligence and genius.

Of course, as Mark Watts' book documents, Pell has been incredibly destructive in the way he has shattered reputations, careers, businesses...in his trade as a scavenger of discarded intellectual property. But what is especially repellent is the glee and delight with which he crows over his victims: people whom he did not know personally and who had done him no harm. Indeed, more often than not he had already made a great deal of money out of them by selling their secrets to Fleet Street. We can all laugh at the humour with which Pell lightens his darkness and the book is genuinely funny, but *The Fleet Street Sewer Rat* is actually a study in comedic evil.

I always knew that Pell controlled his 'seeming' madness far more than it controlled him, but what this book brought home to me is how Pell is actually a very successful, professional criminal who by dint of deploying his nutter act has, for all practical purposes, made himself invulnerable to either the criminal or civil law. This so-called and self-styled 'nutter' earns at least £250,000 a year tax-free out of crime without risk of imprisonment.

Some nutter.

Foreword

Pell by his own admission has never had a friend..nor will he ever have a lover, and despite his gay affectations, he is actually a dormant heterosexual, and will remain so. Nevertheless, he fantasises about the fairytale, and secretly worships any woman he meets who just might see the real beauty behind his ugliness. Marks Watts lists a couple of these but my wife was another.

In 1997 Pell stole a confidential Elton John document, which he put on her website. She was sued and Pell came to her pseudo-rescue. She was repelled by him but, after we married, Pell reacted as if I had stolen his fairytale. He sought revenge by a malicious but ingenious campaign to destabilise our marriage. We were subjected to years of hate mail, anonymous phone calls, fake faxes, poison pen letters, phoney emails, computer viruses... It some ways it was pathetic and ridiculous – my wife even complained to Pell's lawyer about the spiteful banality of what he was up to – but, of course, this vicious, albeit childish, vendetta went to the heart of the man.

It culminated in an 18-inch long rat being put into our flat, through our open letterbox just before Christmas 2004. I spent the whole of Christmas stalking it. Yet, the couple of times I cornered it, the rat held my eyes almost reproaching me for hunting it down. It was odd. Nonetheless, I still thought it was a wild rat that had somehow got into the flat through some crevice or duct in the heating. I even spent an hour on the phone on Christmas morning talking to some pest control adviser (who was on duty!) in Manchester about what to do.

Then, on Boxing Day, I flushed the rat out and clubbed it to death with a wooden pole. As I looked at it still twitching on the floor, I felt sorry for having killed it, then I noticed that it was well-fed, its light-brow fur sleek and unmatted... It dawned on me that this was a pet rat, not a wild one. But I still didn't make the connection until, like in the movies, the rat's features slowly dissolved into Pell's face.

It was Artnik's Christmas present for publishing *The Fleet Street Sewer Rat*.

John McVicar 2005

PREFACE

This book tells the extraordinary story about the person behind some of Fleet Street's darkest secrets. It is the biography of Benjamin Pell, better known as 'Benji the Binman', largely based on a huge volume of raw source material, including around 30 hours of video and audio tapes in which Pell talks frankly, and in great detail, about his exploits trawling rubbish bags for newsworthy documents to Fleet Street.

I have spent many, many hours watching, listening and transcribing these tapes for this book. In fact, I admit that I have not had sufficient time to extract every part of them that would have been worth including in the book. Moreover, much good material has not made it into the book because of constraints of space. McVicar supplied one batch of tapes but these were supplemented by by many hours of footage shot by Iain Jones (see below).

My involvement with Pell began when I obtained one 13-minute video tape, from the Jones stock, in which Pell talked about how he stole confidential 'Bloody Sunday' inquiry documents[i]. This formed the basis of two articles that I wrote for the *Sunday Express* in 2002[ii]. These articles were edited and, unfortunately, a potentially misleading headline was added to the first. Pell sued the newspaper and myself for libel. The *Sunday Express*, fearful of its exposure to huge costs even if it won the case, made a large payment into court three weeks before the trial was due to start in 2003. Pell accepted this payment, resolving the case.

I obtained another Jones video tape in which Pell talked about how he came to raid the bins for documents as well as detailing a broad range of his escapades[iii]. The practice of trawling rubbish for interesting documents – known in America as 'dumpster diving' – is a well-established method of gathering information. Law firms often commission detective agencies to carry out such enquiries as do intelligence services and, naturally, journalists. I have never used this method and I do not believe journalists should raid bins to find information that will merely tittilate the public's interest. If it uncovers fraud or corruption, then it is in the public interest and justified.

The Hollywood-based Jones filmed, for his US production company, Moving Perspective, Pell talking and going about his bin scavenging. There are many hours of such footage. Pell also allowed Jones to copy audio tapes he had made of his telephone conversations with various journalists. Jones filmed these rushes in 1999 to excite interest from a Hollywood studio to back a feature film on Pell's life. As part of that effort, he and his colleague, JC Bennett, made a documentary from this footage lasting just over an hour entitled, 'Thank You for the Rubbish: It's Worth Millions'[iv]. This documentary was first shown, creating much interest, at the Slamdance Film

Festival in 2002 in Park City, Utah, United States. It was one of 12 films, and one of five documentaries, selected from 2,468 submissions to compete in that year's festival. Jones claims to be working on another version of the documentary, incorporating more of the the 'Bloody Sunday' material[v]. I refer to these as the Moving Perspective tapes or material.

Pell subsequently claimed in a High Court case against a British businessman, John Mappin, who had persuaded him to pay £77,500 to help fund the early stages of this project, that he was merely 'developing story-lines' in the Moving Perspective tapes. They were shot, as it were, to become the basis for a fictional account of his life in a feature film. He also claimed that Jones and Mappin specifically told him to 'develop story-lines' for this very reason. Pell successfully recovered £77,500 from Mappin after showing that the businessman had defrauded him.

So, according to Pell, none of the admissions he makes on these tapes to iniquity should be taken as truthful. He was making it up for the camera. Pell maintained the same line during the course of his *Sunday Express* libel action. Nonetheless, it is evident from the tapes that much of what he says on them is true. They actually show Pell brandishing stolen documents that visually confirm his claims: for example, we see him showing to camera confidential 'Bloody Sunday' inquiry documents. Second, as someone who worked on television current affairs programmes and is familiar with the production of drama-documentaries, the idea that a film-maker could direct and instruct Pell, as he so claims, is preposterous. A scriptwriter who dramatises a true story needs to base the work on fact. Pell is only interesting because of what he has done, not for his acting ability.

Jones and Mappin clearly wanted footage of Pell presenting a factual account of his activities. Doubtless Pell bitterly regrets being so candid when Jones filmed him, and he subsequently hoped he might limit the potential damage by denying their truthfulness. The final clincher, however, is I have been able to corroborate many points in the Moving Perspective tapes from other sources.

This brings us to the second, far larger category of tapes to which I have had access for this book. John McVicar first filmed a lengthy interview with Pell in 1998, and the results persuaded Channel 4 to commission a documentary on Benji the Binman, which Victor Lewis-Smith, a journalist and television producer produce made for Associated Rediffusion[iv]. McVicar filmed many further hours of interviews with Pell during 1999-2001 – Pell clearly gave McVicar carte blanche to do what he wanted with this footage as long as the results made Pell a star. Pell often expresses his disappointment on the these tapes over the way Channel 4's lawyers prevented Associated Rediffusion broadcasting any of the truly revelatory material from the 1998 McVicar footage and is passionate to tell the real story. However, no further documentary did not materialise. As with Jones, Pell allowed also McVicar to copy tapes he had recorded of telephone conversations with various journalists – and others. The tapes run to a total of around 26 hours, 15 on video, and 11 on audio. I refer to these as the McVicar tapes or material. Pell talks just as frankly on these tapes as he does on the Moving Perspective material; they proved to be more illuminating simply because I have had access to so much more of them. As Pell later said[vii]: 'During the course of those recording sessions, I was very candid.'

The McVicar tapes are also notable because Pell repeats on them a lot of the claims that he makes on the Moving Perspective material, which Pell vainly tries to claim are fictional. Pell's accounts to McVicar and Jones were recorded many months, even years, apart, often covering in great detail the same incidents or episodes. There are only minor inconsistencies in his accounts of the same incidents: they are accurate accounts. Moreover, Pell is recorded frequently telling McVicar that he should try to obtain the Moving Perspective tapes because, he says, they would be so useful for the Channel 4 documentary. Pell is hoisted by his own words (on this and so much else) because, while Pell is an inveterate liar, it beggars belief that he could attain such detailed consistency if he were simply 'developing story-lines'. McVicar has not seen the Moving Perspective tapes but remains convinced that Pell's account of himself in that he shot is, albeit frenetic, truthful and coherent. Given the similarities with the Moving Perspective material, which was recorded at different times from the McVicar tapes, and having watched and listened carefully to the material and considered it with other evidence, I am certain that these are accurate and reliable accounts.

I am sure that Justice Grey, who heard Pell's case against Mappin would have agreed, too, if he been able to view the McVicar material. He saw only the Moving Perspective footage and ruled:[viii]:

I have already commented that the business in which Mr Pell engaged is contemptible. Whether or nor he was guilty of stealing documents, Mr Pell was dealing dishonestly in other people's confidential information. [Marion] Smith [Pell's barrister] does not suggest otherwise. In his evidence, Mr Pell claimed that much of what he said on tape [filmed by Moving Perspective] was 'creating a story-line'. I think there may be some truth in this: Mr Pell struck me as highly excitable in the manner in which he gave evidence and I think he probably got carried away in what he said during the filming. Nevertheless, I accept that he made admissions of disreputable and dishonest conduct.

When Pell found out that I had obtained the McVicar tapes, he supplemented his claim that they were fictional with the further claim that they were 'confidential'. This is plainly ridiculous because they were recorded with the intention of being broadcast and/or published. Once again, I believe that Pell bitterly regrets being so candid when McVicar taped him.

So, while this is an unauthorised biography of Pell, the book benefits from having an unusually large amount of input from the subject. I must warn readers that Pell frequently swears and is sometimes deeply offensive. In an attempt to keep faith with the full sense of what he says, I have not cut his expletives or offensive remarks. Neither have I corrected his grammatical mistakes, which help paint the picture of this quite bizarre, even surreal, man. He also often recounts conversations that he says took place, repeating the dialogue, but while this may convey the sense of what was said, clearly, these recollections cannot be expected to be precisely accurate. This, of course, applies especially to those conversations in which Pell did not himself take part. Pell's words are often hard to follow, but, in order to give readers a true impression, I have decided against 'tidying up' the quotes as journalists normally do. I just hope that this book does not come to be cited as an example of why journalists must stick to the normal practice!

The third category of raw source material on which this book is based is documents. I have had access to a large volume of documents, including copies of papers that Pell trawled from rubbish and sold. McVicar, again, gave me access to a lot of this material, and Mark Hollingsworth supplied me with further documents.

The final category of raw source material has resulted from Pell's frequent trips to the courts. I have been able to draw on a large volume of affidavits and other papers, as well as testimony, that have been presented to one court or another.

Pell realises that he has a terrible reputation, although he regards it as undeserved. He said[ix]: '

Almost no one in Fleet Street or indeed in any other profession has the correct impression about my past. The reputation that I have acquired, as a result of various articles, which have appeared about me in the Press, is almost completely undeserved and bears little relation to the facts. Going through discarded rubbish is a journalistic method that is as old as the hills. Indeed, it is a source of information used regularly by private investigators, often instructed by leading firms of solicitors.

Of course, it is a method of obtaining stories that involves sifting through refuse sacks that can be dirty and unpleasant. That does not mean that I, as the person doing this work, should be described in those terms.

I get extremely irritated when people still describe me as 'Benji the Binman'. Once again, I cannot be responsible for what people choose to think or write about me.

He told one interviewer[x]: 'I have an important story to tell. I have an important contribution to make. Why do people dislike me so much?' The interviewer said that Pell's 'wails' switched to a different voice but he answered his question: 'Why do people take an instant dislike to you, Benjamin? Because it saves time.'

On completion of this book, I asked Pell for an interview on the broad range of subjects that it documents. Speaking through his solicitor, he declined, even though he wanted, he said, 'to avoid the possibility of your book repeating many of the damaging lies disseminated in the popular press over the last few years'.

His solicitor added on his behalf:

Although there is certain material in the public domain about my client, much of it is inaccurate speculation. There is also, of course, film footage taken by Iain Jones, for the purposes of interesting Hollywood studios in making a blockbuster film about my client. As you are also aware from the recent litigation, that film footage mixes fact and fiction and you would be very unwise to rely on that material without checking your facts very closely first. There is also one further source of information that you may have had recourse to; that being interviews with my client, taped by John McVicar. Much of the contents of those tapes is highly confidential and disclosed to Mr McVicar for the sole purpose of Mr McVicar writing an approved biography of my client.

Pell further threatened to seek a High Court injunction to ban this book, saying through his solicitor:

Any interviews given by my client to Mr McVicar were confidential and only for the purpose of an approved biography to be written by Mr McVicar. To use material supplied to you by Mr McVicar would amount to a breach of confidence. Furthermore, my client is the owner of the copyright in the words spoken by him and recorded by Mr McVicar. The use of my client's words, or any material part of the words spoken by him in those interviews will amount to infringement of my client's copyright. Unless you confirm to me that you will not use the contents of the McVicar interviews in your book, my client will have to consider very seriously whether he should seek an injunction against you and your publisher on a *quia timet* basis for copyright infringement, breach of confidence and breach of his rights [section 8 Human Rights Act].

However, I do not believe that McVicar owed a duty of confidence to Pell over the interviews: they were conducted with the intention of being broadcast and/or published. Pell's Achilles Heel is his desperation to be famous and he has always co-operated with anyone whom he thought could place him, warts and all, in the public domain. In addition, Pell can expect no confidentiality or legal protection over the interviews because of the disclosure of his iniquity, or serious wrong-doing, is plainly in the public interest.

For each chapter, I have compiled a list of relevant references. Much of the source material, as described above, is not available to the general public. I have been very fortunate to have access to such a rich array of revelatory raw source material, and I hope I have managed to convey at least some of its extraordinary depth and flavour. Enjoy.

Mark Watts, 2005

References

[i] "'Bloody Sunday' rushes," Moving Perspective (filmed 1999). Transcript is reproduced in chapter 14.

[ii] Mark Watts, 'This grubby snooper found the names of "Bloody Sunday" Paras in a lawyer's dustbin…' [potentially misleading second clause of headline not repeated here] *Sunday Express* (17.02.02); Mark Watts, 'Dustbin snooper with the names of "Bloody Sunday" Paras is facing MI5 probe,' *Sunday Express* (24.02.02).

[iii] "3½-hour rushes," Moving Perspective (filmed 1999).

[iv] 'Thank You for the Rubbish: It's Worth Millions,' Moving Perspective (first shown 13.01.02).

[v] '14 Dead,' Moving Perspective (to be added to 'Thank You for the Rubbish: It's Worth Millions,' but not shown by time of writing).

[vi] 'Scandal in the Bins,' Channel 4 (first shown 11.01.01).

[vii] Benjamin Pell witness statement, Benjamin Pell -v- Express Newspapers and Mark Watts (08.04.03).

[viii] Mr Justice Gray, judgement in Benjamin Pell -v- John Mappin and Story Master Ltd (19.03.02).

[ix] Benjamin Pell witness statement, Benjamin Pell -v- Express Newspapers and Mark Watts (08.04.03).

[x] David Thomas, 'The binman lifts his lid. For years, he made a living raiding famous people's rubbish bins for confidential documents. But Benjamin Pell, who begins a new career on television this week, is unrepentant: "There's no excuse for not shredding,"' *Sunday Telegraph* (21.04.02).

[xi] McVicar video tape (filmed 08.02.01) DVOO.

Note: the letters following references to McVicar tapes, above and in each of the chapters, are codes identifying the relevant tape. The original logging of these tapes was sometimes inaccurate, so the dates reflect a combination of the original logging together with information gleaned from the tapes' contents.

ACKNOWLEDGEMENTS

First, my thanks go to John McVicar who provided me with a good deal of the extraordinarily rich supply of raw source material – especially audio and video tapes – that I used to write this book. In addition, he edited *The Fleet Street Sewer Rat*.

I am also grateful for the enormous amount of help I have received from several confidential sources. These range from people who provided me with a plentiful supply of raw source material, in the form of yet more video-taped evidence, to others who gave me insight into the thinking on relevant issues within security and law enforcement agencies, from people in the media industry with knowledge of Pell to others who know him in a non-work context, amongst others. Some sources of help have come from the most surprising of places. I must, inevitably, refrain from identifying these people; it is the most basic of journalistic principles to protect confidential sources. Journalists can never confirm or deny that anyone is a confidential source, and nor can we divulge any details that may help lead to their identification. However, you know who you are; you know that I am a hugely grateful; and you know that you have been able to assist me without fear of your identities ever becoming known – no matter what.

Much help has also come from sources on a non-confidential basis. The Hollywood-based Iain Jones gave me some of the knowledge he gathered as a result of working with Pell over a lengthy period on a documentary and feature-film project. Mark Hollingsworth, a freelance investigative journalist and past associate of Pell's, supplied me with some interesting documents. I believe that there are revelations in this book that Mark will not like, but I have been scrupulous about reporting the truth as I have found it, even if at times it is embarrassing to friends of mine.

I owe a great deal of thanks to Kevin Cahill, probably the most enthusiastic investigative journalist in Britain. Kevin, who has that invaluable journalistic ability to be on the scene of a story long before it occurs to any other journalist that it might be worth a visit, has provided me with much support as I have set about my investigations that have resulted in this book.

I am grateful to another journalist who has much enthusiasm for investigative journalism, Yvonne Ridley. Ever since her capture by the Taliban in Afghanistan in 2001 in the wake of the September 11 terrorist outrages, and her subsequent book detailing her experience('In the Hands of the Taliban,' Robson Books, 2001), Yvonne was chief reporter on the *Sunday Express* when I wrote about Pell for that paper.

And I am grateful to Francis Wheen, a columnist on *The Guardian*, who was generous in providing what help he could. I also thank Bill Goodwin, now of *Computer Weekly*, who has become the landmark "journalist sources" case ever since winning his long battle, ultimately at the European Court of Human Rights, over protecting the identity of a confidential source. He provided me with a good deal of wise counsel and support as I successfully beat off pressure from Pell's lawyers to reveal the confidential sources who had given me such devastating material on him.

I must thank my many friends on the *Sunday Express*. I defended a libel case brought by Pell in 2002 against the *Sunday Express* and me, and I drew much support from my colleagues amongst the reporters on that paper, for which I first worked in the early 1990s. I am particularly grateful to Michelle Stanistreet, a writer on the newspaper who has done so much work for me, and for many others, in her role as

Acknowledgements

the principal National Union of Journalists "chapel" official at Express Newspapers. Richard Phillips, as city editor, was responsible for my return to the *Sunday Express* in 2001. Thanks, Richard.

Journalists who dig out stories that others would rather remain hidden inevitably find themselves calling on the assistance of lawyers. I am grateful to the team at Richards Butler – Helen Stanwell-Smith, Emma Lenthall and Michael Skrein – the solicitors who worked so hard on preparations for defending Pell's libel action (over a period of about a year, we were swapping notes until well past midnight, many a time), although their efforts were ultimately made rather pointless by the spineless approach of the *Sunday Express*. I am especially grateful to Geoffrey Shaw QC, our leading counsel on that libel case, who was assisted by a bright young barrister, Ben Mawson. Geoffrey's advice should have encouraged the *Sunday Express* to hold its nerve. A leading libel lawyer and probably the best for newspapers using the relatively new "offer of amends" defence, I always felt that he gave wise advice; it was a pity that the *Sunday Express*, having of course paid a fortune for that advice, foolishly chose to disregard it.

I am also very grateful to Stuart Stevens, a senior barrister who, although ultimately only had to provide me with a little help on the case, did ensure that I held my resolve as I saw the famous *Sunday Express* crusader's sword turn to jelly. And I am grateful to my friends, Julian Bishop and Alison Winward, for their personal support, in particular as I fought that libel case.

CONTENTS

*This book is dedicated to the late
Mark Le Goy, former UK diplomat to Jordan,
who was so supportive of anyone
fighting the good fight.*

Chapter 1

Walk like the 'big Egyptian': Hamilton-v-Fayed

When the *Mail on Sunday* landed on Britain's breakfast tables on February 13th 2000, it broke the story that would dominate the following week's news. AL FAYED 'BOUGHT LIBEL SECRETS' screamed its front-page splash[i]. 'An official investigation has started into allegations that Mohammed Al Fayed paid £10,000 for copies of stolen documents that gave him advance warning of the lines of questioning he would face in his libel battle with Neil Hamilton,' the story began.

And who had taken these documents? The answer, revealed the *Mail on Sunday*, was one Benjamin Pell, 'a 36-year-old unemployed loner'. Suddenly, this Dickensian character, who had been one of Fleet Street's darkest secrets for more than two years, and who had previously avoided coming under such a glaring public spotlight, became known to millions of newspaper readers. Overnight, Benji the Binman became infamous.

The *Mail on Sunday* revelation was a sensational twist on one of the most extraordinary libel battles the High Court has seen. Back in 1994, Neil Hamilton was a trade minister in John Major's Conservative government when *The Guardian* reported claims by Fayed, co-owner of the Harrods department store in London's Knightsbridge, that he had paid Hamilton and another then minister, Tim Smith, to table parliamentary questions[ii]. Fayed, now aged 71, said that he paid £2,000 a time for parliamentary questions when Hamilton and Smith were backbench MPs during the 1980s, when he was battling over an investigation by the Department of Trade and Industry (DTI) into his takeover of Harrods. Fayed said that his lobbyist, Ian Greer, advised him: 'You

1

need to rent an MP just like you rent a London taxi.' While Smith, 45, resigned as a minister immediately and soon escaped from public view, Hamilton, 54, initially held on to his job. Hamilton and Greer, 70, announced that they would sue *The Guardian* for libel, and the MP quit as a minister a few days later. Fayed subsequently turned up the heat on Hamilton by claiming that the Tory MP had collected brown envelopes stuffed with cash. For ever after, 'brown envelope' became a synonym for a backhander or bung. Hamilton and Greer withdrew their libel case against *The Guardian* shortly before the trial was due to begin. It looked as if, like Smith, they had decided to thrown in the towel and spend more time with their families.

A report by the House of Commons standards and privileges committee later accepted the findings of an investigation by the then parliamentary commissioner for standards, Sir Gordon Downey, which broadly endorsed the allegations in *The Guardian* against Hamilton[iii]. Fayed testified in camera, to what was then called the House of Commons members' interests committee, that he had paid £150,000 to Ian Greer Associates for parliamentary lobbying work, which included £28,000 paid to Hamilton. His claims were leaked to a newspaper, which revealed that, according to Fayed, he'd given Hamilton £20,000 cash in £50 notes in 12 instalments between 1987 and 1989 and a further £8,000 in gift vouchers[iv].

Hamilton, recognising that unless he took action his political career and reputation were ruined, decided to gamble on what was, in effect, an all-or-nothing defamation action. If he lost, he would also be financially ruined but, if he won, he would, at least, redeem his reputation if not his political fortunes too. What strengthened his resolve was that while Fayed was litigious, he had always preferred to settle rather than given evidence himself and, actually, had never gone into the witness box. Fayed rather *The Guardian,* therefore, was a much more attractive target. Hamilton sued, claiming that Fayed had defamed him by saying on Channel 4's *Dispatches* in 1997 that the MP had taken cash from him in return for tabling Parliamentary questions[v].

The Hamilton-v-Fayed libel trial in 1999 had in football terms all the colour of a cup final between Manchester United and Arsenal. It was pure knockabout and Fayed, in particular, played to the gallery. He went into the witness box and made mincemeat of Hamilton's barrister, Desmond Browne QC. The press and the jury loved it. To further back his claim that Hamilton was guilty of corrupt practice as an MP, Fayed also presented to the court documents that showed how Hamilton had in 1989 sought payment from Mobil Oil for moving on its behalf an amendment to a finance bill.

The jury found in Fayed's favour just before Christmas in 1999. As the *Mail on Sunday* noted, many legal observers were surprised that Fayed 'ventured into the witness box', expecting him to try to settle the case before the trial started to avoid having to do so[vi]. The Hamilton camp was also surprised by Fayed's 'confidence' while giving evidence. 'He always seemed to know which questions to answer and which to parry,' said one observer at the trial.' The newspaper gave an account of his 'bravura performance', saying:

> Throughout his merciless duel with Desmond Browne QC, the Harrods boss never missed the opportunity to go on the offensive and dispatch even the difficult questions with aplomb... [He] faced up to Browne with a glowering face, repeatedly swearing and unleashing verbal volleys in the direction of any and all his detractors.
> Despite wearing his emotions on his sleeve, the Egyptian millionaire frequently left Browne floundering with his blunt language and crude yet effective parries of awkward questions. When asked about his personal finances, Fayed told Browne to mind his own 'bloody business', adding, 'Get on with the subject and don't waste the time of everybody.

The newspaper noted how Fayed frequently 'pleaded the ravages of time when faced with awkward questions and unpleasant truths, telling the jury he could not remember'. When Browne suggested to Fayed that his claim of 'cash for questions' and 'brown envelopes' was 'another of your inventions', Fayed replied: 'I cannot comment... because you are talking a load of crap.'

In its article of February 2000, the *Mail on Sunday* was offering a startling explanation for Fayed's apparent preparedness for that cross-examination. 'Vital papers – claimed to have come from rubbish bins outside the offices of Hamilton's legal team – are said to have been copied and passed to Al Fayed on the eve of the savagely fought trial,' it reported. The documents, taken from the rubbish bins outside Browne's chambers at 5 Raymond Buildings in Gray's Inn, were 'legally privileged', meaning courts regard them as attracting a very high level of confidentiality and should only be seen by the lawyers and their client. 'An associate of Al Fayed, Mark Hollingsworth, last night admitted he handed over the material and accepted the cash during a clandestine meeting at the Egyptian tycoon's Harrods store. Al Fayed was so delighted that he promised another £10,000 for further material.' Hollingsworth was quoted as saying that the documents gave Fayed 'a bit of a steer' into what he would be asked under cross-examination.

The *Mail on Sunday* said that there was no suggestion that the 'Fayed camp' told its legal team about the material. Indeed, the Fayed camp denied they had received any material to even pass on. An unnamed lawyer for Fayed was quoted as saying: 'There are categorical denials that any of this happened.'

Hamilton, who was facing financial ruin with a £2m legal bill after losing his libel case against Fayed, told the newspaper: 'I will instruct my lawyers immediately to seek to have the verdict overturned and quashed.' The newspaper also suggested that Fayed faced a police investigation. The following month, Hamilton duly lodged an appeal, through his solicitors Crockers Oswald Hickson, to overturn the libel verdict; meanwhile the police mounted an investigation into Fayed, Pell and associates.

Even Michael Heseltine, the former deputy prime minister, chimed in, referring the matter to his former ministry, the DTI (where he was once secretary of state and Hamilton's boss). He was quoted as saying: 'I have written to Sir Michael Scholar, permanent secretary at the DTI, to tell him what I have been told. These are serious allegations, which I had to pass on.'

The article reported that 'scores of pages of stolen

documents' bought by Fayed included 'strategies' devised by Hamilton's legal team for 'attacking' Fayed in the witness box. 'They referred to the tycoon's colourful past and record of dishonesty', and included witness statements.

The newspaper also reported what little was publicly known about Pell. He had 'previously rummaged through rubbish bins for exotic secrets.[...] 'Last year, he was fined £20 for stealing rubbish bags, including 200,000 confidential documents from lawyers (Harkavys, a firm of solicitors whose clients included James Hewitt and Jonathan Aitken, another disgraced former Tory minister: see chapters 10 and 11])' It said that Pell passed the Hamilton documents to Hollingsworth, a freelance journalist, who in turn handed copies to Fayed's then director of security, John Macnamara.

However, it added, Pell and Hollingsworth had fallen out over the deal. Pell claimed that he only received £5,000 and was never paid a further £5,000 that he said was promised by Fayed through Hollingsworth. But Hollingsworth claimed that he paid to Pell all the money he had received from Fayed for the documents. The report added: 'It was because of a row over this money that the allegations surfaced publicly.'

'In conjunction with another contact, Pell set about his revenge. The contact came to the *Mail on Sunday*... Then on Thursday, the contact telephoned Michael Heseltine – without this newspaper's knowledge.'

The story about the Hamilton documents, while revelatory, was, nonetheless, awkward for the *Mail on Sunday*. Two central characters in it, the pair who had obtained and sold the Hamilton documents to Fayed, had previously worked for and sold stories to the newspaper. Hollingsworth was, at the time, on a 'retainer' to the newspaper. This meant that, while he was a freelance journalist, he was contracted to give the *Mail on Sunday* first option on his stories, and so he was a frequent contributor to the newspaper. The *Mail on Sunday* reported that he had written for the newspaper and, in effect, declared this interest. Moreover, the newspaper also had a relationship with Pell. It, like most nationals, had published many stories based on documents that he had stolen from rubbish. Pell had, for example, sold the *Mail on Sunday* material on Aitken (see chapter 10). Pell tells Jones how the *Mail on Sunday* had paid him thousands of pounds for several stories[vii]. One was even about Fayed's passport bid (his application for British citizenship was rejected), although Pell was furious that the newspaper paid him only £150 for that story.

So, who tipped off the *Mail on Sunday*, enabling it to expose the Fayed story? In a twist that is characteristic of 'Benji the Binman' – Pell himself was behind the very story that exposed him and his associates.

Fleet Street's sewer rat is himself a publicity hound. The newspaper's report gleefully blew the whistle on Pell by stating that he 'in conjunction with another contact', was acting in 'revenge' because he believed that Fayed had not paid him all the money that was due. The *Mail on Sunday* said that the 'contact', whom it did not name, had approached the newspaper with the story. That contact was one Richard Murray, a non-practising barrister specialising in media law and a friend of Pell's. Murray was a libel reader for several newspapers, including the *Mail on Sunday*.

Sources at the *Mail on Sunday* say that its associate editor responsible for overseeing the newspaper's news coverage, Chris Anderson, called Hollingsworth on the day before publication to ask whether Fayed had indeed bought the Hamilton documents. Hollingsworth, given that he was on a retainer to the *Mail on Sunday*, believed as he was speaking to colleague that the conversation was off the record. The thought that he was to become the subject of the story did not occur to him until the end of his conversation with Anderson.

Hollingsworth eventually even he began to suspect that he was being set up. He started to stress that he had been talking off the record. Anderson legitimately ignored these after-time attempts to claim privilege and ran the story. Hollingsworth was mortified as it would compromise his reputation as a journalist and certainly damage his relationship with the *Mail on Sunday*.

According to the judgement of Lord Phillips, Master of the Rolls, in Hamilton's subsequent appeal against the libel verdict, Anderson asked Hollingsworth 'leading questions'[viii]. The freelance journalist confirmed to Anderson that Pell had passed him material 'which I did show to Fayed', although he emphasised, 'Virtually all the material they already had,' saying that it had been disclosed to to the Fayed camp by Hamilton's lawyers during the litigation.

He confirmed that on or about November 17th 1999, which was two days into the trial, he had a meeting with Macnamara, but denied that Fayed's then director of public affairs, Laurie Mayer, was there, as the newspaper had been told. Throughout the conversation, Hollingsworth stressed that the material was 'of no real benefit in terms of inside intelligence'. He told Anderson: 'They wanted to know who was funding Hamilton.' The material they had seen 'was kind of interesting and it gave them a bit of a steer...it wasn't what they were specifically looking for'. He confirmed that the material included 'subject areas' for cross-examination.

Hollingsworth said that Macnamara paid him £10,000 there and then. Fayed came in 'later on', but he 'definitely did not...initiate it'. He said that he was promised another £10,000 if more material could be obtained. No further material was obtained, he said. However, Pell wanted more money, so Hollingsworth went back to see Fayed after the trial, in January. He was given the 'bum's rush'.

Hollingsworth did not provide a witness statement to either side in the appeal, but he did not have to as Hamilton submitted the tape of the journalist's conversation with Anderson as evidence.

Pell, now 40, an unmarried orthodox Jew who lives with his elderly parents in Hendon, north London, had his own inimitable version of events. Indeed, every about Pell is inimitable, especially his style of talking. His voice is always in a losing race to express the myriad thoughts in his head. His rapid-fire delivery with its shorthand reporting of what other people say makes him sound like Groucho Marx on speed. Behind his bottle-thick glasses, his eyes swivel like the late Marty Feldman's, his hands move around like Simon Rattle at the end of Beethoven's 5th...and that is not mentioning the spray of spittle that showers everyone in range. Pell on full throttle is a sight to behold. But what he says is generally coherent – especially if one does not challenge his own brand of Talmudic (il)logic – and more often than not funny...

> Anderson had called Hollingsworth because Fayed was denying that he had bought the Hamilton documents[ix]. So, there it is, the story's dead, cos Fayed's denying it on Thursday and Friday. On Saturday he [Anderson] rings up Hollingsworth...he gets Hollingsworth, off the record [some off the record!], to admit everything. 'So, Mark...can you just tell me: is it true that you actually got documents off Benjamin Pell and you passed them on to Fayed?'
>
> 'Well yeah, it's true actually.' Anyway, he was admitting to the whole thing. At the end of conversation, Anderson says to him, 'Thank you very much, Mark. That's going to be our splash for tomorrow.'
>
> 'But, er, that was off the record, you...you can't.'
>
> 'Mark, look, don't worry, you know. It's a great story.'
>
> 'But you can't...'
>
> Of course, the story appears the following day.

Murray was instructed by Pell to tip off the *Mail on Sunday*, but the newspaper did not know that the latter was the prime mover in the plot to betray Hollingsworth. It sent one of of his reporters, Daniel Foggo, up to his Hendon home-cum-headquarters the day before story broke – about an hour and a quarter before the end of Sabbath. Pell took up the story: 'While all of this is happening in Northcliffe House, in Kensington (the *Mail*'s head office in London), here we have in...deepest Hendon, knock on the door at five past five that afternoon... "Oh hello."

'"Oh...I'm sorry for troubling you, Benjamin... We've got a splash in tomorrow's paper about you."

'I said, "I know. It's about the, er...but I thought you couldn't get, em, Fayed to admit it. What's going on here?"

'He said, "You know about it?"

'I said, "Know about it? It's my bloody story" He had absolutely no idea that it was my story. He had a cameraman opposite, trying to catch me out, he was there trying to get me to admit something. And I explained to him, "No, I'm sorry, Daniel, sit down here. You've got it all wrong. I gave this story to Richard.."

'"You know Richard Murray?"

'"Can...can I just make a quick call." I ring up Richard Murray... cos I can't use the 'phone on the Sabbath, I have to get Foggo to actually dial the number for me... I speak to Richard – Said, "What's going on here?"

'"Oh, Benjamin, obviously I couldn't get hold of you the whole of today (because it was the Sabbath), things have got a bit out of hand."

'"Out of hand? I've got Daniel Foggo in my bloody dining room. You know, what's going on here?"'

Pell gleefully says that Foggo was unable to elicit much response from him, although he telephoned the reporter that evening after he left, 'at least ten times' – following the Sabbath, which ends with sunset on Saturday.

The appeal judgement said that the conversation between Foggo and Pell, which the reporter had taped...

>...has its entertaining moments[x]. [It provides] confirmation of Mr Pell's relationship with Mr Murray. Mr Pell telephoned Mr Murray while Mr Foggo was with him and insisted that without confirmation from Mr Hollingsworth and himself there was no story, and he was not going to confirm anything. He complained that the Mail on Sunday kept on wanting more documents from them. The plan was that there would be no story unless Mr Al Fayed could be got to admit it. He expressed concern about the possibility of police investigation. He did complain about not being paid the 'other ten grand'. He expressed a great deal of indignation about the ease with which barristers' chambers allow their rubbish to be stolen.

Pell explained that because of Foggo's visit he could not go to synagogue, which left him 'completely frantic'[xi]. 'There I am, I'm going to appear on the front page of the following...day's newspaper for having committed per... you know, perverting the course of justice. You know, we're talking here much more serious than Aitken and Harkavys (Pell's conviction for stealing documents: see chapters 10 and 11).'

The *Mail on Sunday* had a great scoop. However, everyone involved in the escapade, following the publication of the exposé, denied even attempting to pervert the course of justice. While Pell was reluctant to make full admissions to the *Mail on Sunday*, he gives a frank and detailed account to John McVicar, the sometime hack who helped make the Channel 4 documentary about Pell[xii], although due to the usual gutless TV lawyers the programme shied away from revealing more than the newspaper had already made public about the scandal. At least this book tells the the full story behind Pell's attempt to pervert the course of justice.

He told McVicar[xiii]: 'It is a cracker of a story. But, having said that, cos of the Fayed connection maybe you wouldn't want to be involved in it either, and we'd be both murdered by Fayed.' Pell often claims that someone or other is out to kill him – it another of his knee-jerk boasts that he makes to inflate his own importance.

McVicar replied circumspectly[xiv]: 'It requires someone to incriminate themselves.'

Pell: 'Correct.' Pell, of course, is doing exactly that – incriminate himself – on video. But Pell is a dab hand at extricating himself from the consequences of his incriminating admission by claiming later that he was inventing copy for journalists. His madcap appearance and manner give him a licence not enjoyed by most of us. 'Look, it's an impossible thing to prove without somebody falling on his sword,' Pell clarified.

His part in the saga grew out of his contact with David Leigh, a journalist on *The Guardian*, and currently its investigations editor, who played a leading role in preparing that newspaper's defence to Hamilton's libel action, which the politician ultimately abandoned, and, subsequently, to the case brought by Aitken (see chapter 10). Leigh is another ex-colleague of Pell's whom Pell does everything in his power to discredit.

Pell said[xv]:

I meet up with David Leigh. He introduces me to Mark Hollingsworth. Hollingsworth sits in [Pell's house]. I remember it was a Saturday, so I couldn't make any notes, but... he gave me a list of about 150 names to target. He met me on a Saturday, funny enough, on a Sabbath. And they always say, you should never do business on a Sabbath cos, they say in our Jewish code of law, you will never have any benefit from any business you do on a Sabbath. Well, the first time I ever dealt with Hollingsworth was on a Sabbath and, I can tell you, I've never had any bloody benefit from that arsehole in my whole life. And he sat down with me on that Sabbath, and he said, Yeah, this is very good. I'm going to give you a list here of names, Lord Bell' he said, he gave me a list of all these lobbyists, etc[xvi] (see chapter 12).

I've got all of these bastards on tape. I've got David Leigh on tape, telling me to go to Aitken's lawyers. I've got David Leigh…on tape, telling me to give the stuff to Fayed. I mean…do these fuckers want to end up in prison – just like me? If I go down, we all go down together.[xvii]

Pell told Jones[xviii]: 'I love taping David Leigh.' Asked why, he answered: 'It's just funny, cos he knows what a devious git I am, and when he realises…that I've been taping him, including all the advice he's given me about Mohammed al Fayed…' [xvii]

Pell says that, as he retrieved Hamilton's documents from the rubbish outside Browne's chambers, he supplied them to Leigh over many months running up to the Hamilton-v-Fayed libel trial[xix]. He even found documents showing that Hamilton's solicitors had suspected a leak and hired a private security firm to investigate. 'They were becoming paranoid about security. They thought there was a leak.'

The Guardian, which has taken a sanctimonious attitude towards other newspaper's use of Benji the Binman, will inevitably be embarrassed by the revelations in this book about its relationship with Pell. Journalists at the newspaper say privately that Benji the Binman is a taboo subject in its newsroom. A rare public clue about the secret relationship between Leigh and Pell was contained in a letter from two former *Guardian* investigative reporters, Michael Gillard and Laurie Flynn, about the newspaper's alleged suppression of a story about the Metropolitan police, published in the magazine produced by the

National Union of Journalists for its members. It claimed[xx]: 'He [Leigh] is also the investigations editor who does not disclose the shadowy outsourcing of *Guardian* research to correspondents like Benji 'the binman' Pell.'

Asked about his role in this affair, Leigh replied emphatically: 'I didn't tell him to go and pervert the course of justice by selling things to Fayed. I told him that *The Guardian* was not interested in his stuff about Hamilton-v-Fayed. Whatever he did subsequently is his own affair.' Leigh also added that neither did he tell Pell to target Aitken's lawyers. 'Benjamin Pell,' he commented, 'is a law unto himself.'

Hollingsworth was also in denial: 'My lawyer has advised me not to comment. However, I can state categorically that I NEVER asked Pell to target Hamilton's lawyers.'

Besides taping telephone conversations, Pell says that he also recorded a meeting he had with Hollingsworth the day after the journalist met Fayed and associates on November 17th 1999 to hand over Hamilton documents[xxi], the meeting referred to in the Phillips judgement.

Pell recalled: 'I'm miked up; I tape the whole conversation. And, on there, he actually goes into details about everything, about how it's gone, how he wants to get more stuff off me.' Pell says that he was worried about supplying more documents because he was due in court the following week over the Harkavys theft charge.

He recounted Hollingsworth's response. '"I don't want to put any pressure on you, Benjamin. But, of course, it would be helpful if you gave more stuff."'

In the Channel 4 documentary[xxii,] Christine Hamilton tells an anecdote about Pell's systematic plundering of their case papers. 'We heard a marvellous story… that the security porters at Gray's Inn, where our QC is; they know Pell very well, and for years they've been waving at him as he comes through the door. They thought he was part of the cleaning firm. And he'd been saying, "Good evening" to them.

'And they'd been saying, "Good evening," and they now know that they've been letting him in to rummage through the dustbins.'

Pell also remembered[xxiii]: 'I was once asked for directions by one of the QCs.' Pell also told Jones that he complained about an overly 'aggressive' security guard who asked him to leave one Inns of Court, telephoning his office the following day, posing as a pupil (trainee barrister) working at one of the chambers[xxiv].

Outside Gray's Inn, Pell points out that there is a notice: 'The Servants of the Inn have orders to remove all hawkers, disorderly people and those causing a nuisance.'

'The thing which always cracks me up is, "those causing a nuisance." If they knew the nuisance I'd caused over the last eight months in this chambers, I think they would have removed me a long time ago. Often, I see people coming in late, and they just greet me, say, "Hello, Tarquin," and that's fine. You know, I'm the postman, Tarquin, who cares? I feel like saying to them, "I've been screwing you for the last ten months. Bye."'

Neil Hamilton told the Channel 4 documentary bitterly[xxv]: 'He [Hollingsworth] acted, in effect, as Benjamin Pell's fence. He took the documents to Fayed, got money in exchange, and took it back to Pell. So he wasn't acting as a journalist in that respect. He was acting as a handler of stolen goods.'

Moreover, the ex-minister stressed, the story only broke because Pell and Hollingsworth argued over money. 'I believe that this is why the story actually got out ultimately. The thieves quarrelled amongst themselves, and Pell thought that he should have been paid more for the documents that he provided.' In fact, Hamilton is only partly correct. Pell is a compulsive self-publicist and cannot keep any of his exploits to himself. Eventually, the truth would have come out.

As Pell sat at home, watching a preview copy of this documentary and Hamilton's comments, he screamed to the screen[xxvi]: 'Well I would have sold them to you, you idiot – if you paid me.'

Meanwhile Hamilton continued, even more bitterly[xxvii]: 'I've been fighting this case now for nearly six years, and we've had the most astonishing ups and downs, and twists and turns. And this is the most astonishing of them all. But, you know, I'm the one who's been accused of greed, corruption, dishonesty, lying...'

While watching this, Pell interjected[xxviii]: 'Yes, they're just the nice things they say about you.'

Neil[xxix]: '...and I'm surrounded then by all these crooks and liars...'

Christine broke in: 'And hypocrites.'

Neil: '... just wallowing around in this cesspit.'

Christine: 'Our solicitor calculated that if we'd had to destroy all the paper, all the excess paperwork, just in our case alone, it would have cost an extra £75,000. I hope now that... all the lawyers involved in our case will be doubly careful, even if it means they have to employ somebody extra to do the shredding.'

Neil, himself a former barrister, added dolefully: 'It costs you a fortune to produce the documents in the first place, and then it will cost you a fortune to destroy them... That's what the law's all about, of course.'

Pell explained how he was persuaded to expose Fayed[xxx]: 'At the beginning, when I first did the Hamilton-Fayed thing, I'd never intended to do the dirty on Fayed... I did the deal with Hollingsworth, I knew I'd probably been ripped off, but I never thought that I'd actually decide to go along and sell the story. But then, as Richard Murray said from day one... from the day I read him the Desmond Browne opening statement to the day of the [libel trial] judgement, he kept on telling me, "Look, this is terrible. If Hamilton loses, you do realise you could have cost him the whole decision."

'I thought, "Well, it can't be that..."

'He said, "Well, of course you have. You've given the other side some very important documents. Let's see. Let's see what happens."'

Pell continued: 'Right from the beginning, Richard said to me, "This is amazing. If he [Hamilton] loses, you know, you do realise you're going to be in a very difficult position because you're going to feel guilty for the rest of your life." So then, of course, on 21st December, he loses.'

There is, of course, no indication that Pell felt the slightest tinge of guilt about any undue influence he might have had in the outcome of the case, as Murray suggested he would.

On the day of the verdict, Pell recalled that Murray said to him[xxxi]: 'Benjamin, how can you have a peaceful New Year when you know you've done this to Mr Hamilton?'

Pell recalled reading Desmond Brown's opening speech out to Murray, over the telephone, shortly before the trial was due to start. '"Mr Fayed is a Jekyll and Hyde character. On the one hand, he's this lovable rogue; on the other hand, though, he's a devious man."

'Richard couldn't stop laughing. He said, "Stop it, stop it." And you know what I'm like: if somebody tells me to stop something, I'll continue.

'I was going on and on, then at the end of about 15 minutes of having Benjamin Pell reading him the Desmond Browne [opening speech], I said, "What can I do with this, Richard?"

'He said, "Well, you know you can't do anything with this. It would be a terrible thing to do anything with this. You know, this is outrageous, I have nothing to do with this, I don't want to hear any more of this." And, of course, he was loving it. And then the next call I made was to David Leigh and the rest, as they say, is history: it was David Leigh who advised me to go to Macnamara.'

Pell taped Leigh's description of his theft as an 'awesome coup'[xxxii]. And it was Leigh who encouraged Pell to approach Fayed.

Over in Farringdon Road, in the bowels of *The Guardian*'s head office in London, Leigh picks up the telephone[xxxiii]. 'Hello.'

Pell: David

Leigh: Hello.

Pell (reading from document): 'Members of the jury, Mr Fayed is a Jekyll and Hyde character...'

Leigh: I don't believe it.

Pell: I promise you. 'Mr Fayed is a habitual liar, a man for whom lying is a sickness.' And there are 28 pages of this.

Leigh: You've got 28 pages!

Pell: I've got the fucking opening statement.
Leigh: Well, er, my recommendation to you...
Pell: Well, it's dangerous territory here
Leigh: First of all, put it on a fax to me.
Pell: Yes. Yeah, you see it first. You will love it, you will...
Leigh: If it is as you say, then my second piece of advice is, take yourself round to Mr Fayed pronto, and I am sure he will cross your palm with silver.'

While the libel trial was underway, Hollingsworth at the urging of the Fayed camp was putting Pell under pressure to obtain more material. He discussed this in another telephone conversation with Leigh[xxxiv]. After Leigh said he thought Fayed was on course to win, Pell asked:

So, I wonder why he's giving Mark such a hard time... Yeah, apparently. But, I mean... he [Hollingsworth] expected it. But, er, you know I'm a bit exasperated by the whole situation.
Leigh: What, that he's trying to get you to do more, or what?
Pell: Yuh, exactly, exactly... Is that not surprising? You know, cos, at the time, Mark came to an arrangement. He said, 'Okay, okay, well fine.' I mean, he-he basically doubled what we wanted. And then he said, 'But, of course, any extra information we can get, please, can we have, plus if you can find out who's funding Hamilton.' Now, had these events not happened last Monday [his prosecution for theft of documents from Harkavys], I would have obviously been in a position to provide them with more, albeit it wouldn't have been as good as the original stuff, it couldn't be as good as the original stuff. I think they ripped us off, but, on the other hand though, we still came to a good figure, but, I suppose that's the sort of thing you expect from him.
Leigh: And you and Mark have come to an amicable understanding about it, have you?
Pell: Well, I mean, what can we do?
Leigh: Well, I don't know. I mean, I meant with each other.
Pell: Yeah, yeah, I know. With each other, we're fine. But if you're dealing with a duplicitous bastard like him [Fayed] and he *dips* [cons] you, I mean, what can you do?
Leigh: Well, he's famous for being a duplicitous bastard.
Pell: Yeah. Yes, but he must realise, if he annoys me I can get him put in prison.

Pell's egomania typically manifests itself in the way that he believes that he is not only more intelligent than everyone else but also has more power to harm them than they have to harm him. But Leigh's reply feeds Pell's sense of paranoia in an attempt to persuade Pell against blowing the whistle:

Leigh: Ah, but if you annoy him, he's likely...you might have your head cut off.

Pell: Yeah, that's true. And I could go to prison as well.

Leigh: Yes... Yes, I think, probably...I think, probably, this is a sort of Hamilton-Fayed-type situation [ie both parties having already-damaged reputations].

Pell: Mmm.

However, Pell and Hollingsworth did fall out over the money.

Pell said[xxxv]:

I didn't think that somebody would be that stupid to lie to me about that. I mean, not-not when you're talking about something as dangerous as this. This could backfire against all of us.

This is not the sort of thing where your co-conspirator is lied to. Do you not agree? When you're going to do a deal like this, which is an attempt to pervert the course of justice, normally you are honest with everyone involved.

This is the way that police get criminals, is because when they fall out with each other, and that's how they got us. In other words, the only reason the police were able to get some sort of foot into this story was because Hollingsworth had allowed them to do it by ripping me off over the money.'

Murray now had more purchase with Pell in his quest to expose the way the libel trial had been perverted[xxxvi]. Pell's version was that Murray kept pressing him[xxxvii]. By Christmas 1999, after Fayed won the libel battle, Pell says that he was still telling Murray: 'No, Richard, I've told you, I don't want to get involved.'

In early January 2000, Pell says, Hollingsworth asked him[xxxviii]: 'Any chance of you getting the names, the names of the donors? Now, the big thing is: who funded the Hamilton thing?'

'I said, "...You're supposed to come back now, Mark, and get the rest of the money, you know. What's this business?"'

The organiser of the donors' fund for Hamilton's libel action against Fayed was Lord Harris of High Cross. Fayed wanted the names of those who contributed, so he could pursue them through the courts, too. Pell explained: 'So, I go to Lord Harris, I do him three or four times. I don't get, actually, any of the names of the donors. But I pass that on to Hollingsworth, and he still keeps on telling me, "I need more names"… all the time, "More names, more names."

'And I ring up Richard and I said, "This is outrageous, I'm not going to get any more of the money." Then the meeting [a further meeting planned between Hollingsworth and Fayed] keeps on getting postponed: he's supposed to meet him on the 11th, postponed; the 15th, postponed; finally meets him on the 25th. And that is the final straw.'

Referring to Murray, he said: 'He's quite clever, he puts a bit of psychological pressure on me. He said, "Have you had the rest of the money yet from Hollingsworth?"

'Oh no, no, he's meeting him [Fayed] on 11th January.'

On that day, Pell says that Murray asked him: '"How did the meeting go?"

'Oh, he cancelled it at the last minute.'

'Benjamin, can't you sense that this guy's lying to you?'

'No, no, no. He's meeting him.'

'When's the meeting?'

'25th January.'

'We'll follow him.'

'What?'

'Yeah, I'll follow him.'

'So Richard follows him to Harrods.'

Pell says he later asked Murray: 'How long was he in there?'

'Two minutes.'

'Two minutes? He's supposed to be getting my fucking money.'

'And, it turns out, he [Hollingsworth] corroborates it. That afternoon, Hollingsworth rings me up. "Oh Benjamin, it was impossible. I couldn't get hold of Mo'. He was going in and out of his office, secretaries and everything. I don't think we'll be able to get any more money."'

Of course, Pell tapes him[xxxi]: 'Hollingsworth, by then, is trusting me completely. I mean, he's mentioning Fayed by name, he's mentioning the money, he's crazy. So I just ring up Richard and said, "Bang to rights... fucking bang to rights, he's fucking bang to rights. He's finished."'

Never mind triumphant, Pell can be positively excultant when he springs the trap on one of his enemies.

'And Richard can't stop laughing. He said, "You've got to do him now. He's admitted it on bloody tape; there's no way he can get out of it now." So I said, "Okay, okay, but I still feel a bit guilty about this."'

His justification for exposing the Fayed-Hollingsworth deal was they 'messed me up over the money'[xxxix]. He said: 'What a wanker. Mo' should be angry with him. If it was not to fuck Hollingsworth for ripping me off over the money, I would never have allowed it to happen.'

In fact, there is no evidence at all that Hollingsworth did cheat or con Pell.

Even his fellow worshippers at the synagogue criticised Pell for selling the Fayed story to the *Mail on Sunday*.

People said to me in synagogue, having done a deal with Fayed... 'it's a bit nasty of you, Benjamin, to go back on the deal'...

Everyone I've spoken to, people in synagogue, think I'm a disgrace. They said, 'How could you do this?'

And I said, 'Well, I actually didn't do it directly.'

And they said, 'But you knew that by talking to somebody about it...'

I said, 'Well, you know I've got a big mouth.'

They said, Benjamin, that's no excuse. You do a deal with someone, you don't go back on it afterwards, you know.'

And that is true... It was a shitty thing for me to do, of all the things I've ever done.

He told his fan club at the synagogue: 'Look, if the bastard would have paid me what he promised me, I would never have done it – of course not.'

Whatever the merits of his justification for betraying his erstwhile conspirators, this incident demonstrates how Pell cannot keep anything to himself. His whole persona is of a Scarlet Pimpernel of tabloid news, but without a Baroness Orczy to publicise his exploits he has to do it himself.

According to Pell, 'If Hollingsworth would have paid me what he promised me in advance, I wouldn't have done it. Whatever Richard [Murray] would have said to me, I wouldn't have done it'[xli]. 'And that's when I said to Richard, "Okay then, I'm going to fuck that bastard. He can't even stand up to Fayed over something like this – as serious as this. Okay, I'm now willing for you to go along to any national newspaper, as long as you're discreet etc. Who are you going to go to first?"'

Murray's first port of call was Phil Hall [then editor of the *News of the World*]. He planned to see Hall while he was at Rupert Murdoch's News International plant in east London's Wapping, which publishes the *News of the World* or *Screws* for short, because of its incessant coverage of sex stories. Murray was due that day to libel read at the *Sunday Times*, which News International also publishes.

The *News of the World* had only two months earlier broken the story about how the former Conservative Party chairman, Jeffrey Archer, had attempted to commit perjury in his libel battle against the *Daily Star* in 1987 when he won £500,000 damages, a scoop that torpedoed Archer's bid to become mayor of London in 1999[xlii]. Archer had conspired with a friend, Ted Francis, to create a false alibi to help deny allegations that he had a sexual relationship with a prostitute. The exposé of Archer's false alibi was possible because of the co-operation of Francis. He entrapped Archer at the urging of Max Clifford, so the the *News of the World* ran the story of the false alibi. Archer, 63, was jailed for four years in 2001 after a jury found him guilty on two counts of perverting the course of justice and two of perjury. The jury acquitted Francis.

Pell saw similarities with his Fayed story to the Archer saga in that the Egyptian had also perverted the course of justice albeit so by by acquiring the other side's legally privileged documents but a trumped up alibi. Murray meeting with Phil Hall then was a good omen to Pell[xliii], but Hall's reaction was disappointing:

'Think I've heard that one before, and it's not the sort of thing we're interested in.'

Pell summarised it[xliv]: 'He did say, "It would only work anyway if the person who stole the documents is willing to appear on the front page with the documents, saying, *I stole these documents.*" He wanted me to do a Ted Francis… He needed the Ted Francis in this incident to appear and say, "Hi, I did this. I perverted the course of justice." And I can promise you this, Ted Francis never thought in November 1999 that he would end up being charged as well. Can you believe that? Do you think he'd be stupid enough to give Phil Hall, albeit an exclusive which gave him a new Ferrari, which I got from his affidavit…but nobody knows about that.'

After turning down Murray's offer at the end of January 200, soon afterwards Hall had to leave the *News of the World*, then, ironically, he found employment an employee of Fayed! He oversaw the break-up of Fayed's *Punch* magazine, which ceased publication in 2002.

But after absorbing the bad news Pell says that he was relieved[xlvi]. 'I'm now thinking, "Thank goodness, it didn't get into the *Screws*." And Richard said, "Don't worry. I've got some very good contacts at the *Mail on Sunday*."'

Murray then approached the editor of the *Mail on Sunday*, Peter Wright, who thought the story would make a front-page splash and was worth £50,000. Pell recalled[xlvii]: Two weeks later, he [Murray] meets Peter Wright, and Peter Wright says, "Yup. Fifty grand. No worries, we'll do it the way you want it to be done. We'll get someone to ring up Fayed, we'll get one of our oldest reporters to do it, Peter [sic] Henderson. He's very good, very experienced" and this sort of thing.'

Pell claimed that Murray secured an agreement from Wright that the binman's role was kept 'in the background'[xlviii]. According to Pell, in fact, the plan was for him not to even appear in the story: 'This can only come out if it's not me appearing in the story…we've got to bounce Fayed, in essence. So, Richard's idea – a clever idea – was this: he was going to get the journalist to ring up Fayed and say, "I'm phoning you here from 5 Raymond

Buildings. I haven't been paid yet… for the documents. Here we are, [two] months after the case has finished, and you still haven't paid me. Where's my money, Mr Fayed?"'

The planned script then had Fayed replying, 'What the frigging hell are you talking about? I gave the money to Mark Hollingsworth. What the frigging hell are you talking about?' Murray was supposed to have said to Wright, 'If that doesn't work: end of story, no deal'[xlix]:

However, Henderson had other ideas. He didn't want to stand up the story the way Pell wanted and, when Murray told him that was the deal, he just said, 'Too late now – I've already put in a call. And I want those documents from you.' Doubtless, Henderson had no faith in Fayed replying the way that Pell and Murray had scripted, and that was even on the dubious assumption that he would get through to him in the first place.

Meanwhile, the plot had thickened. Murray had met Michael Heseltine at a Christmas party and told him briefly what had occurred. James Price, Fayed's QC, was also present and he made it difficult for Murray to fully brief Heseltine. However, he followed it up with a phone call in which he described the full story. Murray had wanted to bounce Heseltine to press for a DTI investigation into how Fayed had bought the Hamilton documents[l].

Murray told Henderson of the *Mail on Sunday* about Heseltine. Pell recalled: 'Of course now the DTI are involved, Henderson now has no choice. The story has to appear that Sunday or no Sunday.' Pell and Murray believed that, with the DTI involved, the story would inevitably emerge within a week or so. Pell continues[li]: 'We knew we would lose our exclusivity unless Richard co-operated with Henderson. Henderson said at first, "Just show me the documents." They [Henderson and Murray] met at Stansted airport. This is 7th February [the Monday before publication]; he showed him the documents.

'[Henderson]:"Oh, you couldn't photocopy ten of these pages for me?" Ten turns into 20, turns into 40, and that was the stuff which the police got off the *Mail on Sunday*.'

Pell says that, when the *Mail on Sunday* was struggling to substantiate the story, he considered what further material he could provide to help the newspaper[lii]. He offered a tape of a telephone conversation that he had with Hollingsworth, which provided some detail about how Fayed had bought the documents. In this tape, Hollingsworth referred to Fayed as 'the big Egyptian'.

The newspaper suggested that Pell leave the tape out at the top of his bin... 'I said,"Ah, nobody's going to believe that.They're going to think I did that deliberately." Cos obviously, I'm too intelligent, you see. I want to help them, because he's been good to me, and second of all, I don't want to get my fucking house blown up by Fayed; I don't want to have Macnamara trying to kill me"'

Pell says that he provided the further help to the *Mail on Sunday* by supplying it with the tape of his telephone conversation with Hollingsworth while being careful to make it look as though he did not provide it. By luck, the kind of fortune that can only befall Pell, he was able to take advantage of the fact that one of his uninsured, untaxed vans had been destroyed in a fire-bomb attack by a Hendon arsonist who had nothing to do with the binman.'And the beauty of the bloody fire-bombed van is that I could genuinely leave it [the tape] in there, and they could find it in there.' Pell recorded the conversation onto an Elton John duet tape.

According to Pell, Hollingsworth says in the taped telephone conversation: '"I've picked up the money; and I've passed on the documents." And in the second one, he says, "We've had a result; I'm meeting the big Egyptian next Thursday." That's all.'

However, Pell's version is that Fayed's camp doubted the story of how this tape found its way to the *Mail on Sunday*.'Fayed's lot are going mad over it... "We don't believe you."'

They were indeed right to be sceptical: Pell admits that the story was false. Pell continues: 'I think the way I did it was brilliant...I had the brainwave of doing it on an Elton John cassette. I think it's brilliant.'

Brilliant! Of course, for all his savant-like intelligence, the Talmudic logic can go...well, Pell-mell.

Pell says that while the tape he supplied, in a round-about route, to the *Mail on Sunday* was important in helping the newspaper substantiate the story, the key factor was Hollingsworth's admission to its associate editor. 'They had Hollingsworth anyway; they had Hollingsworth talking to Henderson… All I've done is given them a connection between the binman and Hollingsworth – that's it, without risking myself being blown up by Macnamara. It's unbelievable, he's effectively admitted that I've committed the murder and here's where the weapon is.

'"Well obviously this is Benji, you know, Benji the Binman, and I got the documents off him, and you know I gave him the money and, er…"

'"Oh thank you, Mark. We've got our splash for tomorrow."
"

Pell was working with Hollingsworth on an Elton John story until very shortly before the *Mail on Sunday* exposé was published[liv]. 'We're dealing with each other right up to the day of publication. And, of course, I haven't spoken to him since… He never rang me. I always assumed that he'd at least ring me up once, and say, "You bastard."'

Hollingsworth also frequently worked for the *Sunday Times*, but it was upset with him after the *Mail on Sunday* broke the Fayed story, says Pell. 'Why were the *Sunday Times* angry with him? Not because he's perverted the course of justice. "Why didn't you give the story to us?" Doesn't that tell you so much about Fleet Street?'

The case also tells us much about Pell and the 'phoney Pharaoh of Harrods, and not a little about Fleet Street.

References

[i] Paul Henderson, 'AL FAYED "BOUGHT LIBEL SECRETS,"' *Mail on Sunday* (13.02.00).

[ii] David Hencke, 'Tory MPs were paid to plant questions, claims Harrods chief,' *The Guardian* (20.10.94).

[iii] House of Commons standards and privileges committee, 'Complaints from Mohammed Al Fayed, The Guardian and others against 25 Members and Former Members,' (volumes I-III 08.07.97 and volume IV 24.07.97), the first volume of which includes, 'Memorandum Submitted by the Parliamentary Commissioner for Standards,' (03.07.97).

[iv] Mark Watts, 'Letter reveals Al Fayed paid £150k for lobby work,' *Sunday Business* (17.11.96).

[v] 'The Question of Sleaze,' *Dispatches*, Channel 4 (first shown 16.01.97).

[vi] Paul Henderson, 'AL FAYED "BOUGHT LIBEL SECRETS,"' *Mail on Sunday* (13.02.00).

[vii] "3½-hour rushes," Moving Perspective (filmed 1999).

[viii] Lord Phillips, 'Judgement as approved by the court: Mostyn Neil Hamilton-v-Mohammed Al Fayed,' (21.12.00).

[ix] McVicar video tape (filmed 14.01.01) DVRG.

[x] Lord Phillips, 'Judgement as approved by the court: Mostyn Neil Hamilton-v-Mohammed Al Fayed,' (21.12.00).

[xi] McVicar video tape (filmed 14.01.01) DVRG.

[xii] 'Scandal in the Bins,' Channel 4 (first shown 11.01.01).

[xiii] McVicar audio tape (recorded 2000) MDOB.

[xiv] McVicar audio tape (recorded 09.11.00) MDRY.

[xv] McVicar audio tape (recorded 03.01.01) MDOV.

[xvi] McVicar video tape (filmed 14.01.01) DVRG.

[xvii] McVicar audio tape (recorded 12.11.00) MDRG.

[xviii] "3½-hour rushes," Moving Perspective (filmed 1999).

[xix] McVicar video tape (filmed 14.01.01) DVRG.

[xx] Michael Gillard and Laurie Flynn, 'Win over police a blow for press freedom,' *Journalist* (January/February 2004).

[xxi] McVicar video tape (filmed 14.01.01) DVRG.

[xxii] 'Scandal in the Bins,' Channel 4 (first shown 11.01.01).

[xxiii] McVicar audio tape (recorded 12.11.00) MDRG.

[xxiv] "3½-hour rushes," Moving Perspective (filmed 1999).

[xxv] 'Scandal in the Bins,' Channel 4 (first shown 11.01.01).

xxvi McVicar audio tape (recorded 12.11.00) MDRG.

xxvii 'Scandal in the Bins,' Channel 4 (first shown 11.01.01).

xxviii McVicar audio tape (recorded 12.11.00) MDRG.

xxix 'Scandal in the Bins,' Channel 4 (first shown 11.01.01).

xxx McVicar video tape (filmed 14.01.01) DVRG.

xxxi McVicar audio tape (recorded 09.11.00) MDRY.

xxxii McVicar video tape (filmed 14.01.01) DVRG.

xxxiii Extract of Pell-Leigh telephone conversation shortly before the Hamilton-v-Fayed libel trial starts in November 1999, 'Thank You for the Rubbish: It's Worth Millions,' Moving Perspective (first shown 13.01.02).

xxxiv Extract of Pell-Leigh telephone conversation, McVicar tape (recorded 24.11.99) MDOO.

xxxv McVicar audio tape (recorded 30.12.00) MDRI.

xxxvi McVicar video tape (filmed 14.01.01) DVRG.

xxxvii McVicar audio tape (recorded 30.12.00) MDRI.

xxxviii McVicar video tape (filmed 14.01.01) DVRG.

xxxix McVicar audio tape (recorded 30.12.00) MDRI.

xl McVicar video tape (filmed 14.01.01) DVRG.

xli McVicar audio tape (recorded 30.12.00) MDRI.

xlii Neville Thurlbeck and Robert Kellaway, 'Archer quits,' *The News of the World* (21.11.99).

xliii McVicar audio tape (recorded 30.12.00) MDRI.

xliv McVicar video tape (filmed 14.01.01) DVRG.

xlv McVicar audio tape (recorded 30.12.00) MDRI.

xlvi McVicar video tape (filmed 14.01.01) DVRG.

xlvii McVicar audio tape (recorded 30.12.00) MDRI.

xlviii McVicar video tape (filmed 14.01.01) DVRG.

xlix McVicar audio tape (recorded 30.12.00) MDRI.

l McVicar video tape (filmed 14.01.01) DVRG.

li McVicar audio tape (recorded 30.12.00) MDRI.

lii McVicar audio tape (recorded 30.12.00) MDRI.

liii McVicar video tape (filmed 06.01.01) DVRY.

liv McVicar audio tape (recorded 30.12.00) MDRI.

Chapter 2

It Wasn't Me,
says Fayed

Fayed, as we know, denied any role in receiving documents taken from the rubbish outside the chambers of Hamilton's barrister. The Harrods co-owner knew nothing about legally privileged documents. This – from a businessman who had boasted of bribing MPs – did not wash with uninterested parties, never mind the interested ones. Consequently, the obvious suspects – Fayed, the binman and his middle-man – were feeling the heat.

Pell's solicitor, Paul Graham, made clear to his anxious client just how compromising was his role in taking the documents and selling them to Fayed. Pell says[i]: 'Paul has always said to me, "Of all the things [you] could ever do, this is one of the more serious ones." He said, "Unless, Benjamin, you suddenly become a murderer overnight, perverting the course of justice is as serious offence as it gets."'

Graham – a fine criminal trial solicitor and one long-accustomed to Pell's Talmudic logic chopping – defined the crime as free of self-exculpatory wriggle-room as he could: 'If you buy the A-Z which is used by the bank robber to... rob the bank, you can be guilty of conspiracy... that's the way the law works in this country.'[ii]

'Paul said to me, "This is much worse than Aitken (Pell's theft of documents from Harkavys: see chapters 10 and 11)," He said, "This is you being done for perverting the course of justice and conspiracy"'

The publication of the *Mail on Sunday* article[iii] also sparked panic in the Fayed camp. Fayed called in Max Clifford, who was then handling the publicity for another of Fayed's acquisitions, Fulham Football Club, as troubleshooter. The small but turbo-powered Clifford rang up Pell and tried to establish what was behind the *Mail on Sunday* story[iv].

Pell, of course, recorded the conversation.

Clifford began by reminding Pell that he had previously committed perjury to protect him in a High Court case brought by the manager of Elton John against Pell and *The Mirror* (see chapter 5). On oath, Clifford denied knowing that Pell was responsible for stealing confidential documents about the singer's finances. Clifford had sold the documents to *The Mirror*, when he was acting in effect as Pell's agent. He gave evidence in the High court to the effect that he did not know the true identity of the source of the documents.

During their telephone conversation, Pell tried to deflect the blame onto Hollingsworth. 'You've got to speak to Mark Hollingsworth; he's the person who gave the story to the *Mail on Sunday* – not me.'

Clifford: No, but all I want to do, Benjamin, is to get to the heart of it because I'm going to, you know... I'm – I'm advising Mohammed. That's my interest.

Pell: See, Hoilingsworth is your guy. He's the one who gave Chris Henderson 17 minutes of... of confession. I've never spoken to Anderson in...well, I've not spoken to Henderson.

Clifford: No, but that's not the answer.

Pell: Yeah.

Clifford: What I'm saying is, did you get to this information for Mohammed?

Pell: Look, I've never spoken...I've never spoken to Mohammed in my life.

Clifford: No, no, no, no, hold on. That's a clever answer. That is not you speaking to me. I just want you to mark me card.

Pell: I've never spoken to Mohammed in my life. I've dealt with Hollingsworth... But that's something which Hollingsworth can answer. I've never spoken to the Mail on Sunday.

Clifford: No, I...I don't know Mark Hollingsworth, and I've got no interest in talking to him, Benjamin. I know you, and I like you, so I want just you to mark me card as to the truth of it.

Pell: Yeah, well the truth is..' [Of course, with Pell, the truth as he avows it never is the truth.]

Clifford: Not [unintelligible] you. I mean, Jesus Christ, I went in the bloody High Court and lied for you. [In fact, Clifford lied for himself more than Pell, but that is another story.]

(Pell laughs excitedly, ostensibly in agreement but actually at the ease with which he had entrapped Clifford.)

Clifford: I'm not going to let you down.

Pell: Yeah, yeah. (Pell is fully aware that the only person Clifford doesn't let down is himself.)

Clifford: But I need you to mark me card so as I know what's gone on.

Clifford, given his experience with the binman, should have known that Pell lives by lies and, on principle, would rather lie than tell the truth. He takes another tack: 'I'm obviously concerned cos the last thing you want to do is make an enemy of Fayed. And everyone tells me that...you crazy man, here you are making an enemy of somebody who...can blow your house up.'

Pell told Clifford that, after the story broke, he asked his 'civil lawyer' to contact Fayed's camp. 'He actually rings up Macnamara that morning, this is the morning... the Monday morning. Within an hour the 'phone rings, his 'phone rings and it's Ian Burton – he's Fayed's criminal lawyer. Very anxious, of course, to know what this whole thing is about. We arrange a meeting immediately; I think we meet at about three o'clock that afternoon... It was an absolutely crazy meeting... We sit there for an hour, talking bullshit to each other.'

On the tape, Pell recounts how the conversation at that meeting went, and, even by his own account, he is as disingenuous as ever.

Pell said of the meeting:

This is all nonsense. This is all mad, but we spend a whole hour saying this. Now, as Paul Graham said, in retrospect, this was a terrible thing for me to have done. Cos had we been, as we should have been, charged with perverting the course of justice, this would have been wonderful: there are the conspirators meeting two days after the newspaper article appears having this meeting. Paul said to me, 'How the hell can you be so stupid to meet Ian Burton, his criminal lawyer, two days after the article appeared?'

'I said, "I was scared about Fayed blowing me up." So, it was a…terrible mistake to make. And, I made matters even worse at the end – there's always a Benjamin Pellism which has to come into any meeting, you know. I always have to make some sort of fuck-up.

'So, at the end of the meeting… I turn round to Ian Burton, and I said to him, "Look, I'd like you to pass on my sincere apologies to your client for having…you know, for the embarrassment I've caused him."

'"But, Mr Pell, you haven't caused him any embarrassment, you had nothing to do with it."

One trusts that Burton had gleaned enough of Pell's act to have meant this ironically. But clearly Pell didn't think so as he replied: '"No, no, sorry… For him to be associated with somebody like Benjamin Pell must be terribly embarrassing. Please pass that on to the client."

'We all knew… we'd been talking bullshit for 60 minutes… He [Burton] even offered to pay my legal costs. I thought, "This is sounding a bit odd." But it's obvious, here, they were shitting themselves.'

Pell summarised the import of the whole incident: 'I think, in essence, it's John Macnamara who saved me, Hollingsworth and Fayed from going to prison cos this was… a much more serious crime than what Jeffrey Archer is going to court [and was subsequently jailed] for. We were perverting the course of justice, for goodness' sake.'

He then remembered that David Leigh funnelled him into Hollingsworth and he recounts Leigh's favourite refrain whenever he told the *Guardian* journalist about one of his stories[vi]. 'He used to say to me about all my stories, "amazing if true." … His biography should be called, *Amazing if True*. Well, I'm telling you this, it's amazing and true, Mr Leigh, that you committed…that you've perverted the course of justice, darling, and that's going to come out in the wash.' (Pell looks directly at the camera. When he is being recorded, Pell has the habit as he is betraying someone of addressing them directly, anticipating them watching it.)

While journalists' willingness to use the results of Pell's trawls may sometimes be understandable, clearly Leigh's and Hollingsworth's actions in this case were indefensible – Fayed's, of course, were beyond the pale.

Meanwhile, the Hamilton camp was also active. Following a court hearing four days after the *Mail on Sunday* story, Hamilton was given copies of the documents that the newspaper had acquired from Murray, examples of material supplied by Pell to Fayed via Hollingsworth, as set out in the appeal judgement[vii]. There were nine documents, totalling 54 pages, as follows:

1 'Desmond's shopping list': a detailed list of inquiries from Browne, Hamilton's barrister.
2 A list of unidentified credits in Hamilton's bank and building society accounts.
3 A paper setting out legal argument about tax on unsolicited commissions.
4 A draft witness statement of a former security guard at Fayed's Park Lane home, who was giving evidence for Hamilton, showing his home address and current place of work.
5 A letter from Hamilton to Browne, mainly on financial information about Fayed.
6 A fax to Hamilton's solicitors containing a draft response to objections to Hamilton's witness statements.
7 A fax to Hamilton's solicitors listing potential sources in the media for cross-examination.
8 A fax from Hamilton to his solicitors commenting on transcripts of taped conversations between Fayed and the late Tiny Rowland, his adversary in the battle for control Harrods.
9 A draft diary of principal events created by one of Hamilton's barristers.

Documents 2, 3, 6, and 9 were served on Fayed's lawyers before trial, as had the former security guard's witness statement (although this would, of course, have been the final and not the draft version) and the tapes referred to in 8. In addition, a list of subjects for cross-examination for Fayed was served shortly before trial. Thus, from Fayed's point of view, the documents were hardly the Crown Jewels.

As set out in the appeal judgement, ten days after the *Mail on Sunday* story Murray approached Hamilton's solicitors. He told them that Pell had described to him how he had delivered copies of stolen documents to Hollingsworth in five brown envelopes by posting them through his letter-box late one night and, then, the following morning, how Hollingsworth took them to a meeting attended by Macnamara, Mayer, and, for some of the time, Fayed himself, where the journalist was paid £10,000 in new £50 notes. Five days later, an unsigned draft of a witness statement by Murray was served on Fayed's lawyers. This was later replaced by a signed statement dated March 1st.

Pell told McVicar that he left the brown envelopes of documents late one night with a security guard at a building near to Hollingsworth's then office in London's Mayfairviii. Pell said he was attempting to compromise Hollingsworth, in that it was reminiscent of Hamilton's collecting Fayed's brown envelopes of cash. Pell wanted the security guard to be a witness who could verify that Hollingsworth had collected the envelopes of documents. However, this wheeze cam to nothing as the security guard later told the court that he could not remember the envelopes being left with him.

In Murray's statement, as set out in the appeal judgement, Murray described a telephone conversation he had with Pell the day before the Hamilton-v-Fayed libel trial began. This is apparently the same telephone conversation as described by Pell in another of his taped interviews with McVicar. According to Murray, and in line with Pell's account, Pell read over the draft of Browne's opening speech and referred to proposed questions or topics for Fayed's cross-examination, and 'Desmond Browne's shopping list'.

Murray said that Pell told him that a journalist hostile to Hamilton had suggested he give the material to Fayed. Murray said that he tried to persuade Pell not to do so. At some point, said Murray, Pell told him he had been collecting documents relating to the case from outside 5 Raymond Buildings for some time and copying them to a large number of journalists. These included a copy of the draft witness statement of Fayed's former security guard, which he found two Sundays before trial and which he had faxed to several journalists, including James Steen, the then editor of *Punch*, a magazine that Fayed owned at that time.

According to the statement, Pell told Murray that Hollingsworth telephoned Pell later to say that he had just had a meeting with Fayed, Macnamara, and Mayer and that they had promised £20,000 for the documents. Hollingsworth was given £10,000 there and then, but the documents were not exactly what they were seeking and they were keen to know what else Pell had obtained.

Pell telephoned Murray the following day to say that Fayed had refused to pay any more money. Subsequently, Murray said that he tried to interest the *Mail on Sunday* in the story. He had obtained copies of certain documents from Pell and passed them to the newspaper. Pell told him that he had mislaid other 'particularly sensitive documents', including 'a manuscript document on lined paper in neat hand writing entitled something like "Topics for Cross-Examination"', and the draft of Browne's opening speech. Murray said that journalists on the *Mail on Sunday* were reluctant at first to believe the story. However, they decided to run it after they learned that Murray had told Heseltine about it and Hollingsworth had confirmed its essentials.

Pell was questioned as part of the police investigation into the supply of Hamilton's legally privileged documents to Fayed. Unfortunately for the police, they never found out about the McVicar tapes. As Pell later tells a journalist from a Jewish newspaper in an interview that was also filmed by McVicar[ix]: 'They arrested me on 6th March over this...'cos, of course, this is perverting the course of justice...'

The police also raided his home. He says that he gave police a statement[x]. 'I said, "The stuff you got out of the garage, I would like to explain to you that that stuff all comes from last year before I was convicted for theft [in 1999 over documents from Aitken's solicitors]. Now that I realise, of course, that it's an offence to go through rubbish, I no longer take rubbish."'

Pell would often later claim to have stopped his bin-raiding activities, although he has never really given this up. It is doubtful, if he could since his compulsive-obsessive personality has made this virtually an addiction (see chapter 16).

The police told Pell's solicitor at the beginning of July that he was no longer on police bail, which suggested that their investigation was going nowhere, although they reserved the right to resume investigating Pell.

Asked what his motives were for helping to expose the story about Hamilton's documents, Pell told McVicar[xii]: 'It wasn't a question of motives; Hollingsworth ripped me off over the money', adding that Fayed 'shouldn't have let us down over the money'. Only doublethink can square these claims with the facts as we know them: Hollingsworth split with Pell the ten thousand. Similarly, Fayed wanted the names of the donors for the further ten thousand. As with much of what Pell says to justify his actions, it does not meet the facts that he himself has put into the public domain.

He returned to the subject of his motives three months later, telling McVicar[xiii]: 'There were three reasons why I decided at the beginning of last year, 2000, to finally dish the dirt on Fayed, cos, even though I hadn't been paid properly, I wasn't that upset… Firstly…I saw that Hollingsworth was a complete madman, he was messing up all my stories and Elton John was one of the final straws (see chapter 7). Second of all, of course, I felt angry that I hadn't been paid the complete amount, and… Richard Murray was putting pressure on me.'

He has already listed three reasons and now he adds a fourth that he calls his third (unless it is money, counting is not Pell's forte): 'But the third reason was on 5th January… I was there at quarter to midnight, suddenly, as I'm going through the bins of 3, 4, 5 Raymond Buildings… suddenly, the light goes on at 5 Raymond Buildings… I stop doing what I'm doing and I walk around. And then the light is still on five…ten minutes later, so I decide, "No, err on the side of caution, I'll leave."' He saw someone from 5 Raymond Buildings talking to a security guard. According to Pell, this person later challenged him, but let him go after he claimed to be there working as a cleaner. For Pell, it was a narrow escape, and he says he had not been back since.

Thus, his final reason was that he thought it might be his last chance of getting a scoop out of 5 Raymond Buildings. In fact, his real reasons were the money and the publicity that would add lustre to his cultivated image of the Scarlet Pimpernel of Fleet Street scoops.

Nevertheless, he remains bitter over the *Mail on Sunday* exposé of him... 'That was disgusting – especially when they had about a hundred stories off me... They had no proof. Yet they made me a splash... they had no evidence, yet they still went for me.'

He believes the newspaper calculated that he would not sue. 'They know I'm just an eccentric... It's outrageous, this is the *Mail on Sunday*, who'd had story after story from me.' As with many things that outrage Pell, he reaction was more a product of his own Talmudic (il)logic than the facts of what happened.

Two weeks before Hamilton's appeal was due to start, the *Mail on Sunday* reported that the Crown Prosecution Service (CPS) was considering whether Fayed should be prosecuted[xiv]. Police had sent a file to the CPS.

But, on the eve of the appeal, the police announced that their investigations had turned up no evidence on which a successful prosecution could be mounted. They had not even interviewed Fayed[xv]. Indeed, four days before the appeal hearing, a police inspector informed Fayed's solicitors: 'Following my investigation and the provision of an advice file to the Crown Prosecution Service, I have decided not to interview your clients in relation to this matter. Additionally, I have decided not to charge any person with any offence.' The alleged offence was, understandably, not high up on the Met's lists of priorities. The shenanigans of Fleet Street were not part of its remit.

Hamilton's appeal went before Lord Phillips, the Master of the Rolls, Lord Justice Sedley and Lady Justice Hale. Hamilton, represented by Anthony Boswood QC, wanted the jury's verdict in his libel case against Fayed set aside and damages awarded to him or, at least, that a fresh trial be ordered. He also sought the reversal of the order that he pay Fayed's costs. He accused Fayed of gross misconduct that perverted the trial procedure, making it unfair. He also claimed that had the jury been aware of Fayed's conduct it would have damaged his credibility and that of other witnesses called on his behalf.

Hamilton filed witness statements dealing with the time when Browne's draft opening speech and cross-examination notes were written. The appeal judgement recorded[xvi]:

> Browne said that he always put documents for shredding in the red bins next to the shredder and never in waste paper bins. Another barrister at his chambers said that he sometimes put documents for shredding next to the red bins if they were full and expressed the fear that the cleaners may have mistakenly put such papers out with the rubbish. Later statements from the cleaners, however, deny this, saying that they would never throw anything away that was not in the ordinary waste paper baskets.

Hamilton's lawyers, according to Pell, had approached his solicitor, Paul Graham, asking whether Pell would give evidence[xvii]. 'Paul said, "What?" (Pell's tone indicates that Paul Graham was expressing incredulity.)

'Then they said to Paul, "We'll get him immunity (from prosecution)."

'Paul said, "You can never get immunity in English law."'

Pell claims that Hamilton's lawyers even approached the director of public prosecutions, David Calvert-Smith, in September 2000 about giving him immunity from prosecution. But Pell says that he would not have given evidence at the appeal anyway, partly because of his cultivated paranoia. 'The last thing I want is Fayed murdering me,' he said. 'And he would, he'd kill me… If he knew I was going to give evidence, he'd kill me.' As always Pell colours his predicament with threats to kill.

Fayed, represented by Michael Beloff QC, resisted the appeal. He filed evidence from himself, his legal adviser, Stuart Benson, and others, including three key witnesses who had testified at the trial and supported his account of giving 'cash for questions'. According to the appeal judgement, Fayed described how he had employed Hollingsworth to write his biography and, although this had been taken over by someone else, he continued to employ the journalist from time to time to conduct various investigations for him[xviii]. This included help in relation to: his long-running battle with Tiny Rowland that dated from Fayed's takeover of Harrods; the death of his son, Dodi, in the car crash that also killed Princess Diana in Paris; and his nationality application, which was unsuccessful. Fayed said that he had met Hollingsworth in October 1999 to discuss the Hamilton case and asked him to conduct some background research into the former MP's activities and associations. The results of this, he said, was faxed to Macnamara on November 17th, which made no reference to any meeting that day. Fayed said that he also saw Hollingsworth on November 29th, but could not recall what they discussed.

Fayed was cross-examined. The judgement recorded:

> He maintained that he knew nothing of any theft of privileged documents and had no involvement at all in the alleged receipt of these documents. Mr Boswood made little headway with cross-examination. When questioned on detail, Mr Al Fayed replied either, 'I can't remember,' or, 'It's a possibility.'

Journalists counted the number of times he said 'I can't remember' – it was over seventy times. There was none of the bravura spark of his evidence at the trial. Instead he cut a pathetic, lacklustre figure who because of the threat of a perjury charge could only lie by evasion not confrontation. In a word, his evidence was embarrassing. One thing he did admit was that his security officer Macnamara would not have had authority to pay Mr Hollingsworth £10,000 without his express permission.

The judgment concluded:

> There were developments shortly before and during this hearing that would not have been out of place in one of John Le Carré's early novels. On November 22nd 2000, Mr Hamilton's solicitors learned from the Crown Prosecution Service that they did not intend to

pursue any criminal charges in relation to thefts from the dustbins outside 5 Raymond Buildings. They sought out Mr Murray in the hope that further information could now be obtained from Mr Pell. On November 17th 2000, Mr Wheeler, an assistant solicitor with the firm, was taken by Mr Murray to a place in Hendon where they found a cassette tape in a fire-damaged Ford Transit van. This was a tape of duets by Elton John, part of which had been recorded over. On Thursday December 7th, in circumstances which are unexplained, Mr Vaughan, a trainee solicitor with the firm, acting on information from Mr Murray, again went to the burnt-out Transit van and retrieved three tapes, one of which contained recordings. Finally, on the penultimate day of this hearing, December 14th 2000, we received a witness statement from Mr John McVicar, a freelance journalist, who was until last month a columnist with Punch, exhibiting a third tape.

All three of these tapes appear to contain recordings of messages left on Mr Pell's answering machine, or recordings of one side of telephone conversations with Mr Pell, whose own contributions to the conversation have not been recorded or have been expunged. There are indications that other editing has taken place in that the recorded messages appear to be out of chronological order.

The first tape contains messages from both November 1999 and January 2000...'

In his judgement on behalf of the court, Phillips began: 'This application is about a load of rubbish.' He wasn't being ironical: the evidence not only came from rubbish most of it was rubbish.

Pell had stolen a tranche of case-related documents from Hamilton's QC, which he sold via Hollingsworth to Fayed for £10,000. The documents did not amount to much more than were disclosed to the Fayed camp in the run-up to the trial. Although Fayed intimated that he would pay another £10,000 for anything really valuable like the list of Hamilton's backers, nothing else was forthcoming. Pell, however, concluded that he had been robbed by Hollingsworth and Fayed, and decided that he would gain his revenge by exposing them to the newspapers and the courts, earning in the process £50,000. With a couple of cat's paws – Murray and McVicar – he put all this into the public domain and into the hands of Hamilton's solicitors. But this was the sum of it.

Phillips said that the court had to answer four questions:

(i)   Was Mr Al Fayed party to the purchase of documents protected by legal professional privilege which had been stolen from the dustbin of the chambers of Mr Hamilton's [then] counsel? If so:

(ii)   Is there a real danger that those documents gave Mr Al Fayed a procedural advantage at the trial to which his success in the action was attributable?

(iii)   Had the jury been aware of Mr Al Fayed's conduct, might this have had such an effect on his credibility and that of his witnesses that the jury would have found against him rather than in his favour?

(iv)   Has Mr Al Fayed's approach to this litigation had so serious an effect on the trial process that he should be disqualified from advancing a positive case?

Phillips said that the jury at the original trial considered two issues: whether Fayed paid Hamilton for asking parliamentary questions; and whether Hamilton sought payment from Mobil, the oil company, for moving a parliamentary amendment. The case against Hamilton regarding the second of these two issues relied entirely on evidence, said Phillips, 'which depended not at all upon what one can call the Al Fayed camp'. In addition, Phillips said the judge made a clear warning about the strength of Fayed's evidence in relation to the first issue. The judge, Justice Morland, had told the jury:

> You may have come to the conclusion that Mr Al Fayed's evidence in detail is inconsistent and unreliable, that he has made many wild and unsubstantiated allegations about all manner of people, and that at times he has been vindictive towards those whom he thinks have let him down or double-crossed him. You may have come to the conclusion that Mr Al Fayed's obsessional attitudes and beliefs have distorted his perception of truth...
>
> By his own admission, his recollection for detail and his memory of events is defective. His versions of events and occasions when he alleges payments were received from him by Mr Hamilton have varied and been markedly inconsistent one with another.
>
> All those matters mean, you may think, that Mr Al Fayed's appreciation of what is fact and what is fiction, and what is truth and what is falsity is warped.
>
> Therefore, I strongly advise you that it would be very dangerous to accept even those parts of Mr Al Fayed's evidence that you find credible, and indeed would be very unwise to do so, unless you are satisfied on evidence independent of Mr Al Fayed's evidence

which you find highly convincing and find confirms Mr Al Fayed's evidence in a material way.

Although confused, inconsistent and varying in detail, the main thrust of Mr Al Fayed's evidence was that Mr Hamilton received payments from him for his parliamentary activities. This is of course denied by Mr Hamilton.

If you find that main thrust of Mr Al Fayed's evidence credible, my strong advice to you is that you only act upon it if you are satisfied by highly convincing evidence, independent of Mr Al Fayed's evidence, which confirms that evidence of Mr Al Fayed.

Phillips said that the judge had crystallised the issues at the trial by a single question that he put to the jury: 'Are you satisfied, on the balance of probabilities, that Mr Al Fayed has established on highly convincing evidence that Mr Hamilton was corrupt in his practice as a member of Parliament?'

The jury answered, 'Yes' and so found for Fayed. Phillips said that in considering its answer to this single question, the judge had directed the jury to treat Fayed's evidence with great caution.

Turning to the quality of evidence for the Hamilton's appeal, Phillips made clear that the court was unimpressed.

We doubt whether a court has often, if ever, been invited to make a finding of misconduct equivalent to fraud on evidence as unsatisfactory as that placed before us. Much of Mr Murray's evidence consists of quadruple hearsay – what Mr Murray has said that Mr Pell told him that Mr Hollingsworth had told Mr Pell. Added to this are tape recordings, which are for the most part of uncertain provenance and heavily edited.

He went on to consider the answers, as shown by the evidence, to the four questions he posed, as set out above. To the first question, Phillips said: 'Evidence from all sources combine to drive us to the firm conclusion that Mr Benjamin Pell stole documents from the dustbin outside 5 Raymond Buildings.' He referred to a successful appeal by Express Newspapers against an order that it disclose the source of a document, concerning Elton John, that he said had probably been discarded as rubbish from barristers' chambers in what the court had thought of as a one-off infringement of professional legal confidentiality. However, Phillips said:

The evidence in this case suggests to us that this was more probably but one droplet in a particularly free-flowing source of Press information. It seems that it was Mr Pell's practice over a considerable period to scour the dustbins outside counsel's chambers and to attempt to sell the fruits of his labours to the Press.

On the balance of probability, we find that Mr Pell supplied to Mr Hollingsworth some of the documents that he had obtained from the dustbin outside 5 Raymond Buildings and that Mr Hollingsworth handed these to Mr Macnamara.

The court of appeal concluded that Hollingsworth took documents to the Fayed camp. It found the silence of Macnamara to be significant.

On Mr Al Fayed's own evidence, Mr Macnamara acted as his right-hand man, at least in relation to dealing with the Hamilton litigation. If the allegation that the privileged documents had been handed to Mr Macnamara is a complete fabrication, we can see no reason why Mr Macnamara has not provided evidence to that effect. We think it a legitimate, and indeed a powerful, inference from Mr Macnamara's silence that he is not in a position to rebut that allegation.

Phillips made some trenchant personal criticisms of Macnamara who as an ex-Detective Chief Superintendent of Scotland Yard had found it necessary to be in South Africa during the appeal. He continued:

The evidence has not satisfied us that Mr Al Fayed was present at the meeting where Mr Hollingsworth handed over the documents to Mr Macnamara.

We find, on balance of probability, that Mr Macnamara paid £10,000 for these documents. Pell and Hollingsworth agreed on this point. Mr Al Fayed gave evidence of other payments made to Mr Hollingsworth for other services, which appears to have been on a generous scale. It is entirely credible that he would have received some payment for providing documents from a source who would himself expect to be paid.

Mr Al Fayed, in his written and oral evidence, denied any involvement in or knowledge of payments being made for stolen documents. He also stated emphatically that Mr Macnamara had no general authority to make payments on his behalf. Mr Al Fayed was not an impressive witness... Whether or not Mr Al Fayed had expressly authorised this particular payment to Mr Hollingsworth, we are satisfied that in making that payment Mr Macnamara was acting on behalf of Mr Al Fayed and within the scope of his authority.

But the court accepted that Fayed did not initiate the theft of the documents. 'Documents from that dustbin were offered to his camp, and he was party to their purchase. The evidence suggests that the principal reason why Mr Al Fayed may have been interested in these documents was because they might indicate who it was who was funding Mr Hamilton's action. We in no way condone Mr Al Fayed's conduct, which was discreditable.'

So, the answer to the first question was yes. However, the answer to the second was no: 'We do not believe that he [Fayed] would have derived any significant benefit, by way of preparation for cross-examination, from sight of any documents that might have found their way into the dustbin of 5 Raymond Buildings, and from there into the hands of Mr Pell.

'The reality is that, whatever papers may been sold to Mr Macnamara by Mr Hollingsworth, there is no reason to believe that they will have given any significant procedural advantage to Mr Al Fayed.'

Turning to the third question, Phillips said: 'The judge gave the jury as strong a warning against giving credence to Mr Fayed's uncorroborated evidence as it is possible to imagine. We do not believe that evidence that he had been party to the purchase of the stolen documents would have done any harm to his credit. He had no credit. Indeed, the very case that Mr Al Fayed was seeking to establish was one that was damaging to his general credit, for it was that he had bribed a politician to behave corruptly. The jury might have thought that the purchase of the dustbin documents was on a par with such behaviour.'

Given these conclusions, Phillips said, the fourth question 'does not arise'. And with that, Hamilton's appeal was totally dismissed and his attempt to restore his reputation failed. Nonetheless, in the course of the case, the reputations of Fayed, his then security chief, freelance journalist, and binman, were trashed.

Pell was predictably astonished by the judgement, particularly the decision not to consider the fourth question about the impact of the effect of Fayed's actions on the trial process. He says[xix]: 'It was proved to the satisfaction of three judges of appeal that there had been, here, theft of information, that it had been passed on to Fayed. The only thing is, under English law, even if there's an abuse of process like this, it still doesn't affect the decision, which I think is outrageous.' However, Pell says that he did not think the documents helped Fayed secure the trial verdict in his favour[xx]. Nonetheless, for himself, he believed that he was lucky not to have been sent to prison.

After the appeal judgement, the remaining issue for Pell was payment by the *Mail on Sunday* for the story about Hamilton's documents. When McVicar asks him in January 2001, 11 months after its publication, whether Murray had secured an agreement with the newspaper that it would pay as promised, Pell replies[xxi]: 'Funny enough, I spoke to him only a moment ago. I spoke to him only an hour ago. And he's going to be meeting Wright [the editor].

'We'll get the money... Today's the first day back after Christmas, but he's of- of- of no doubt, they have to pay. So, he's not concerned at all... In fact, it's a good sign that his main concern today was how he wanted to get the money over to me. He wanted me to think of some sort of name I can make it out to, or something.'

Eventually payment was forthcoming. Murray said that the newspaper's reluctance was that it could not be seen to be paying someone who was so roundly condemned in an article it had just published previewing the documentary, which described him as a "dishevelled loner", eccentric and a thief[xxiii]. Of course, they are only the nice things they say about Benji the Binman.

References

i McVicar audio tape (recorded 30.12.00) MDRI.

ii McVicar audio tape (recorded 09.11.00) MDRY.

iii Paul Henderson, 'Al Fayed bought libel secrets,' *Mail on Sunday* (13.02.00).

iv Extract of Clifford-Pell telephone conversation, McVicar audio tape (recorded shortly after publication of *Mail on Sunday* story on 13.02.00) MDOO.

v McVicar video tape (filmed 14.01.01) DVRG.

vi McVicar video tape (filmed January 2001) DVRV.

vii Lord Phillips, 'Judgement as approved by the court: Mostyn Neil Hamilton-v-Mohammed Al Fayed,' (21.12.00).

viii McVicar video tape (filmed 14.01.01) DVRG.

ix McVicar video tape (filmed 24.01.01) DVOR.

x McVicar audio tape (recorded 30.12.00) MDRI.

xi McVicar video tape (filmed 14.01.01) DVRG.

xii McVicar audio tape (recorded 09.11.00) MDRY.

xiii McVicar video tape (filmed 08.02.01) DVOO.

xiv Paul Henderson, 'Police send Al Fayed file to CPS,' *Mail on Sunday* (03.12.00).

xv Mark Watts, 'Blow to Hamilton over appeal,' *Sunday Business* and *Scotland on Sunday* (10.12.00).

xvi Lord Phillips, 'Judgement as approved by the court: Mostyn Neil Hamilton-v-Mohammed Al Fayed,' (21.12.00).

xvii McVicar audio tape (recorded 09.11.00) MDRY.

xviii Lord Phillips, 'Judgement as approved by the court: Mostyn Neil Hamilton-v-Mohammed Al Fayed,' (21.12.00).

xix McVicar video tape (filmed 14.01.01) DVRG.

xx McVicar audio tape (recorded 09.11.00) MDRY.

xxi McVicar audio tape (recorded 03.01.01) MDOV.

xxii McVicar video tape (filmed 14.01.01) DVRG.

xxiii Claudia Joseph, 'How I tricked the Elton John judge into thinking that I was a real nutter,' *Mail on Sunday* (07.01.01).

Chapter 3

Benji and the Bins:
how it all began

Benjamin Gerald Pell was born on December 23rd 1963 at what was then called Bearsted Memorial Hospital in Stoke Newington, London[i]. He was born to orthodox Jewish parents living in Hendon, David Pell, then a wholesaler of travel goods, and his wife, Rita (née Hepner). David Pell was 34 and living in Clapton when he married Rita Hepner, a 23-year-old shorthand typist of Golders Green, in 1955 in Maida Vale[ii]. Pell, now 40, still lives with his parents, in a semi-detached house in Hendon.

His father escaped from Austria in 1939; his mother came to Britain with her family from Leipzig, Nazi Germany in 1938[iii]. Pell tells McVicar[iv]: 'They both left their respective countries just after the rise of Hitler; my father lived in Vienna, which was the heart of Naziism.' Pell says that his father initially escaped to Canada, and still has a Canadian passport, and then moved to Stamford Hill in London where he met Rita. Pell adds that only two relatives in his extended family were killed in the Holocaust. His father went from being a wholesaler of travel goods to work in property, but is now retired[v]. However, he still heads a family property company called Pula Investments, of which he is the lone director, and which he controls with his wife, who is its company secretary, and in which Benjamin and his three brothers each has an 11% stake[vi].

By his own account, Pell started out as a bright, but odd child. He says that he edited the school magazine when he was at primary school[vii]. And, he says, his first brush with the Sunday Express was when he was about seven or eight years old: he entered an essay competition, and was one of the top five entries. 'I've always had that bug, the writing bug... and the fact I could have some sort of input into the media.' He also had the legal bug. As a child, he says that he would sit in court rooms watching long, complicated cases[viii]; he was doing the same thing at least as recently as 2003.

Pell and his family were devastated when an older son, Daniel, died at the age of 21 in a road accident one Sabbath in 1977. Dany died soon after Pell's bar mitzvah. His loss was utterly traumatising for Pell. He says that having consistently come top of the class, he could no longer concentrate on school work following the loss of his brother.

Pell told Iain Jones, the Hollywood-based film-maker, that his father arranged for him to see a psychiatrist[ix]:

> When I was 16, he just thought I was going completely barmy. He just felt that, because my 'O' Level results weren't very good and, er, I hadn't performed very well in my first year in- at lower 6th, he just felt that something was going wrong in my life. My father, don't forget, comes from Vienna, and he studied Sigmund Freud all his life. So, he thinks everything can be resolved by seeing a psychiatrist.

Jones asked Pell why his father thought you had gone completely mad and he replied, 'Well, my brother died… My elder brother, his name was Daniel, and he was 21.' It was a road accident and Pell was 13… 'I happened a week after I had come out – not as a homosexual, but as a man… 13 is when you have your bar mitzvah… all Jews have that… I did admire him, he was very popular – with everyone.

'He was much more sociable than I or my other brothers have ever been. Basically, I wasn't the same thing ever again. Until then, I had always come top of everything. In my first year at school, I literally came top in all nine subjects – in the whole year of 127 pupils; and in the second year, I came top in only about two subjects. And ever since – after…after that event I became completely obsessional because, don't forget, this happened a week after what was supposed to have been, 'til then, my happiest day of my life. So, a week after the happiest day of my life, my brother gets killed.

So from then on, I always had to have much more than anyone else… If the teachers recommended buying two course books, I would have to buy all 20 of them. Anybody who told me to spend three hours preparing an essay, I would have to spend six hours preparing the essay. Everything I was asked to do, I would have to do double. It was a sort of way of compensating for the loss of my brother. It can't just be coincidence that, 'til then, I was a happy-go-lucky character who was just successful as a student and didn't have any problems at school.' In fact, his parents tell a slightly different story: Benji was a problem long before Daniel died.

Significantly, he told McVicar[x]:

I was always- from the first time I went to school, I was always the outsider. I would never- I've never had – still to this day, I don't have any real friends.'

Pell still has an older, and twin younger brothers. Asked what his older brother does, Pell says:

He's the vice-president of the Republic Bank of New York. But that doesn't mean anything 'cos the cleaner is the vice-president of banks in America. Still, a reasonably impressive position. He was an accountant in this country, but he went off to the States five years ago like my brother- younger brother is going off next week. I mean, basically, it seems that my parents have encouraged my brothers to leave the country. Not surprising when you see the way they treat me.

And his problems continued into university, where he studied law. Pell had decided on a career in law, having ruled out his initial choice: he had wanted to be a rabbi. Pell told the Channel 4 documentary[xi]:

I was a good student until I became obsessed with gambling and because... I was always alone at university; I hated making friends. Nobody liked me. Nobody ever used to speak to me and everything, so the only excitement I had in my life was actually the gambling, and so I got obsessed with it.

Pell told McVicar that he suffered from kleptomania while at university, the manifestations of which included shoplifting at Foyles, the bookshop[xii]. But he helped with the university magazine, saying[xiii]: 'I wrote Elton a letter, a fan letter, in 1985 'cos I wanted to interview him for the university magazine. And John Reid[Elton John's manager] never responded, and his punishment came 15 years later (see chapters 4 to 7).'

However, he says that his problems, particularly with gambling, led him to fail his degree. He told Jones[xiv]:

I was the black sheep of the family when I failed my degree. For the first year, when I failed my university degree... I obviously couldn't admit that to my parents, so I actually pretended to be going to the

Institute of Advanced Legal Studies in Russell Square. So, every day, I used to leave the house at half past nine with a big bag, come home at night with a big bag. And the big bag my parents assumed was full of law notes was actually just full of newspapers, which I was going to read on the Tube. And there were some days where I, literally, just drove, drove round and round on the Tube.

However, Pell was soon caught out with this lie.

My uncle, Leo Hepner, started getting suspicious. He had a good sixth sense. He realised that I was lying my arse off. He got a private investigator to follow me in 1986 and, I'll always remember this, November, it was about second week of November 1986, it was the same day as the Breeders' Cup... I overheard... a phone call to my father to Leo Hepner – he's a bachelor, mid-50s, horrible man, my m-my mother's brother, you can tell he's my mother's brother because he's a bastard – and I could overhear the conversation from this end, and my father said, 'What? He hasn't passed?' And not only that, I'd actually forged the certificate, to make matters worse, cos my father, cos of the Austrian compensation scheme, he was basically able to get all of his children money from the Austrians, 'cos he was in the Holocaust, you see. So, at the early part of July of that year, I had to prove that I was now doing this post-graduate course and, of course, cos I'd failed I wasn't able to do that, so I'd actually forged the documents to give to my father to pass on to the Austrian authorities. Can you imagine that November, he realised that I'd lied to him: I'd forged documents.

Pell told McVicar[xv]:

I had to re-do the exams. I knew I was going to fail, so I cheated in my exams. In '87, me, Benjamin Pell, who never thought... he would never steal a Tipp-Ex from somebody's desk, cheated in all his exams. I wrote all the answers down, cos with law, it's basically memory work. So I, literally, had pages and pages of notes, and I would never have done it had I still been a normal student. Walked into the exam room with about that much of notes, hidden of course under... cos you're allowed to take books and statute books into the exam room with you. And, cos funny enough, cos-cos I was right at the back, I was re-doing it, I thought the invigilators are never going to watch me anyway. And even if they did, who gives a fuck anyway? My life is all over; nobody's ever going to employ me anyway cos I've only got a third-class degree if I graduate. Cos if you re-do an exam, you can't get more than a third. So, I thought, 'Who gives a fuck?' So, I cheated in all the exams and passed, so I actually managed to graduate in '87.

He repeats that he lied to his parents about failing his degree and, in another interview with McVicar two years later[xvi], that he cheated in his re-takes

Pell, while complaining about lawyers with whom he had clashed, told the documentary[xvii]: 'I got the same education as they got. All the difference is...between me and them is that I messed up my exams and they didn't. That's all. And look at them now... so-called highly qualified lawyers... too stupid to appoint an office manager to look after the running of their business.'

The McVicar tapes provide an insight into Pell's relationship with people. While watching a preview of the Channel 4 documentary with him and the now dead comedy writer, Debbie Barham, Pell talks about his plans for the future, including a documentary series about him, but he is worried about Victor Lewis-Smith's commitment[xviii]. Pell commented:

He wants the fourteen-and-a-half minute-fame syndrome – he can then write about me, and say, 'What was Benjamin Pell doing a year ago. Where has Benjamin Pell disappeared to?' That's what he wants. He doesn't see long term. He's not a journalist like you and me. I mean, he's a columnist, there's a big difference. Debbie is a... What are you exactly?

She does not reply immediately, and Pell continued: 'Exactly – you don't even know.'

McVicar picked him up on his put-down, and Pell replied: 'No D-Debbie is good. No, that's just... that's just a gratuitously... that's just a gratuitous insult because I'm so self-conscious about my own incapability.' This, undoubtedly, explains much of Pell's behaviour towards others. He likes to claim superiority but when he is called he folds...especially when, as in the case of Barham, he doesn't have a hand that can compete.

He was later to ask McVicar if Debbie if would go out with him. Given that she was an extreme anexoric and looked like a holocaust victim, Pell toyed with the idea that two talented but dysfunctional people would make a go of it. When McVicar mentioned it to her, she replied: 'Fuck off. I write and sell jokes for a living but I couldn't give that one away. It ain't funny.'

With Pell's ambition to becoming a lawyer ended, in 1991 he found a job distributing brochures for a cleaning company, which led to a career as a cleaner

> Then, what I had to do, and I did for the next seven years, was deliver brochures for a cleaning company called Global Cleaning. And what I had to do was deliver the brochure, get a compliments slip with the name of the company on it, and keep a record and send that to them, so every compliments slip I got, I got 50 pence. And I got obsessive about that as well, because it was my aim to basically target every single company in London.
> I realised, as I was doing the rounds, that there were lots of companies moving all the time. And, just by chance, I happened to be walking down Southwark Street one day, and I noticed that outside one of the big firms of surveyors in that area, called EA Shaw, were six orange rubbish bags. And I- I don't know why I did it, because I didn't realise, because, of course, at that stage I hadn't become a cleaner, so I didn't actually know what people put into bags, and I just thought, that's a bit odd, you know, middle of the morning and they've got bags outside their building, I wonder what's in there.
> So I took one of them, went into a building called Tower Bridge House, to this day, I remember, took the lift up to the second floor, opened one of them, and within about five minutes I was discovering all of the transactions they were doing that week, all the deals which they were currently doing, and this was the leading firm of surveyors... in the London borough of Southwark.
> Within about two weeks, I was starting to do about ten of the largest firms of surveyors in the country, and I was being able to compile, for all of my friends in the cleaning industry, lists of people relocating."And that's how it really started. So I started off with EA Shaw, and then within about two years I was doing about 40 surveying companies.

Pell started all this in 1993. It led to him trading information with surveyors... 'I was dealing with about 25 good friends who are surveyors; I was dealing with about ten firms of estate agents. And, of course, I was actually known... at that stage I used to have an alias for the cleaning company, which was Paul Lewis, I had an alias for the, er, petitioning company, which was Andrew Beckett, Peter

Jeffrey was my alias for the, erm, property company, and John Langley, hence Langley Management Services [Pell's trading name].'

The reason for the aliases was that I was so ashamed to admit to anyone who knew me what I was doing, I just could not admit to having any associations with a cleaning company. Oh, I forgot to tell you one of my names, David Probert… And this is the list of all the companies, these were basically companies looking to move… All of these names emanated from the dustbins.

I was being paid… £250 a month to supply them with about 60 names a week, and then, in addition, they were giving me three per cent of any price which they were able to negotiate with a company who used their services for petitioning. So, it was very, very lucrative business – very lucrative.

I was dealing there with some of the top developers in the country. Who am I? I was phoning them up; they think I'm some sort of arsehole. They don't realise- I mean, they know the information is good, but because I have no name, because John Langley is a complete nobody, people didn't take me seriously. I needed, even in those days, in property, middle men… and do property transactions for me.

Pell talks about one particular middle man. '[He] was basically buying information off me. And he was meeting the clients directly, cos I can't meet clients directly; I couldn't because they wouldn't take me seriously. I mean, somebody dressed like me, with my mannerisms and everything, I'd probably put them off. And he was doing brilliantly, I mean he had a successful practice for three years, half-based on my information.

'After four or five years of going around collecting brochures, I was collecting compliments slips and everything, I told you I was beginning to get an affinity to what was happening in the… property industry. So, I was able to find out about companies moving offices a long time before they actually did so. So, I actually started to be able to provide a cleaning company… with a list of companies looking for cleaners. But they were so incompetent, like everyone I've ever dealt with in my life, it's always carried out with in- completely incompetent. Journalists were incompetent; doctors were incompetent; cameramen I've dealt with have been incompetent; basically I'm surrounded by incompetent people. This guy… (I ended up, of course, having to take him to court because he owed me so much money) he wasn't turning up at appointments… So, I was losing money on commission because this guy was too stupid to realise I was giving him brilliant information. And don't forget, already at that stage, I'd started going through people's rubbish as well, I mean, you know, surveyors' rubbish. So I started to get into cleaning places, by winning the contracts. Then, of course, who's incompetent at the next stage? The cleaners are incompetent; they don't turn up. So I ended up having to do the cleaning as well. So that's how I got into the cleaning business myself.'

The Channel 4 documentary reported[xx]: 'His nocturnal foraging started in 1991… he began plundering the bins of estate agents for personal information about their clients.'

While watching this, Pell corrects the commentary, saying[xxi]: 'Well, chartered surveyors rather than estate agents.'

Pell also tells McVicar how, after discovering the 'bin bag loophole', he sold information gathered from rubbish to a network of people in the property industry[xxii]. Thus, around the time that he turned his bin-raiding into a lucrative sideline, Pell also began using aliases and found his first use of the law. All these activities were to dominate his life for the next 15 years.

Pell told McVicar that he began after noticing that EA Shaw left rubbish bags outside its office during the day. He looked in the bags and found documents containing… 'Pretty useful information', he says. 'So, I started doing EA Shaw from them on. And then, I thought, let's do one or two other local firms. And then: everyone, I started doing everyone. By the end of that year, I was doing about 20 firms of surveyors: finding out from their details about who was moving, passing that information on… By the end of '92/'93, I was then passing on information to 25-30 surveyors. I was basically taking the rubbish from 20 surveyors and passing the information on to 25 other people, and getting money as a result. Then I had petitioning companies paying me for information. And so, basically, I was becoming obsessed, at the stage, with property… And that is a continuing obsession cos it's still happening. I'm still doing firms I've been doing for nine or ten years.'

He told McVicar that he still does estate agents… 'I still do- I still do them. Obviously, I don't do as many as I used to… I was giving [one company] information as well as going through his bins. And often I was giving him the information which he actually had from his own rubbish and he was paying me for his own information… So no, the property industry was about four or five years and I still do it… I'm now- now able to say to people, "Look, you've got to give me a retainer to do this because I haven't got time any more." So I've now- I've got a petitioning company paying me 250 quid a month just to give them names, you know, of people moving, which is fine.'

Pell even found hope for his aborted legal career in the rubbish. He told Jones[xxiii]:

'I was going through the rubbish… of a firm… [in] SW19. As it turns out, they have a sub-tenant… a firm of solicitors… I have actually, inadvertently, taken their rubbish bags by mistake… Being a kleptomaniac, I decided to look through it, just to see, I don't know why, what I could find. In that list, they had a CV, curriculum vitae, from this girl, whose name escapes me, and… in this part of her CV, she says, "I currently work for the legal practice committee of the Law Society in… south west London." And of course, I had her home number. I thought, "I'm desperate, I'm trying to get back onto this course, if she actually works for the College of Law, maybe she can help me." And she turned out to be the foot in the door which I needed. She was able to swing a few things for me, put in a few names, and within two years, I was back on the course… normally, there's a five-year waiting list to get on to the College of Law legal practice course.'

Pell summarised for Jones his operation: 'In the simplest terms, it means taking the bags from outside their building. But often it means much more than that; it actually means researching who to do… I don't just target everyone. I could target everyone and be here all day and doing just one Inn of Court. So, I've basically been targeting the major Inns of Court, the major firms of entertainment lawyers, the major of firms of music lawyers, and… for about a year, I have been targeting some of the major commercial lawyers as well. So… that's what it means, "doing" them. It means finding them. And then, of course, targeting entertainment PR consultants, people who are in the music industry, managers, promoters, concert artists, that sort of thing.' When he was asked if this is against his religion or whether it would hurt his parents, he replied[xxiv]: 'My father's never said he wanted me to be a rabbi.' But is this acceptable? 'It never comes up... It's not as though I'm selling pig's meat...Don't forget I've been doing this for ten years. For the last ten years, every time I go out with my parents and we drive past a bag, my father will invariably, not remembering he's told the joke hundreds of times before, "Benji, get out now, you can take those bags[xxv]."' One of Pell's few redeeming features is that he always tries to squeeze humour out of any situation.

Another defining characteristic of Pell is how his obsessiveness propels him into the small print of everything:

> I've always been interested in the minutiae side of anything to do with the music industry. I mean it's always been my one passion. And the way I got into this actually was- in fact, we should really go over to the offices in Baker Street of the tip sheets owned by Jonathan King, one of the biggest pop eccentrics in the world. And I wrote for their magazine under the alias of 'Peter Jeffrey' for a period of a year, and actually was in contact with Jonathan King, and was actually going through his rubbish for six months to try and get my way into his affections.[xxvi]

Pell was aware of King's predatory homosexuality but this did not affect his affection for the pop impresario who at the end of 2001 was sentenced to seven years for raping young men.

Pell used his cleaning business to expedite the marketing of his stolen documents. Once when filming Pell outside an office at night-time, Jones asked him what was going on. Pell told him that this was an office in Southwark... 'Somewhere where I go through my stuff, make 'phone calls. This is a very important spot. Course, they don't know that I'm in their cellars. This is probably the safest place in the whole of London to talk, I mean, any of my offices, cos there's no way they'd be bugging my offices. Normally, what I do is make a few 'phone calls from here as well...'

Jones asked: 'Phone calls about what?'

Pell: 'Well, just generally, 'phone people, no not business ones...

but generally, you know. I've got to 'phone people, I'd rather 'phone them from here than at home.'

Jones: 'So show me the... stuff.'

Pell: 'Well there's nothing to see... it's a boring office.'

Jones: 'But it's your office, is it?'

Pell: 'No! Course not.'

Jones: 'Oh, it's not. What is this place then?'

Pell: 'It's a company... we clean for.'

Outside another office at night-time, Pell told Jones:

They have a very nice kitchen here as well. They always have lovely food here. Oh, and it's not too hot. I'll just, er, switch the alarm off. Now you may ask how come I have the keys to so many of my cleaning clients? Well, obviously, I do that on the assumption that if the cleaner doesn't turn up, I can cover for them; but the real reason I do that is because I want to keep as many safe places throughout London as possible. I'll just show you through to the kitchen. Now, this is the fastest photocopier in London... Wonderful 'phones: I've made many trans-Atlantic 'phone calls from here. When I had my first ever interview, when I interviewed Barry Mann and Cynthia Weil, something which you have to hear about, and they thought I was some journalist from the *Musical Express*, all the phone calls were made from here. I've done some of my best work in this office. And, as you can see... it's a very clean office cos my cleaners do a very good job. I can have my breakfast here. I can have my tea here. I can have a coffee here. This [fridge] is always well stocked; have a bit of wine. Maybe we could drink to celebrate a successful evening. All the glasses are nicely here. So, we won't pour out too much in case they notice when they come in tomorrow.

Jones: 'How many of these places do you have around London?'

Pell: 'Safe houses? I have about 20 safe houses throughout London, plus I have another 50 people who I can actually hide stuff with, and that's not forgetting friends and family where I have had stuff safe. So, in other words, it would be a logistical nightmare for anyone to try and get stuff from me.'

Pell also tells how he delights in fooling staff at client companies where he cleans. Referring to a firm of architects in Waterloo, he says: 'They thought the cleaner was called Rose. They didn't realise that, for three years, their cleaner, Rose, was me. They didn't realise that every time on Christmas they were leaving me a £10 box, I was cursing them thinking, "Ten quid! I'm worth more than that!"

'And, of course, towards the end, when the cleaning got even worse than it was towards the beginning, [the firm's boss] rang me up, said, "Paul, I'm really sorry, but has Rose had a death in her family?"

'So, I said, "Why?"

'And he said, "Cos her cleaning has been totally disgraceful these last few weeks." I said, "Well, it's funny you should mention that. She's just lost, tragically, both her twin brothers in a car crash; it's tragic."

'He said, "Oh, I'm really sorry." … To this day, we still do that job. But what happened was… I couldn't do the job anymore, so I just gave it up. I told him by the way, I said Rose had gone to- back to the Caribbean. Now ever since then, he's had a different cleaner which is fine.'

'They used to leave me chocolates, and I used to leave them presents. "Dear Rose, thank you for the chocolates, you are very kind and generous," that's me. "Say hello to Chris," that was a made-up name of my son so-called, "Kind regards, Nigel."

'I also used to look through their diaries and everything. Can you imagine? I arrive in somebody's office in the middle of the night; [laughs] they don't have to be famous, I was just looking through everything. So, for example, [the boss's] wife had a birthday, I would leave him a note the night before, "Dear Jeffrey, please give your wife my best wishes, love Rose." He'd have thought it was a highly intelligent cleaner who just loves being nice. He didn't know, of course, it was me taking the piss out of him for three years. This is how I used to clean [laughs]. Well, they're only Pakistanis. They wouldn't notice anyway.'

Pell told McVicar the same story about how he responded when a client complained about the standard of cleaning[xxvii]. 'I said: "Really sorry… but she had a death in the family."

'"Oh, that explains it…"

'"Yeah, and he'd been ill for a few days before…"

'Left her a note that night, which obviously I get: "Dear Rose, heard from your boss, Paul, about the death in your family. Please, if you need to take some time off, please, it's okay, we can cover for you… anything you need, our thoughts are with you." And, for the next year-and-a-half, I was able to get away with murder.'

He told Jones[xxviii]: 'In the early part of 1994, I was actually a very aggressive, cleaning contract developer.' Then, as the camera was rolling the telephone rang, which Pell answered. It was a journalist trying to buy a story, which Pell told him he'd already sold.

He said to Jones:

You have to be quicker than that. You see? We haven't got have enough time in the day to be polite to people, as you can see from this letter. I used to go round a building in Vauxhall… unfortunately, I was rather aggressive in my methods. I was trying to get a rebellion against the landlords. I wanted all the tenants to kick out the landlords, and replace them with my company. Hence the following letter, 'Re: security at 68 to 70 South Lambeth Road. It has come to my attention that a certain character,' even then I had character, 'has been allowed access to 68 and 70 South Lambeth Road. This gentleman, who has so far gone by the name of both Mr Lewis and Mr Williams, purports to know the management company. He freely quotes information from internal documents, 'cos, of course, I was going through their rubbish, that's where I got this letter. 'I am led to believe that this person is after cleaning contracts within the building...' Ooh, what a crime that is… So, here we have a cleaning developer who's being criticised for wanting contracts. 'However, he dishonestly claims to have established existing contracts within the building. This is simply not the case. I would be extremely grateful if this person causes any further menace,' and I love the following phrase, 'you should pander to him.' See that's the lesson which the rest of the world should have learnt, pander to Benjamin, whatever the fuck that means, '...pander to him for a contact name, meanwhile, get another member of staff to urgently contact the police.'

Pell says that some of his cleaning clients are prestigious, such as the National Association of Schoolmasters, Union of Women Teachers, the teachers' union, and that he was earning many thousands of pounds. 'My cleaning company's still owed about 40 grand, which I'm still chasing up.'

Pell also hates losing business. Referring to one client, he said: 'When he gave my cleaner the sack… I threatened to blow up his bloody building.

'And when I left saying, "You bastard, I'm going to blow up your office building." He had to call the police.

'I'm so cuntish. If somebody falls out with my cleaners or falls out with me, they will suffer.'

For self-proclaimed physical cowardice, Pell undoubtedly has a vindictive, malicious streak towards anyone whom he thinks has crossed him.

As for being homosexual, he is more likely to be repressed heterosexual. McVicar wrote in an article published in Punch of his first telephone conversation with Pell[xxix]: 'Over the phone, his piping voice and fussy diction confirmed it – a mummy's boy. He is Jewish, homosexual and lives with his mother.'

Pell denies that he is gay.

Jones asked him[xxx] if he had ever had a girlfriend and he replied: 'No. But I've never had a male friend either. I've never had a friend.'

Jones: 'Have you ever kissed a girl?'

Pell: 'No.' And at that, Pell laughs in his manic cackle that invariably showers anyone facing him with spittle. Yet, for all Pell's affected homosexuality, which took McVicar in at the beginning of their association, the latter now thinks that he was tricked:

> With Pell, nothing is as he says it is. He can be truthful, but he is *never* truthful for its own sake. Just as there is always a reason for telling the truth, there is always a reason for lying. If the reason for lying is a better one than telling the truth, he lies. Pell is as simple as that.
>
> The key to Pell is that he believes he is a star but the world never gave him a fair shake. Thus everyone who isn't prepared to correct that injustice is up for grabs, is fair game...even members of his own family.
>
> To get Pell, understand him, you have to look what he does and, as there is a pattern to the lying, at what he says over time. As regards women, for example, I have seen him utterly intoxicated with the notion that some women like Anne Pounds, Debbie Barnham, my wife Valentina would see the star in him and love him for it.
>
> When they don't, he turns into a malevolent, spitting viper. He can be vicious about men but never as vicious as he is with women, whom in his own head have not recognised his genius and loved him for it.

When I first spoke to Pell, he affected being gay because he wanted to distract me from the other big lie he was telling me at that time, that he was a hacker not a binman[xxxi].

McVicar has his own axe to grind in respect of Pell because of the way Pell has attempted to damage his marriage, nonetheless he probably has more than a point in his take on Pell's' character.

References

i Birth certificate for Benjamin Pell.

ii Marriage certificate for David Pell and Rita Hepner.

iii David Pell witness statement, Benjamin Pell -v- Express Newspapers and Mark Watts (25.04.03).

iv McVicar audio tape (recorded 03.01.01) MDOV.

v David Pell witness statement, Benjamin Pell -v- Express Newspapers and Mark Watts (25.04.03).

vi Annual return for Pula Investments (06.08.01).

vii McVicar video tape (filmed January 2001) DVRV.

viii McVicar video tape (filmed 24.01.01) DVOR.

ix "3½-hour rushes," Moving Perspective (filmed 1999).

x McVicar audio tape (recorded 03.01.01) MDOV.

xi 'Scandal in the Bins,' Channel 4 (first shown 11.01.01).

xii McVicar video tape (filmed January 2001) DVRV.

xiii McVicar video tape (filmed 24.01.01) DVOR.

xiv "3½-hour rushes," Moving Perspective (filmed 1999).

xv McVicar audio tape (recorded 1999) MDRV.

xvi McVicar audio tape (recorded 03.01.01) MDOV.

xvii 'Scandal in the Bins,' Channel 4 (first shown 11.01.01).

xviii McVicar audio tape (recorded 12.11.00) MDRG.

xix "3½-hour rushes," Moving Perspective (filmed 1999).

xx 'Scandal in the Bins,' Channel 4 (first shown 11.01.01).

xxi McVicar audio tape (recorded 12.11.00) MDRG.

xxii McVicar audio tape (recorded 1999) MDRV.

xxiii "3½-hour rushes," Moving Perspective (filmed 1999).

xxiv Frances Welch, 'Rubbish is fine – except on the Sabbath,' Sunday Telegraph (04.02.01).

xxv McVicar video tape (filmed January 2001) DVRV.

xxvi "3½-hour rushes," Moving Perspective (filmed 1999).

xxvii McVicar video tape (filmed 21.01.01) DVRI.

xxviii "3½-hour rushes," Moving Perspective (filmed 1999).

xxix John McVicar, 'HACKING OFF THE MUSIC BUSINESS: ALL THESE STARS ARE BEING TARGETED BY ONE MAN. Who'll be the next victim on the hit list of Benjamin Pell?' Punch (01-13.08.98).

xxx "3½-hour rushes," Moving Perspective (filmed 1999).

xxxi telephone calle to McVicar 13.7.04

Chapter 4

The Queen of Rock: Sir Elton John

When Sir Elton John's long-time manager, John Reid, moved to a new office in Hammersmith, west London, little did he know the disaster that was set to unfold. A property industry specialist who was familiar with the music manager's company, John Reid Enterprises (JRE), was a friend of Pell's. And this accidental link led Pell from raiding surveyors' bins for clients in the property industry into the world of show business; it triggered acute embarrassment for Elton John, now aged 56, and sealed the end of Reid's relationship with the singer, breaking up one of the most enduring and, for Reid, lucrative partnerships of the pop industry.

Iain Jones filmed Pell outside the office in Hammersmith that was once home to JRE explaining how he targeted Elton John.

> So, this is where it all started. Diana died in August [1997]. A friend of mine…who happens to be an estate agent… knew I was an Elton John fanatic. He told me just after Diana's death, 'Benjamin, it's all very well going through the rubbish of surveyors, estate agents etc; why don't you go find- try going through Elton John's rubbish?'
>
> I said: 'What d'you mean, go through El- I couldn't go all the way to Windsor [where the singer has a mansion] to go through Elton's rubbish… I don't want to get bitten by dogs or- or by him, you know, he's a buggerer.'
>
> He said: 'No, no, no. John Reid's got an office… at 32 Galena Road in Hammersmith in 1996.'

Although Elton John was the most important client of John Reid Enterprises, the company also managed other stars, including Michael Flatley of Riverdance fame and Andrew Lloyd Webber, the musical composer.

All around the world, Princess Diana's death was a cataclysmic event for nutters and Pell was no exception. He told McVicar[ii]:

The day of Diana's death was quite a revolutionary day in my life…
And I've always been a bit of an Elton John fan, but never more than
that. Anyway, basically, Elton John, in one of his 1980's albums…
predicted Diana's death to the minute, and I tried selling this to the
newspapers. He talked about somebody dying in Paris, a 'rose', at
four o'clock… I tried getting it into the papers, and everyone ignored
me. From then on, I started targeting the rubbish. [For about a year
he had been trawling the rubbish of the PLO (see chapter 12), which
had an office across the road from Reid's new premises and a friend's
suggestion began doing Elton John's manager.] In those days, all I
did was financial companies, removal companies, I used to do office-
related companies for my own property business[iii]. So, I went along
there that week, and I thought, 'No, nothing here. Nothing here.' So,
I 'phoned up [his friend] and said, 'No, there's nothing here.'
He said, 'No, no… I know where the rubbish is kept. It's kept
behind…' No, listen to this, this is the whole joke of course, cos when
I was in court of course in February of [1998], I had to say under oath
where the rubbish was. And I lied of course; because I actually got
the rubbish… I had to open up a cupboard to get the rubbish. I actually
said…which, I suppose, is trespass. I actually said on oath that the
rubbish was left in front of the building, which wasn't true.'

Pell regularly committed perjury over his dealings with Elton
John's rubbish. But Pell's trawls at JRE proved highly effective. He
says[iv]: 'Within a week or two, you were getting amazing things. I was
already getting bank account statements from Elton: those were from
day one. Then, within about a month, I got that letter from Branson
to John Reid and the letter from John Reid back, you know, about the
Diana thing. So, I thought, "Fucking hell, this is amazing." And,
being Benjamin Pell, I sent it to about 100 people; all my friends got
it; I sent it to GLR radio, on which I used to appear every morning.'

He had found copies of confidential correspondence between
Reid and Sir Richard Branson, 53, the tycoon who was owner of V2
Records that released the Diana Tribute Album, which featured tracks
from a range of artists. Branson wanted to include on the album Elton
John's re-worked song, 'Candle in the Wind', which the singer
performed at Princess Diana's funeral in Westminster Abbey.
Branson was upset when the singer released it as a single. The album
and single raised money for the Diana, Princess of Wales Memorial

Fund. However, Branson felt that releasing the single would damage sales of the album and cost Princess Diana's favourite charities millions of pounds, although events proved that the separate releases were very successful, raising tens of millions of pounds and more than double the original target.

As Pell told the Channel 4 documentary[v]: 'Within about two weeks, I'd already found *the letter*, the letter from Richard Branson to John Reid saying, you know, "Please can you allow 'Candle in the Wind' to be on the album?" and John Reid writing back... to Richard Branson saying: "I've been asked by Elton John to tell you to fuck off."'

Back at the office in Hammersmith, in full megalomania he told Jones[vi]: 'These are the famous gates that I opened; and these gates literally contained all the treasures sitting behind them. These were the gates which opened up the treasure trove of Elton John's bank accounts, his statements going back five years, everything about his AIDS charity, the letters from Richard Branson to John Reid asking him permission to include "Candle in the Wind" on his Diana tribute album, the letter back from John Reid to Richard Branson saying, "I'd like to tell you please to piss off, don't hassle me again." All of that stuff is literally from here.'

Pell rang up Ally Ross on *The Sun*, who, at that stage, was one of the two journalists who worked for 'Bizarre' [showbiz column]. In those days, 'Bizarre' was actually edited by Andrew Coulson, who [became] deputy editor of *The Sun*... 'I rang Andy Coulson on his home mobile. How did I have his home mobile number? Because one of my clients, Absolutely Productions [a television production company], who I cleaned for... who we still clean for, I had a whole list of all the 'phone numbers of all the people in the place. So I was able to contact the Press, but I'd never done it before in my life. Rang up Andrew Coulson on his mobile.

'He said: "Why don't give my Ally Ross a ring at *The Sun*."

'I rang up Ally Ross. I said, "I'm Jeremy Kennedy." And my name since then has always stuck. If you ever hear Ally Ross leaving me a message, he always leaves a message for a "Jeremy", he still calls me "Jeremy Kennedy".

'"Jeremy Kennedy – I'm Jeremy Kennedy. I own a second-hand record shop in Willesden High Road. Somebody's just walked in... with some letters from Richard Branson to John Reid, and from Elton John to Richard Branson. I don't know whether you'll be interested in them cos I think they're very funny."

'He said, "Well, can you fax them over to me?" So I faxed them over to him, this is on... Monday January 12th, and he got back to me immediately, within a minute, I think, of me faxing them.

'He said, "And who, exactly, are you?"

'I said, "I'm Jeremy Kennedy." I mean, I knew the stories were valuable; but I didn't realise, of course, at that stage, how valuable they were.

'He said, "Yes, I think we would be interested in this story."

'When he got back to me – just to show you how these people in Fleet Street lie – I said to him... "Is the Elton John story worth money?"

'He said: *"I think I could just about get you a four-figure sum for that story."*

Famous last words. I mean that story was worth at least £50,000.

Anyway, so he's now got these documents. I'm thinking to myself, 'Shit, he said these are worth a four-figure sum.' I can see now, I wasn't stupid, because I'd never dealt... with Fleet Street before; I just didn't know what to do. Suddenly, I had this brainwave, and I rang up Max Clifford... rang him up that afternoon and I told him, basically, I've given this story to *The Sun* and whatever.

Pell told a similar story to the Channel 4 documentary team. 'All of a sudden,' he says[vii], 'I've had this brainwave – **Max Clifford**. You know, this is the sort of thing where maybe...no, he's not going to be in the 'phone book, is he? So...but let's have a look, just in case. And, of course, he's in the 'phone box because Clifford, more than anyone, needs idiots like me to ring him up.'

Pell told Jones[viii]:

He said, 'Well it's a bit too late now, I'll get a hold of *The Mirror*.' He told me half an hour later, 'I've spoken to the editor of the *News of the World* [then Phil Hall]. If you would have given this story to the *News of the World*, left it for a Sunday newspaper-' I mean Max Clifford, he taught me my first ever lesson in the journalism industry.

He said the Sunday papers will pay much more than the daily papers. The Sunday papers are waiting for big exclusives, while the dailies can rely on the daily news. Anyway, he said to me, 'You've just lost yourself, Benjamin Pell, £20,000 because basically *The Sun* aren't going to give you anything anyway – more than about £1,000. *The Mirror* would have loved it exclusively; cos you can't give it to them exclusively, they'll offer you £3,000 for their first edition.'

Clifford said on the Channel 4 documentary[ix]: 'Benjamin, like a lot of other people, came to me, initially, to try and help him through the media minefield. Benjamin is- is no ordinary person by anybody's stretch of the imagination...

In January 1998, the story broke[x]. *The Mirror* (which has since been returned to its name of the *Daily Mirror*) reported on its front page:

Elton John and Richard Branson were involved in an astonishingly bitter row over the Diana tribute song 'Candle in the Wind'. Sensational letters between the duo, leaked to *The Mirror*, reveal how they clashed angrily over the best way to celebrate Diana's life musically after she died. Virgin boss Branson claimed the singer's decision to release the song as a single and not include it on the all-star Diana Tribute Album would harm sales and cost her memorial fund millions.

[The story, continued inside the newspaper, quoted Branson's letter of the previous November to Elton John.] He started by saying: 'I have always liked and admired you. However, since these sentiments are in danger of being lost, I felt it important to write to you.' He said he was writing in his capacity as chairman of the record industry's efforts on behalf of the Princess Diana Foundation to raise as much money as possible for her charities. Branson carefully explained the background of a possible musical memorial, which he hoped would have Elton's song at its heart. He said of the 'Candle In The Wind' single: 'I knew that the decision would cost Diana's charities tens of millions of pounds because, instead of The Fund being guaranteed the biggest-selling album in history, it would just be the single. I could see your motives for doing so, but they saddened us. Later that day, I rang you at home and was told by an embarrassed girl that you were "busy". I'm beginning to see a different side of you, and that saddens me too.'

'Almost every major artist in the world has given up time and energy to make sure this album is the best ever released. You personally pledged the track for the album.' He added: 'Are you really going to go back on that, knowing the damage it will do?' In hindsight, Branson's forecast was wrong. His letter to Elton continued: 'Right now the world thinks the world of you. Please don't let them down.'

Elton was furious when he read Branson's three-page letter and ordered manager Reid to send back a firm reply, copies of which were sent to Earl Spencer and Diana's sister, Lady Sarah McCorquodale.

Reid insisted there had been no discussion about a tribute album. He said he had told record bosses and the Memorial Fund that it wasn't fair to put the song on the album because 'it would be asking people to buy it twice.' Reid also pointed out the album had already been completed when Branson wrote. He added: 'The fact that the recording of Candle In The Wind '97 has resulted in an unprecedented sale of over 32 million copies, I think is a tribute to Elton's ability to channel the focus of grief around the world for this most unfortunate event. For you to question his integrity and motives and indeed behaviour throughout this time is uncalled for.' Reid signed off the reply to Branson by adding: 'The implied threats in your letter are extremely distasteful, and I would caution you to be wise about anything you might wish to say in the future.'

Branson claimed in his letter that he arranged for Elton John to sing 'Candle in the Wind' at Princess Diana's funeral in Westminster Abbey. 'We drew up a shortlist of artists and songs that we felt would be good for the album and for the service. The first on the list was yourself and we felt that "Candle In The Wind" would be perfect. I 'phoned John Reid, and he suggested I speak directly with you. I asked if you'd like to perform at Westminster Abbey. Over the next 48 hours, I and my colleague Stephen Abbott [head of Branson's V2 record company] put everything else aside to try to arrange for you to play at the Abbey. Initially we had to persuade the choirmaster, then the Dean, then the Spencer family, then, with the help of Tony Blair, the Royal Family. During that process I asked if you could arrange a rewrite of the song since the family was not happy with the words "hounded by the press".'

Elton John, however, said that Lady Sarah McCorquodale asked him to sing at the funeral.

A spokesman for Branson tried to dismiss the significance of the tetchy correspondence, and was quoted in *The Mirror* as saying they were 'very old letters'.

But, despite the characteristic Branson spin effort, as Pell told Jones[xi]: 'That was basically the beginning of the end for Elton John's manager, John Reid. Cute story, I mean, involving some of the biggest names in the world: Diana, Elton John, Richard Branson... *The Mirror* did a bloody good job. I mean, they re-printed my letters in full. So, here, you have the letter from John Reid Enterprises Limited to Richard Branson, as you can see there from the date, 6th November 1997; I started second week of November.

'In open, they were saying about each other, "We've never had any arguments," etc, etc. But I was told by... everyone I knew in the press that he was absolutely furious.

'He thought that John Reid deliberately leaked this correspondence to embarrass him; well, obviously, Branson looked like a complete fool in it as well. Nobody came out of this looking good – apart from Diana, and she's dead.'

The leak mystified Reid, who wondered, wrongly, whether Branson was responsible. Reid told the Channel 4 documentary[xii]: 'There was a- a letter that had- that I'd written to Richard Branson. I wrote a very strong letter, which turned up in the *Daily Mirror*. It was very odd, and at the time I didn't know where it had come from. I wasn't sure whether Branson had leaked it or... somebody had leaked it.'

Asked whether he pursued the leak, he said: 'I can't remember the sequence because I've been chasing them[Fleet Street] all for years, but, yeah, I did chase them up about it. And they said it was dead and they wouldn't reveal their sources, as usual. And I didn't really think any more about it. It kind of went away, and you get used to these things from time to time. But they'd printed it [the letter] in full. It was, you know- it was an odd thing to do.'

But Pell soon found even more in Reid's rubbish about Elton John. Clifford told the documentary: 'I broke one story and it was obviously- checked out and stood up. And then he came to me with another story, which- the same thing.'

As Pell watched a preview of the documentary, he said of Clifford[xiii]: "He's so arrogant. I hate that man, and he thinks I like him, that is the weird thing. He thinks I like him.'

Pell explained on the documentary[xiv]: 'I walk into Max's office...

with about 30 black plastic bags… Came into his office… met two guys from *The Mirror*, and we went through all of the stuff together. I had some fuckers of stories. I had stories about shagging. Because he [Reid] does Michael Flatley as well. I had a great Michael Flatley shagging story. I had at least 20 great stories from that office, but the one brilliant story which anybody… a blind man could have noticed, was *the letter*.

> This was the letter, basically, which changed my life. It was a very, very recent letter. 'We have a serious cash-flow problem. We are running out of money. If you don't get this sorted out soon, John Reid, your whole business empire is going to collapse.' It's a huge story. Elton John's then accountants, Price Waterhouse, had written the document.
>
> Anyway, we were sitting there, you know, me and The Mirror and stuff, we were looking at it, and they were saying to me, 'It can't- it can't be the case. It can't be the case. You know, you… cannot be happening – somebody like Elton cannot be in financial trouble. I mean, John Reid cannot be, he's a multi-millionaire. Elton John is…'
>
> 'But look at- look at the evidence.'
>
> 'But what do you mean, "look at the evidence?"'
>
> 'I've got other stuff as well.'
>
> 'What do you mean, "You've got other stuff?"'
>
> I said: 'I've got his bank accounts.'
>
> They said: 'Fucking hell! You've got all his bank account statements?'
>
> I said: 'Yes, of course. I've got more at home as well.'
>
> Then they were able to get the connection between Elton John spending all his money and John Reid going belly up. The 26th of January, front page: 'Elton John in cash crisis.' I was gazumped there… because the fucking Queen Mother had to break her hip the-the same evening, so in the second and third editions I was only a bubble on the front page. But inside it, I had three pages.

As Pell says, his story lost its splash slot in later editions after it emerged that the late Queen Mother had broken her hip[xv].

The rabbi at his synagogue was appalled by what Pell said on the programme, this part especially. Pell recalled[xvi]: 'Rabbi David said, "Benjamin, you're a disgrace, the language you use, the Queen Mother's a personal friend of mine."' The rabbi only decided against expelling him from the synagogue, says Pell, because the video showed him observing Jewish orthodoxy in making a blessing before drinking from a glass.

The Mirror splashed[xvii]:

An amazing insight into the spending habits of superstar Elton John is given by The Mirror today, as his business empire faces a cash-flow crisis.

A senior member of his circle has revealed that accountants have written to his management team, warning that his companies are running out of funds.

The source also told in detail of the singer's massive shopping sprees – one of which produced a bill of more than £500,000 in a day. Elton's monthly credit card bill is usually about £250,000 and he once paid off £1m in eight days after a particularly lavish spell.

The reference in *The Mirror* to 'a senior member of [Elton's] circle' was of course a red herring: the source was none other than Reid's trusty dustbin as revealed by, as the *Mirror* well knew, Benji the Binman.

The report continued:

When the singing legend is home in England, his love of fresh flowers has two florists preparing 240 arrangements a week for his houses in Windsor and London.

The Elton source was so worried by his extravagance that he provided an in-depth rundown on the Rocket Man's soaring expenditure.

He said, 'For shopping, Elton prefers a Bentley – he has them in black, blue, silver and azure – because there's plenty of room in the boot for his bags.

'Before he makes the 25-minute journey into London, an aide telephones his planned destinations to alert them that Elton will be calling.

'It's all hands on deck when Elton arrives in your store.'

The source who spilled the beans on Elton's spending described the day he got through half a million – £527,849 to be precise.

'It was amazing, even by Elton's standards,' he said.

'First, he paid two sums to Sotheby's auction house – one for £43,125, the other for £59,743.

'He then had another splurge at Christie's and forked out £174,981 on various items.

'But he still hadn't finished. Later in the day, he paid his favourite interior designers Fred Dilger and Monique Gibson £250,000 for work they were doing for him.'

The source added: 'It was a truly staggering amount to spend in one day and typical of the way he likes to do business.

'But for Elton, when the going gets tough, the tough go shopping – and he loves every second of it.

'That kind of money is a drop in the ocean for him.

'He has admitted before that it's an addiction, that's just his personality.

'Thankfully, it's not a destructive addiction like his drink and drugs problems. It gives him a great deal of pleasure.'

[The report continued] The source disclosed how Elton ran up a £38,000 florist's bill in a month from New York's exclusive Bloomingdale's.

'Elton loves fresh flowers around him at all times,' said the source. 'He has had a fascination with flowers since he was a boy. It makes him feel happy just looking at them.'

For a dustbin, the source was remarkably lucid!

The Mirror quoted from the letter sent to Andrew Haydon, then managing director of JRE, by the accountants: "As you know the latest cash-flow projections show available headroom running out by substantial sums by April of this year.

"As a matter of urgency, during the course of this month we need to consider means by which this anticipated shortfall can be filled."

Reid said[xviii]: 'Well, Elton went ballistic – quite rightly. It turned out that Max Clifford brokered this story. I remember having a conversation with my lawyers and the people that worked for me, and saying that this kind of stuff could cost me my relationship with Elton, and ultimately it did.'

And with management fees from Elton John of around £5m a year under threat, and with a 26-year business relationship set to crumble, Reid was determined to identify the source. This was going to be difficult because *The Mirror* regarded the source of its story about Elton John as confidential, and so felt duty bound not to disclose any details that might help identify the source or sources.

The golden rule of journalism is protect your sources. Journalists' right not to disclose confidential sources is recognised in law as a fundamental tenet of a free Press and of a true democracy. British journalists have the limited protection of section 10 of the Contempt of Court Act 1981, but, much more important is article 10 of the European Convention on Human Rights.

This article concerns freedom of expression, and the European Court of Human Rights has interpreted it as meaning that a journalist must have the legal right to refuse to disclose confidential sources. The law was tested by Bill Goodwin, when he was a journalist on *The Engineer*, a specialist business magazine. After receiving confidential company documents, the company concerned asked the High Court to order the journalist to identify his confidential source or sources, claiming that the information was needed to find out who had allegedly committed a crime by leaking the information. Despite the Contempt of Court Act, the company succeeded in its application. In line with the codes of conduct of both the Press Complaints Commission and the National Union of Journalists regarding the protection of confidential sources, Goodwin refused to comply with the order and was fined £10,000.

He appealed, ultimately to the European Court of Human Rights, represented by the specialist media barrister, Geoffrey Robertson QC. In a landmark decision for Press freedom, the European Court of Human Rights overturned the British ruling, which showed that UK law provided inadequate protection for journalists and their sources.

Nonetheless, Reid succeeded in finding out who provided the information for the story about Elton John in *The Mirror*...

References

i "3½-hour rushes," Moving Perspective (filmed 1999).

ii McVicar audio tape (recorded 04.10.98) MDRO.

iii McVicar audio tape (recorded 1999) MDRV.

iv McVicar audio tape (recorded 04.10.98) MDRO.

v 'Scandal in the Bins,' Channel 4 (first shown 11.01.01).

vi "3½-hour rushes," Moving Perspective (filmed 1999).

vii 'Scandal in the Bins,' Channel 4 (first shown 11.01.01).

viii "3½-hour rushes," Moving Perspective (filmed 1999).

ix 'Scandal in the Bins,' Channel 4 (first shown 11.01.01).

x Richard Wallace, 'BRANSON'S FEUD WITH ELTON OVER DIANA, ELTON JOHN AND RICHARD BRANSON IN ROW OVER PRINCESS DIANA RECORD,' 'BRANSON: I'M BEGINNING TO SEE A DIFFERENT SIDE OF YOU. RIGHT NOW THE WORLD THINKS THE WORLD OF YOU. PLEASE DON'T LET THEM DOWN. ELTON: THE IMPLIED THREATS IN YOUR LETTER ARE EXTREMELY DISTASTEFUL, I WOULD CAUTION YOU TO BE WISE ABOUT ANYTHING YOU MIGHT SAY. *MIRROR* REVEALS WAR OF WORDS BETWEEN ELTON JOHN AND RICHARD BRANSON,' 'BRANSON: I WAS SECRET MR FIXIT BEHIND ELTON'S FUNERAL SONG TO DIANA. ROW OVER ELTON JOHN'S PERFORMANCE AT FUNERAL OF PRINCESS DIANA,' *The Mirror* (14.01.98).

xi "3½-hour rushes," Moving Perspective (filmed 1999).

xii 'Scandal in the Bins,' Channel 4 (first shown 11.01.01).

xiii McVicar audio tape (recorded 12.11.00) MDRG.

xiv 'Scandal in the Bins,' Channel 4 (first shown 11.01.01).

xv Gerard Couzens And John Todd, 'QUEEN MUM BREAKS HER HIP IN FALL,' *The Mirror* (26.01.98).

xvi McVicar video tape (filmed 24.01.01) DVOR.

xvii Clinton Manning And Graham Brough, 'ELTON'S EMPIRE IN CASH CRISIS. ACCOUNTANTS TELL SHOPAHOLIC STAR: MAKE MORE MONEY. ELTON JOHN FACES FINANCIAL RUIN,' '£527,849 IN 1 DAY – WHAT ELTON SPENT ON AMAZING SHOPPING SPREE, ELTON JOHN'S BUSINESS EMPIRE FACES CASH FLOW CRISIS,' *The Mirror* (26.01.98)

xviii 'Scandal in the Bins,' Channel 4 (first shown 11.01.01).

Chapter 5

Don't Go Breaking My Heart...
the split

The Mirror and Max Clifford were at the centre of legal action in the wake of the newspaper's articles about Elton John's financial crisis. The singer's manager, John Reid, took legal action against them to try to unearth the source.

Reid later told the High Court, in a case brought by Elton John against his former accountants and Andrew Haydon, by then the ex-managing director of John Reid Enterprises (JRE), that the star suspected his management company of the leak. Reid and Elton John, who declared in 1976 that he was bisexual and in 1992 that he was gay, were lovers for five years in the 1970's. Reid told the court[i]:

> I was in New York, and Elton 'phoned me at 7am, and he was incandescent with rage. He thought someone from JRE had sold the information to the newspaper and told me in no uncertain terms to find out how it had happened.
>
> I arranged for a firm of private investigators to see how this could have happened. I was very angry about it too... and for a couple of weeks there was a terrible tension between myself and Elton, and within the office structure because everyone was under suspicion of having somehow leaked this letter to the press.
>
> Elton started to become a bit frosty with me and I could sense things were not right, and I tried to put that right by finding out about the letter, but we really didn't get any satisfactory answers until much later.

Reid told the court that, in February 1998, his mother died while he was in Los Angeles. 'I came back to England, and Elton came back on the same flight in order to go to Buckingham Palace to be knighted,' he said. 'He didn't invite me to go with him, which upset me.' They then flew to Australia to start a tour. Reid continued,

'Things by this time were really frosty, and I had heard that Elton had been asking if people thought I was dishonest.' For Reid, 1998 truly was his annus horribilis. He explained:

> I went to his suite and asked him if he had been asking people if they thought I was dishonest, and he said no, he didn't think I was dishonest, but he was concerned about where all his money was going, and he had appointed KPMG [an accountancy firm] to do an audit.
>
> I said, 'In that case, I will go back to England to ensure that everything that should be done was being done.'
>
> That was the last time I spoke to him. That day was March 18th

Soon after, Elton John fired Reid, alleging that the audit showed he had lost millions of pounds because of financial disarray at his management company. For Reid, it was devastating. He had lost his biggest client, on top of losing Michael Flatley, the Riverdance star, as a client the previous year.

Reid told the court:

> At the time I knew I was fired, I was concerned that at least I should like to attempt to salvage some of my personal relationship with him and that indeed I could have a friendly relationship with him in the future because we had spent almost 28 years together. But, sadly, that did not happen.

Despite the hurdles he faced, Reid succeeded in finding out that the source of the material was Pell... The first Pell knew he had been rumbled was when Reid's lawyers knocked on his front door one day in early February 1998 with a court order allowing them to enter his house to seize documents.

Reid said on the Channel 4 documentary[ii]: 'I got a name and address... of Benjamin Pell, and we put him under surveillance.'

And he told another interviewer[iii]: 'I investigated, brought in surveillance people, to find out how the letters got out, and months later the truth came out. But by that time, it was all over.'

Pell says that he had expected *The Mirror* to give no clue that might help identify him as the source[iv]. Pell, however, opportunistically changed his attitude about this issue when he wanted to find out the identity of confidential sources who provided a newspaper with information about him (see chapter 17).

The first clue to *The Mirror*'s source appeared the day after the story about the row between Elton John and Branson. And it was in the *Daily Mail*, which reported[v]: 'The row might have remained a private disagreement between two creative people (Elton John and Branson) until the entrance of publicist Max Clifford, sleazefinder-general of public relations.

'Yesterday, he maintained he gave the story to *The Mirror* newspaper, saying: "It came from someone close to Elton John who has fallen out with him, someone who had a grudge against him."'

Extraordinary how dusty the dustbin should hold such a grudge against Elton John.

The *Daily Mail* continued: 'But one senior Mirror person said last night that the leak came not from a disgruntled ex-confidant, but from "a cleaner".'

Pell was furious with the 'senior Mirror person', saying[vi]: 'Fuck you... why did you have to say that?'

He continued: 'I was fearful more of my name coming out than of John Reid as much. I just didn't want anyone to know what I was doing at that stage. I was lying to everyone about what I did.'

Initially, he says, *The Mirror* was refusing to name its source. Pell said on the documentary that Clifford had told him about Reid's legal steps to try to find out the source[vii]. 'Max rang me up and said: 'I don't want to alarm you, Benjamin, but I've got to go to court this morning and swear an affidavit saying, "I've never heard of you. Your name is Doris." And this has obviously stuck ever since, "You're Doris, and I never met you. You've rung me up from a 'phone box and that's it. Okay? As long as you know what I'm saying." So, basically, Max committed perjury for me.'

Clifford confirmed this in a telephone conversation with Pell, which Pell taped. McVicar, while interviewing Clifford for the Channel 4 documentary, pressed him about how he had lied to the court. Clifford said: 'All I was concerned about, quite honestly, at that time was that we were going in the High Court, and I needed to know exactly, you know, why- or where things were so that when I stood up in the witness box I knew what was coming.'

McVicar interjected: 'Yeah, but you knew his name then.'

Clifford: 'Yeah, I mean, yes, I knew his name. Yeah.'

McVicar: 'So you committed perjury?'

Clifford: 'Yeah, yeah. No, well, no. No, John. Because in the early days I-I explained, when I went to court, that I knew him as lots of different names.'

But Pell contradicted this in his interview on the documentary, despite the fact that he had often used aliases with other people, saying with regards to Clifford: 'For the first time ever, I'd actually given my real name.'

Clifford added: 'I know I finished up in the High Court, being asked to reveal my sources, which, I didn't.'

And Pell added: 'I will never say that Max Clifford is a complete shit because, at the end of the day, he could've easily, at that stage, shopped me.'

But Pell claimed on the documentary that while Clifford protected him as the source of the story about Elton John's cash crisis, he took most of the spoils from *The Mirror*. 'Four grand. I- I was able to get four grand for that story. Well, now I know, Max took ten grand. He ripped me off.'

When McVicar started putting to Clifford the claims by Pell on how the money was divided, the slick PR man lost his cool. 'Look, John, I'm not talking about money. I've said I'm not talking about money. I'm not going to continue this interview, okay? I've given you background on Benjamin Pell. I was asked to give background on Benjamin Pell, the guy that I know. I've given you plenty of that, and I've answered your questions. That's all.'

McVicar persisted as Clifford walked away from the camera. Clifford could not contain his anger any longer, saying:

> Thanks, John, very much. You're a load of crooks. Fuck off out of it, the lot of you. Clear off. You're not welcome up here. If you want to do a straight interview, you tell me what you want to talk about. Don't come up here trying to con me because it's not clever.

Channel 4 lawyers cut from the documentary some of the scenes in which Clifford erupted, fearing that to broadcast them might be considered by television regulators to be a breach of his privacy. How lucky for Clifford that he escaped the exposure that he helped heap on Elton John and John Reid.

Pell told an interviewer from a Jewish newspaper that he was planning to sue Clifford[viii], whom he describes as 'a horrible character'. And he planned to exploit the fact that he had Clifford on tape admitting to perjury. 'When I take him to court, the first thing... my barrister needs to say to the judge, "Well, excuse me, we can't really believe Mr Clifford's evidence: he's an admitted perjurer."' The irony of this statement, given Pell's perjury, including his taped confessions seems lost on him.

However, he decided against suing Clifford. He told Jones[ix]: "If I make an enemy of somebody like Max Clifford, all he needs to do is go up to John Reid and say... Cos, don't forget, the money I got for the story has never been disclosed to John Reid's lawyers. He'd (Clifford) be fully capable of saying to them, "Oh, he got seven grand for that story, do you want to get that money now?" Cos one of the orders from the court was if I ever got any money for the story I would have to hand it over to John Reid's lawyers. So no, no, it's not worth making an enemy of Clifford.'

But at the time when Clifford had to swear an affidavit, Pell was panic-stricken. He told McVicar[x]: 'On the Friday afternoon, I was getting really scared cos Max had had to do the affidavit the day before. So that Friday, I rang Martin Cruddace, who's the [then] head of the legal department of *The Mirror*, and I had a chat with him. I said, "You know, it's five minutes to go before the Sabbath [which starts at sunset on Fridays]. I mean, I've been trying to get hold of you all day, at least now I've got hold of you." Cos I was desperate. I said, "Can you tell me what's going on here? Cos I've heard that Max is being dragged into the office. You're not going to give away my name, are you? Cos you know that's unethical."

'So, he said to me, "Oh Benjamin, I wouldn't worry. I would never give away your name. You should know that."

'I said, "I've got the Sabbath beginning now. Do I have to worry about these people coming round to my house?"

'Martin Cruddace said to me – this was five minutes before the Sabbath on... 30th January – "You've got nothing to worry about on that score." Famous last words.

'So, you may ask, how did I get discovered in the end?'

Pell thought that Kelvin MacKenzie, 57, then deputy managing director of *The Mirror* and the legendary former editor of *The Sun*, leaked his name. Pell believed that Reid told MacKenzie that *The*

Mirror could have an exclusive interview with Elton John, and to be able to follow him around his next world tour.

Pell's account, which is a pack of lies, goes at follows:

> Clifford told me, the reason is, [MacKenzie] doesn't want to be sued. You know, he felt that by giving the name away, he wouldn't end up with being sued by John Reid Enterprises. As it turns out, we were all sued by John Reid in the end. I was sued by him, Clifford was sued by him… and *The Mirror* was sued by him, and, in the end, came to a £2m settlement out of court with him four months later, which I wasn't even allowed to talk about.

In fact, Reid was given the name by another journalist, who worked for *Punch* magazine. This journalist pressurised one of the then deputy editors of *The Mirror*, for a name... The deputy editor just wrote 'Benjamin Pell' on a piece of paper and left the room. The *Punch* journalist gave the name to Reid both as a favour and for an undisclosed sum.

Ever after he was told the truth, Pell refused to credit it. It makes a better story to say it was Kelvin McKenzie. To support his version of events, Pell cites the fact that *The Mirror*, after its brush with Elton John, was fawning in its reporting on the singer.

Certainly MacKenzie had previously fallen foul of Elton John: he was editor of *The Sun* when it ran an entirely untrue story linking the singer to rent boys. The newspaper subsequently ran an apology to Elton John as a splash[xi], and paid him £1m to settle his libel claim, earning a rebuke for both sides from a High Court judge[xii].

Pell was predictably outraged that his identity as the confidential source of the Elton John stories had emerged, saying[xiii]: 'I'd been basically grassed up by a fucking newspaper, who bought the story off me for fucking chicken feed; it's absolutely disgraceful.' Again Pell knows the truth. Clifford, who does not sell stories for chicken feed, took twenty grand from *The Mirror* for the Elton splash and gave Pell four. As John Reid laconically put it in the aforementioned interview when he was asked how the conspirators cut up the spoils: 'I believe Max Clifford got the lion's share.'

Pell says that the first he knew that Reid had found him out was a knock on the door in February 1998: Alan Watts of Herbert Smith, accompanied by a supervising solicitor, announced that they had an anton pillar order (now called a search-and-seizure order) against Pell and explained that it allowed them to conduct an immediate search of his home for documents related to Reid. Pell says that he already knew about anton pillar orders from his law degree.

'The first people who anton pillared me was John Reid. He would face further anton pillar orders from solicitors representing other celebrities, including All Saints (see chapters 8 and 9).

'I lied at first. Oh yes. "Is Benjamin Pell here?"'

'So, I said, "No, no, I'm sorry Benjamin Pell isn't in at the moment."'

'So they said, "Well, I think you better get him. How soon could you get him here?"'

'And I already knew then- by then, John, cos I had done my reading on it. I knew that anton pillars, you can't deliver after half past five. So, I thought, "Fuck, if I can play for time 'til half past five, I'm okay and I can hide everything tonight."'

Of course, Pell also knew that hiding or destroying documents subject to an anton pillar order is acting in defiance of that court order, so is a contempt of court that is punishable by jail.

'I said to him, "Well, he's not here at the moment."' After about ten minutes, Pell says, he admitted to them who he was.

'I knew my next priority was basically to get them out of the house as soon as possible that night, and hide the stuff... which, by the way, is a criminal offence, so this mustn't come out on camera. Though, we'll get lawyers on that, cos I'd like them to know that I fucked them. But, apparently, it's contempt of court.'

Pell says that they asked him whether there was anything that he did not think they should be allowed to see. He told them that they could not see his Elton John music collection, giving them the false impression that it had been signed by his source. In court they asked me on oath, 'Why did you ask us- why did you say that would give away the source?'

'I said, "Well, I thought, maybe, you know, I'd written down once on there." I know, I was talking rubbish, course they knew by now, I was fucking well bullshitting them."' More perjury...

Pell continued his account of the Reid anton pillar: 'By now, my dad is home. So, I've now wasted so much time. And I knew, as soon as my dad is home, cos he's deaf as well, this is going to be complete mayhem. It's going to be like a *Carry On* movie.'

He says that his mother overheard Alan Watts calling a private detective who was to keep watch on Pell that night. 'By then, I knew I was being watched, 'cos I originally thought, "Fuck, if they go at half past seven, eight o'clock, we hide the stuff tonight."'

A confidential source in the Elton John camp told me later: 'It was clear that the man is an absolute fantasist.' Referring to the attempt to serve on Pell the anton pillar order, the source added: 'For the first fifteen minutes, he pretended to be his brother... Then he was telling... how he studied for a law degree. He was just a very, very odd character.'

Pell also tells Jones about how he frustrated the anton pillar order[xiv]:

I was frantic of course... They have to have a supervising solicitor... [The supervising solicitor] obviously knew that I was going to hide stuff. Cos I come into the house... knock at the door, five lawyers at my door. I'm immediately panicking because I've actually got four full Royal Mail bags in my fucking bedroom 'cos I'd never believed in a million years I would be anton pillared.

So what did I do?...

I said to [the supervising solicitor], who's Jewish by the way, so obviously he was a bit sympathetic, 'I've really got to pray now, it's the afternoon service,' ... He allowed me out unsupervised, and, I must admit to the Lord, I didn't pray. I ran up the stairs, and then I spent five minutes hiding everything in my parent's bedroom. And he must have known. He should have been – as the supervising solicitor, – watching me. And those five minutes saved my life because, had they found those documents, I wouldn't have any proof of this gross negligence, and, of course, those documents are now still in my safe.

Jones asked Pell why didn't the supervising solicitor go into his parents' bedroom? Pell replied: 'They can, of course they can... What he should have done when I said to him, "... I'm going off to pray now", he should have followed me. That is the point. And Alan Watts was an idiot cos Alan Watts should have said to [the supervising solicitor], "How do we know that he's praying? How do we know that he's not hiding documents?"

'I left the room, pretended to go into the dining room; then, a minute later, walked slowly, quietly up the stairs. And the bags were, conveniently enough, reasonably close to the bed. So, I just took the bags, ran into my parents' bedroom, put them in there and ran back down the stairs again."'

Pell knew that they could only search until 5.30pm, so he stalled them in his own bedroom until then. 'Of course, definitely, that night was the night of being like in Nazi Germany, going through the undergrowth into the neighbours' gardens, getting thorns... but it was worth it, just to bloody well fuck these people.'

When, in the case he brought against John Mappin (see chapter 13), Pell was cross-examined in 2002 in the High Court by Adam Wolanski about these confessions that Jones had filmed, Pell said that they were untrue[xv]. Wolanski put to him that in the summer of '99, he tricked solicitors from discovering the relevant documents.

Pell replied: 'Untrue. Completely untrue. Since I haven't actually been anton pillared since 18th August 1998... I don't quite understand what you're talking about.'

Wolanski: 'Well, what I am talking about is your evident delight in recounting the story of how you managed to conceal documents from solicitors who you knew had anton pillar orders to search your home for those documents, is that correct?'

Pell: 'But the story isn't true, so I don't understand what I'm... I'm delighting in giving a yarn to somebody (Mr Jones) who I think is a Hollywood director and he'll take it back to Hollywood and make a story out of it, that part of my life.'

Wolanski: 'Well, what I suggest is that that is not the case, and that in fact you recount on this footage something that took place and follows an anton pillar order that was obtained against you by solicitors acting for John Reid, is that correct?

Pell: 'That is correct.'

Wolanski: 'And you knew what that meant when those solicitors turned up to your house – that the High Court had ordered a search of your home for certain documents, yes?'

Pell: 'That's correct.'

Wolanski: 'Thank you for that. When those solicitors turned up with their anton pillar order you hid the documents?'

Pell: 'No, I didn't.'

But Pell also told the same story to McVicar that he told Jones. He said that when the lawyers left his house, he said to his parents[xvi]: '"I've just got to get certain stuff out of the house."

'So then, my mother said, "I don't think we should get it out of the front because I think they've got a detective watching you."

'So, my father says, "Don't be silly, Rita. There's no way."

'I said, "Look, I don't want to take the chance." And, as it turns out... they did [take a chance].'

My father says, 'Look, the only thing we can do is: neighbour's garden.'

So, it was like fucking being in bloody Colditz or like being in Nazi Germany. We took all this stuff from upstairs, walked outside, all the lights were off. The fucking neighbours got... these holly bushes and stuff. My hands were all bleeding both – just as well... Herbert Smith didn't check my hands the following day. My father was holding the torch; I was able to get all... my neighbour's garden, which looked like a fucking jungle, a jungle... that's even messier than my bedroom. So, I thought, 'Thank goodness for that.'

Basically, by 9.30, I got all of the stuff out of my house in the neighbour's garden – hopefully without being watched. I was getting paranoid, of course, cos I thought, fuck, you know, you could have helicopters or whatever. So, I felt much better then; I felt much better then. And then of course we had to decide what do I say, you know: what do I say to them the following week? Do I tell them my method? Do I tell them who my source is, you know, what do I do next?

Pell revels in breaking the law and is not concerned about embroiling his parents in aiding and abetting his criminal acts.

I know there were fucking private investigators cos my mother heard Alan Watts from Herbert Smith ringing them up... That night- that was the night we hid all the documents in the neighbour's garden. It's cos we knew they were in the fucking front of the house. That night, I went with my dad, cos... I was still doing my cleaning jobs; I went with my dad to all of my cleaning jobs. Every time we got out of the car another car was following us.[xvii]

McVicar filmed Pell proudly showing a sodden clump of Reid's documents that he had been hidden in the neighbour's garden – and were subject to the anton pillar order. Pell said[xviii]:

> Why do you think that night was the night I hid all of John Reid's documents in the neighbour's garden. These are they – still in existence. I know, [cackles], yeah, but you can still read them; you can still see them. You can still see the dreaded word: this was Aida, the thing written by Tim Rice and Elton John, with the word 'shred' on it. Who knows, that could... be John Reid's handwriting. Still in pristine condition... Still bits of Elton John's bank account details here in the rubbish.

Pell also re-enacts for Jones's camera how he hid the Elton John documents. Filmed in his garden, he says[xix]: "These are the two John Reid boxes still, which- I... was supposed to put them back. I mean, this is what I said to the Evening Standard: I've hidden them. What I've actually done is hidden them next door in the garden. I mean, basically what happened is... 'Can we re-enact this now?'

Pell demonstrated how he his hid about 'twenty-five black bags' full of the Reid stuff. He said, 'Here, some of it's still in there... And, obviously, every time the house was raided, this was my hiding place.'

Showing Jones some of the hidden documents, he continued: 'This is some of my Elton John stuff, which obviously I shouldn't have because it's all contempt of court. This is the stuff which was hidden next door. This is one of my favourite little possessions: it's the 'Royal Ascot Enclosure John Reid Esquire 1993'. Well I don't think he'll be able to afford to get into Royal Ascot ever any more. And this is just an example of the sort of devious nature I had. These were the envelopes I was filling up and hiding in the synagogue, and these were all his.

'To show you what a bastard Alan Watts is, when I was swearing my affidavit the following day or so, he of course was claiming Benjamin Pell has hidden these documents because there's no way we're ever going to find them in the house; he must have got rid of them... Anything I said to them they would argue with. I'm going to the synagogue with a bag and it's got some of my books in there, I come out empty-handed. The truth is of course I was actually handling documents ha, I was actually hiding documents, but he wasn't to know that.' Pell also re-enacted for Jones who he transported the Reid documents to the synagogue.

Pell's next-door neighbour, Linda Cohen, became used to seeing piles of rubbish in Pell's back garden, although even she had not become accustomed to having her own garden used by Pell as a hiding place for documents that the High Court had ordered he must return. Interviewed on the Channel 4 documentary, she said[xx]:

> There was a day last year when we were having a barbecue in the garden, and I stood up to go and get something from the kitchen, and I just glanced over the garden wall and there were piles of black sacks, some of which had split open, and coffee dregs were coming out, old sandwich packets. Okay, there was masses and masses of paper as well, but there was all the usual sort of debris that you would find in a rubbish bag. And I thought, 'My God, this is disgusting... If you keep bringing these back you're going to get rats because they love rubbish.'
>
> All night long you hear him walking backwards and forwards, backwards and forwards, backwards and forwards, up and down the garden, bins slamming, the doors slamming, and shouting and screaming going on. I just assumed he was in paper recycling. I suppose he is really. It's what he recycles it to, isn't it?
>
> He was very proud of what he'd done. He said he'd hidden some of the important documents in the synagogue because a place of worship couldn't be searched. He is hurting people's lives. He is causing human misery to people. That is so against the kind of morals that one believes is right for Judaism.

Pell claimed later that he was joking when he told his neighbour that he had hidden documents at the synagogue[xxi], yet when he saw Cohen's interview in a preview of the Channel 4 documentary, he didn't say this. Instead he screamed abuse at her, saying[xxii]: 'I don't even know her name, I hate my neighbours anyway... No wonder she hasn't spoken to me for two years. I better be careful what I say about my neighbours cos that's one thing my mother wouldn't allow me to do... What a bitch... stupid woman. Ha, ha, that's your five minutes of fame, now piss off.'

To her comment that his activities ran contrary to Jewish morals, Pell said: 'That is disgraceful, that is so not true, the woman is just pathetic. Not that she knows anything about Judaism anyway, she's a bloody reformed Jew who's married to a non-Jew...

'You can't pick your neighbours, can you?'

Unfortunately for Elton John and John Reid, they couldn't pick their binman either.

References

i Nick Craven, 'Bitter end of my 26 years with Elton. Former manager tells how star began to lose trust in him,' Daily Mail (05.12.00); Sean O'Neill, 'Elton "kept lover from investiture,"' Lewis Smith, 'Sir Elton's former lover tells of hurt at Palace snub,' The Times (05.12.00); The Daily Telegraph (05.12.03); 'Elton's 'rage' at spending revelations,' The Daily Telegraph (06.12.00); Cathy Gordon, John Aston and Cathy Mayer, 'I WANTED TO STAY FRIENDS WITH SIR ELTON, SAYS SACKED EX-MANAGER,' Press Association (04.12.00).

ii 'Scandal in the Bins,' Channel 4 (first shown 11.01.01).

iii Valerie Grove, 'Elton chose to just cut me off. I had seen him do it to others in the past,' The Times (21.04.01).

iv McVicar audio tape (recorded 1999) MDRV.

v Paul Harris, 'War with Elton over tribute to Diana,' Daily Mail (15.01.98).

vi McVicar audio tape (recorded 1999) MDRV.

vii 'Scandal in the Bins,' Channel 4 (first shown 11.01.01).

viii McVicar video tape (filmed 24.01.01) DVOR.

ix "3½-hour rushes," Moving Perspective (filmed 1999).

x McVicar audio tape (recorded 1999) MDRV.

xi 'Sorry, Elton,' The Sun (12.12.88).

xii Kelvin MacKenzie, 'Taking the chopper to the whoppers: ex-Sun editor Kelvin MacKenzie on the day that Rupert Murdoch ordered an end to the spiralling libel bills his tabloids were handing him,' The Guardian (11.03.02); Frances Gibb, 'Judge rebukes Sun and Elton John,' The Times (13.12.88).

xiii McVicar audio tape (recorded 1999) MDOR.

xiv "3½-hour rushes," Moving Perspective (filmed 1999).

xv Transcript of evidence of Benjamin Pell, Benjamin Pell -v- John Mappin and Story Master Ltd, (11.03.02).

xvi McVicar audio tape (recorded 1999) MDOR.

xvii McVicar audio tape (recorded 03.01.01) MDOV.

xviii McVicar video tape (filmed 21.01.01) DVRI.

xix "3½-hour rushes," Moving Perspective (filmed 1999).

xx 'Scandal in the Bins,' Channel 4 (first shown 11.01.01).

xxi McVicar video tape (filmed 24.01.01) DVOR.

xxii McVicar audio tape (recorded 12.11.00) MDRG.

xxiii McVicar video tape (filmed 24.01.01) DVOR.

xxiv McVicar audio tape (recorded 12.11.00) MDRG.

Chapter 6

Something About the Way You Look Tonight

After Sir Elton John's lawyers finished raiding Pell's home, Benji the Binman went out that evening on his cleaning round and raiding rubbish as usual. Pell told McVicar[i]:

> I can't use the car because Herbert Smith [solicitors' firm acting for Elton John's manager] has said I'm not allowed to go into my car because my car is full of rubbish, and they want to search the car. So, basically, I couldn't use my car. So, my dad took me out that evening, okay. So, we went to three cleaning jobs and whatever; I was able to pick up Searles [solicitors then acting for All Saints: see chapters 8 and 9] bags that evening, Lee & Thompson [solicitors whose clients included The Spice Girls: see chapter 9] bags that evening, okay. So, I still did my normal rounds with my dad.
>
> We didn't know we were being followed. I thought that I had a detective, John, opposite my house – maybe – maybe. And I'd be on the safe side in hiding the stuff, but I'd never thought they would fucking follow me.
>
> Following morning, half past eight, Lawrence Abramson [Pell's solicitor] rings me up, and says, 'I've just had Herbert Smith on the 'phone this morning. Apparently, last night...' they've just sworn an affidavit, '...apparently last night, you were seen hiding stuff in a building in Putney, a building in Battersea, you were taking- seen taking a bag outside a building in Fulham.'
>
> I said, 'What, you know, what do you do?'
>
> 'I've already spoken to you, Benjamin, about your... Peter, whatever your name is, what exactly were you doing last night? I hope you weren't hiding anything?'
>
> I said, 'No, I've got a cleaning business.'
>
> He said, 'Well, they're not going to believe that.'
>
> They thought that evening, when I was doing my cleaning job, I'd been hiding stuff. So, their affidavit the following morning was hilarious. 'We followed him with his father going into various

buildings in London. Also, he was seen taking black bags from somewhere.'

Under the anton pillar order, Pell had to disclose to Reid the source of the documents. Speaking to McVicar, Pell said[iii]:

As you know, with an anton pillar, immediately you've got to tell them who gave you the information, okay. So, that Wednesday morning, I had a long chat with Lawrence, cos, for the first time, I was going to have an honest chat with him, he thought it was being honest at the time. So, we had to go through everything I did. So, I told him, I'm a freelance journalist, I'm an investigative journalist, I appear on the radio and stuff.

I, in common with colleagues in the industry, regard Pell's frequent claim to be a journalist to be risible. As for him appearing on radio. When?! Nonetheless, Pell's desire to be recognised as a journalist is another window onto his character. Given the number of front-page stories that he broke, he would often express the view that he deserved to be named 'journalist of the year'. Yet, Pell was essentially a respondent – he was the source of a lot of scoops but never the actual journalist. In fact, he could never be a journalist as he cannot organise facts or strands of an argument into a coherent linear form. His mind does not work that way. The way he talks is a indicator to the way he thinks. His mind connects everything up into a mesh topology, in which everything is connected to everything else. This is why when he talks he jumps around all over the place at a bewildering rate, making the most seemingly odd associations, which, nevertheless, from Pell's perspective usually make sense.

His solicitor asked him if he was willing to divulge his source? Pell replied 'No, I can't divulge my source.' Why? 'Because I'm a journalist. I don't want to give out my source. If I give… the name of my source to Herbert Smith, that person would get the sack, and I don't think that's fair.'

Lawrence said that was OK and assured Pell that he would be able use section 10 of the Contempt of Court Act 1981, which regulates the rights of journalists to protect confidential sources. Lawrence then told him that they were in court that afternoon. In fact,

Pell's lawyers applied for a stay on the part of the anton pillar that required him to disclose his source.

In his judgment on Pell's application, the High Court judge said[iv]:

The plaintiff [John Reid Enterprises] obtained an anton pillar order against the defendant [Pell] which, inter alia, required the defendant to disclose to the plaintiff's solicitors the name and address of everyone who had offered to supply him with certain information about the affairs of Elton John and other clients of the plaintiff. The defendant applies to stay that part of the order on the grounds that he was a freelance investigative journalist and he claimed the protection of section 10 of the Contempt of Court Act 1981. The defendant's evidence was that he had a large number of sources and that it was very important to him that he should not reveal their identities. Having been given the information in question by one such source, he had approached Max Clifford who had approached *[The Mirror]*.

The judge referred to a draft affidavit put before him on behalf of Pell by his barrister, Timothy Corner. The judge said:

The essence of that is that the defendant is a freelance investigative journalist with some four or five years' experience, and he works under different names. He says that most of his work is in the property world, and more recently in the music world. He says that he relies on a huge network of sources, including some 85 sources in the property industry and 15 to 20 in the music industry. He does not pay his sources for information, but people are prepared to let him have information because, as he says, they enjoy the feeling of letting people know something is going to happen before it happens. He says it is very important to his activities that he should not reveal his sources, and he would find it difficult to get anyone to trust him if he did. Accordingly, in his affidavit, he does not identify the person who supplied the information to him.

Having been given the information by someone he defines as 'X', he approached a Max Clifford who then approached [*The Mirror*]. He was able to demonstrate to [The Mirror] that the source was genuine and, accordingly, it was arranged for him 'to work with a couple of Mirror journalists in order to complete the story.

The judge ruled:

The information in question looked as if it had come from an insider, an employee or officer of the plaintiff or someone else with direct access to the information. It was of the essence of the plaintiff's business that it should be able to assure the well-known figures for whom it acted that it could protect their confidentiality. Accordingly, the plaintiff needed to be able to identify the person responsible and take appropriate measures. Furthermore, as a small business, unless the particular person was identified, everyone would be under suspicion, and that would affect the conduct of the business in a serious way. On the other hand, no one could suggest that there was a great public interest in Elton John's finances being published. While it was generally desirable to protect sources this factor had less weight where the information appeared to have been taken unlawfully, as here. Furthermore it did not appear that the identification of one employee of the plaintiff would have a dramatic effect on the defendant's legitimate business. Accordingly the balance favoured requiring the defendant to disclose the information sought.

Pell described how he got the news[v]: 'Half past six, Lawrence rings me up and said, "We've spent all afternoon in court, Benjamin. I'm afraid I've got some bad news for you... We've lost. You know, you have to divulge your source."'

Pell protested that he was a journalist but Lawrence pointed out that the judge had decided that this was such a serious breach of confidence, which was ruining Reid's company, this took priority over preserving the confidentiality of Pell's sources.

But Lawrence then told Pell, 'But, of course, if you don't mind going to prison, you don't have to divulge your source.'

Pell thought about this, then after twenty minutes rang Lawrence and said: 'Well Lawrence, there's something I have to tell you that I haven't told you before...there was actually no source.'

Lawrence asked whom he was protecting and Pell told him that he got this information from Reid's rubbish. The flabbergasted lawyer replied:

Benjamin, do you know what you've just done? You made me spend the whole day in court today, arguing over something... you can be done for perjury. You've sworn an affidavit, saying you can't reveal your source because if you reveal your source this person will lose their job. Do you realise what you've done?

'And of course my parents go mad with me as well, cos my mother immediately says to me, "You better have your toothbrush for tomorrow cos you could end up going to nick for this." You know, I committed perjury basically because my affidavit was complete bollocks.'

'I thought I was being clever because, actually, when I saw the affidavit, I thought to myself just in case things do go wrong... I never thought I would have to reveal my source, so when Lawrence rung me I did think it was a complete shock to me that I would- So, I actually used the word "source", and "reveal my source", and I always thought the word "source" could cover "source of information", how I get the information. But, I'm afraid... Talmudic logic didn't work with a Jew like Lawrence Abramson; it may have worked with a gentile... but not with him.

'He said, "Look, Benjamin, don't try to be clever with me, you know. It's bad enough...never lie to your own lawyer." And of course, Anne Pounds [then a friend of Pell's], when I rang Anne that evening, she said to me, "Of course, Benjamin, I've always said to you... you've always got to tell your own lawyers everything, you know, it's your own fault, and you should have done it before," and whatever.

'Cos Lawrence was upset with me. I wrote him a three-page letter... "I'm really sorry, but, you know, this is very close to me, I've been doing this for years in the property industry, and... going through people's rubbish is my livelihood and I don't want people to know about it."

'So Lawrence said to me, "Well, first of all, they can't tell anyone else because that's part of the anton pillar order. And second of all, I'm sure that Herbert Smith and John Reid aren't interested in anybody else you do."'

Pell added[vi]: 'Lawrence, you've got to realise I've been going through rubbish for eight years, I've only been doing showbiz rubbish, or Elton John's rubbish, for three months.'"

Pell summarised[vii]: 'So, he said to me, "Well, there's a big problem, Benjamin. We've committed, you know, you've committed – you've sworn an affidavit that was false, we've argued the whole day in court, you know, I'll have to go to 'phone them up, see how they react Thursday morning."

It's driving my parents mad, I'm being followed everywhere. I can't even go to synagogue without being followed. Oh, by the way, on Wednesday morning, there were certain bits which I'd forgotten to put next door. So, basically, I had about six envelopes to get rid of. So, for the first time... in ages, I'd gone to synagogue in the morning, I don't normally go to synagogue in the morning, cos normally I get up too late, so, I went to the synagogue and I had a plastic bag with me and I went to the synagogue. On the way out, I had an empty plastic bag with me, and somebody else came out with a plastic bag. That was in the bloody private detective's report... And I- I knew [my] excuse: it was my- some of my Jewish books or something.

'Lawrence rings me up... "You're going to have to appear in court tomorrow, okay? And you're going to have to be on your best behaviour tomorrow, you're going to have to tell the truth to the court. Cos, basically, Herbert Smith don't believe you, John Reid don't believe you. You've sworn this affidavit which now is completely false. You're going to have to... – the only way out of this outrage is to bargain with them."

'As my mother said, bring my pyjamas with me as well.

'I go along to court the following morning... I've got an umbrella with me, an Elton John umbrella with me, I've got the Elton John hat with me, and that's important. Basically, I looked like a complete nutter. I go in there with reams and reams of papers about Elton John... not the paper I'd taken from John Reid's office, but stuff about Elton John. So, I go in the witness box about quarter to ten. I want to come across, basically, as an Elton John fanatic, or whatever, who's been going through the rubbish.

'Anne said to me, within about ten minutes, she could overhear [Reid's] QC saying to his junior, "That guy's a complete nutter, isn't he?" So, already by then, at least they got that message.'

This is another of Pell's strongest cards – playing the nutter. He is emotionally disturbed and dysfunctional, even teetering on the edge of madness, but he is sufficiently in control of it to be able turn it on or off. And when he turns it on, and verbally that is probably 300 spittle-drenched words a minute, people react like they have turned the corner and been confronted with a rabid dog. Most just want to get out the cross and the garlic, then run for cover. Pell told the Channel 4 documentary[viii]:

I went in there as a complete Elton John fanatic. I went in there with an Elton John umbrella; I went in there with all my Elton John merchandise, you know, I went- you know what I'm like with my bags. I had all my bags at the court. I had all this Elton John stuff, all the magazines about him, all the tapes and everything. I came across as a complete nutter. I said to the judge, 'I'm completely obsessed with Elton. I love him, you know. When Diana died I-' You know, all of that stuff. And, of course, the judge did believe me.

Pell showed the umbrella in question to Jones on camera[ix].

Here's my Elton John umbrella, which I actually haven't ever – literally – ever used. All I did was stand up in court like this, showing off my Elton John umbrella. So let's take it apart: I was an honorary member of the Elton John Fan Club. Here, Elton John Fan Club, Hercules, which is his middle name. 'She passed like summer rain,' bit like me... All I did was stand up in the witness stand in the court, and I opened it up and said, 'I'm sorry, but I'm such an Elton John fanatic, I feel much safer with this umbrella next to me. Do you accept that, your honour?

He said, 'Fine, if it makes you feel comfortable.'

He continued:

I'm there in the courtroom; they're saying to me, 'And not only that, not only do you know these people on this list here, Mr Pell, if you are saying that you don't know anyone on this list and you've been going through our rubbish, which you of course deny completely, why did it say in the article, "A senior member of his circle had revealed." That implies that somebody from the office had given you these documents.'

I said to him, 'Excuse me, I didn't write this story.'

'Oh, so you're now...' be fair, these are QCs; these are highly trained people; they are trying to twist me up in knots. So then, he immediately said to me, 'You have said in your affidavit, Mr Pell, you're a journalist; now you're telling me that you're not a journalist.'

I said, 'Excuse me-' I turned round to the judge, I mean I basically- this is where my insanity does come in quite useful. I basically said, 'Look, I'm sorry your honour, I don't know what to say to this guy here. I've got these documents from the rubbish; if they don't believe me, they don't believe me; I don't know whether you believe me.'

At one point, Pell tells Jones:

I am obsessive, and the courts like hearing about obsessive people. It gives them an excuse to deal with them, you know, reasonably sympathetically. (See chapter 11 on how Pell visits a psychiatrist in the hope of lenient treatment in another court case.)

 Anyway, I ended up having to give evidence for one-and-a-half hours; I was being pummelled by the QC acting for John Reid. I won, of course, in the end. The judge thought I was completely barmy.

Reid, who watched Pell's performance in court, said on the Channel 4 documentary[x]:

He was very tricky in court. He played a kind of... somewhere between a simpleton and a- and a kind of madman and a lunatic, you know, an oddball.

In the Mappin trial, Pell claimed that in the passages filmed by Jones in which he admits to trying to fool the court in the Elton John case by playing a 'nutter' he was 'developing story-lines' (see preface and chapter 13 on how Pell explained his filmed admissions to Jones). Wolanski cross-examined Pell on what he was filmed telling Jones about playing the nutty Elton John fanatic[xi].

Wolanski: 'Another thing which you are particularly proud of on that footage, Mr Pell, is your ability to fool judges and others into thinking that you are more mentally unstable than in fact you are because you think that by doing so you will receive lenient treatment. That is something which you discuss at length on the footage, is it not?'

 Pell: 'Your question implies, Mr Wolanski, that I'm mentally unstable, which I deny.'

 Wolanski: 'Well, Mr Pell, I will ask the question again, and perhaps you can answer it this time. You are very proud on the film of your ability to fool judges and others into thinking that you are much more mentally unstable than in fact you are because you think that by doing so you will receive lenient treatment. Correct or not correct?'

 Pell: 'Well, let's go through the facts here. I don't think Justice Garland, Justice Langley and Justice Hordern were ever given an impression by me of being unstable, mad, any impression, so I don't understand what the question means. It's complete nonsense. It's another myth. I don't know who invented it, your client or yourself, but it's absolute nonsense.'

Wolanski [after describing another filmed scene in which Pell explains how he fools the courts]: 'So, Mr Pell, what you are describing there is attempting to give the impression to the judge and the court during that hearing that you are an absolute nutter in order to evade the questions of the QC?'

Pell: 'Well the whole story is a complete invention. You can ask Justice Garland himself, he's in court this week. Justice Garland was my judge. I was in court for eight minutes being cross-examined by (John Reid's barrister) and I never once put my umbrella up. I never once had to discuss my sanity because it wasn't an issue. The only issue was whether John Reid had left Elton John's documents out for two and half months. So the story is a complete fiction.'

Wolanski: 'And you say again on this footage, Mr Pell, "I am obsessive, and the courts like obsessive people because it gives them an excuse to deal with them, you know, reasonably successfully but sympathetically." Do you recall saying that?'

Pell: 'I recall saying it.'

Wolanski: 'You see, Mr Pell, it is yet another example of your delight in showing how much cleverer you are than judges, lawyers and other professionally qualified people, is that right?'

Pell: 'That's a complete misinterpretation of what I'm saying. What I'm saying here is a development, once again, for Hollywood of my story, and since the umbrella incident never occurred, since the insanity incident never occurred, I don't quite understand the points you're making, Mr Wolanski.'

Wolanski briefly returned to the subject with Pell the following day in the High Court[xii], but with no more success. He had plenty more examples from the footage shot by Jones, but Pell's answer to each was the same – he was developing story-lines. And Wolanski neither had the McVicar tapes to put to Pell, nor did he challenge Pell's answer with his comments in the Channel 4 documentary. Nonetheless, he continued to cross-examine Pell on his evident pride in telling Jones that he had hidden Elton John documents.

Wolanski: 'Now, you were very pleased when discussing that case with Mr Jones that you had managed to find a place to hide away the documents that the court had ordered you to return, is that correct?'

Pell: 'It's actually not a correct version of events. What I'm doing here is re-enacting with Mr Jones the story which appeared in *The Evening Standard* on 13th March 1998 (by John Sturgis), exactly four years ago this week... I didn't hide any documents, ever. Not in 1998. Not in 1999. I don't know whether you want me to give you the background to that story?'

Wolanski, probably much to his regret, did just that.

Pell: 'Okay. On March 12th, 1998 at half past seven I left my house to go to synagogue for the Purim festival. A journalist called John Sturgis was outside my house asking me, "Benjamin, what's this about you and Elton?" I came back at half past ten, it was a long service, and he was still there. Now, I didn't really know in those days how to deal with the Press, so he said to me, "Look just give me some good quotes, and I'll let you go."

'So I gave him a completely fictitious story about having hidden documents, about having gone into the synagogue with bags, and I couldn't believe that he printed it the following day. It was the headline in the *Evening Standard* City Prices Edition on 13th March 1998, "Elton John sues hacker." Also, another lie I told him, I told him I was a computer hacker. I mean once again I didn't believe that a journalist would just run a story without any proof, and my lawyer, Lawrence Abramson, got a letter from Herbert Smith, from Alan Watts.

'He said, "We've read the article in the *Evening Standard*. Can you clarify please whether it's true or not?" Lawrence Abramson wrote me a letter. I clarified to Lawrence that it was a made-up story. He wrote back to Alan Watts, and that's the last we ever heard of it. I'm sure if Alan Watts thought the story were true he would have gone further, and that's how the story went into Pell folklore if that's the way you want to describe it.'

Meanwhile Pell lied to every newspaper that doorstepped him...*Daily Mail*, *Daily Express*, *Evening Standard*, *The Independent*... The latter was so desperate for a headline it printed every bit of nonsense spouted by Pell:

> 'I couldn't believe my eyes when I saw how easy it was to get hold
> of this stuff,' Mr Pell, who also works as a freelance music journalist,
> told *The Independent*. 'I went through their rubbish and I got some
> very clever computer nerds to hack into the system for me. Getting
> into the computer system was even easier than getting into the
> rubbish. I am a fan of Elton's, and I wondered whether I could find
> anything out after Diana's death. I certainly don't usually go through
> people's rubbish or hack into their computers.'

Pell said[xxiv]: 'And of course the rumours were going around Fleet
Street cos I'd admitted to Steve Boggan from *The Independent*; the
headline was, "Computer hacker went through rubbish."...I was
admitting to one or two people, it was the rubbish, cos... nobody was
believing me anyway. So I thought if I tell them I'm a hacker, it's the
rubbish, just basically confuse them – tell them anything.'

Boggan and *The Independent* subsequently became clients of Pell
as well. Within a week, this newspaper bought Pell's next Elton John
story: based on correspondence with Sotheby's, the auction house.
The Independent reported[xxv]:

> Elton John has been asked to return a piece of an ancient Roman
> sarcophagus which he bought at auction following the discovery that
> it had been stolen. Sir Elton bought the piece at Sotheby's in London
> four years ago for about £8,000, believing its provenance to be
> completely sound. However, late last year, the auction house
> contacted him to ask for the piece back when it emerged that the sale
> may not have been lawful. There is no suggestion that either party
> knew there was a problem with the piece, but the need for its return
> has resulted in Sotheby's conducting a world-wide search to find a
> replacement for him.

Pell admits to McVicar that he also lied to him about how he was
obtaining confidential documents when the journalist interviewed
him for *Punch* magazine[xxvi]. He claimed that he was a computer
hacker. Pell admits: 'I lied to you.' He again refers to the *Daily Mail*
failing to run the story about how he had obtained the Elton John
documents from rubbish. 'So then, I thought, "Fuck it. In future, I'm
not going to tell the truth."'

As Pell did not tell the truth to the court, he was aware that Reid could still pursue him. He told the Channel 4 documentary[xxvii]: 'In theory John Reid could be pursuing me. Of course he's not going to sue me for two reasons, (a) he's got no fucking money left, [again Pell turns to the camera as if he is talking to Reid] you fucking wanker, and (b) you know, what's he going to get out of me anyway? I'm penniless.' Pell is actually rich but he does hide his money to stop anyone claiming any of it (see chapter 13).

As Pell watches a preview of the documentary, he shows his worry – and paranoia – about this passage being broadcast, saying[xxviii]: 'But me telling John Reid he can go to... he's not going to kill me for that?' Pell is also incredulous that Reid allowed the programme to interview him, saying: 'How can you agree to be on the programme, you utter idiot. I ruined your life... oh no, I better not say that.'

What Pell did not know was that McVicar, who conducted the interview, secured Reid's co-operation by handing over to him a copy of the recorded interviews in which Pell tells the truth about how he plundered Reid's offices and ruined him. Reid, though, was too demoralised by the whole episode to use them to go after Pell for perjury and contempt of court. He also had no confidence that the courts would not fall for Pell's nutter act again.

Pell is triumphant about ruining Reid's life. When he adds 'oh no, I better not say that' he is not retracting his glee at breaking Reid, he is merely paying lip service to the convention that we don't crow over our defeated opponents. But it is just lip service. Pell does see himself as wronged by the world and any victory over people, who by being successful, famous or powerful personify the world, he views as justice for himself. Reid had done nothing to him but to Pell he represented a means to make money and inveigle himself in the lives of celebrities. Thus he was legitimate and fair game and, in Pell's Talmudic [il]logic, ruining Reid was vindication of his unrecognised genius and compensation for the way the world has wronged him.

Wolanski was far more perceptive than he understood when he put to Pell that his nutter act was 'yet another example of your delight in showing how much cleverer you are than judges, lawyers and other professionally qualified people, is that right?'

In fact, the Reid episode puts Pell's character in stark relief. Pell is hellbent on outwitting the world and he acts without scruple, morality or conscience in his crusade to prove that he is cleverer and superior to everyone else.

My confidential source in the Elton John camp told me that Alan Watts warned other solicitors firms about Pell and his activities. But far from stemming the tide, Pell was just finding his stride. And the warning did not reach Brick Court chambers, one of the leading sets of barristers' chambers in the UK...

References

[i] McVicar audio tape (recorded 1999) MDOR.

[ii] "3½-hour rushes," Moving Perspective (filmed 1999).

[iii] McVicar audio tape (recorded 1999) MDOR.

[iv] Mr Justice Carnwath, 'John Reid Enterprises Ltd -v- Pell,' High Court, Chancery Division (04.02.98).

[v] McVicar audio tape (recorded 1999) MDOR.

[vi] McVicar video tape (filmed 17.01.01) DVRB.

[vii] McVicar audio tape (recorded 1999) MDOR.

[viii] 'Scandal in the Bins,' Channel 4 (first shown 11.01.01).

[ix] "3½-hour rushes," Moving Perspective (filmed 1999).

[x] 'Scandal in the Bins,' Channel 4 (first shown 11.01.01).

[xi] Transcript of evidence of Benjamin Pell, Benjamin Pell -v- John Mappin and Story Master Ltd, (11.03.02).

[xii] Transcript of evidence of Benjamin Pell, Benjamin Pell -v- John Mappin and Story Master Ltd, (12.03.02).

[xv] McVicar audio tape (recorded January 1999) MDOI.

[xvi] John Sturgis and Sandra Laville, 'ELTON SUES OVER "STOLEN" SECRETS. STAR ACCUSES "HACKER" OF SELLING DETAILS OF CREDIT CARD SPENDING SPREE,' *Evening Standard* (13.03.98).

[xvii] McVicar audio tape (recorded January 1999) MDOI.

[xviii] "3½-hour rushes," Moving Perspective (filmed 1999).

[xx] McVicar audio tape (recorded January 1999) MDOI.

[xxi] *Daily Express* (14.03.98).

[xxii] "3½-hour rushes," Moving Perspective (filmed 1999).

[xxiii] Steve Boggan, 'Hacker stole secrets of stars from dustbins,' *The Independent* (14.03.98).

[xxiv] "3½-hour rushes," Moving Perspective (filmed 1999).

[xxv] Steve Boggan, 'Elton John asked by Sotheby's to return stolen sculpture,' *The Independent* (20.03.98).

[xxvi] John McVicar, 'HACKING OFF THE MUSIC BUSINESS: ALL THESE STARS ARE BEING TARGETED BY ONE MAN. Who'll be the next victim on the hitlist of Benjamin Pell?' *Punch* (01-13.08.98); McVicar audio tape (recorded 03.01.01) MDOV.

[xxvii] 'Scandal in the Bins,' Channel 4 (first shown 11.01.01).

[xxviii] McVicar audio tape (recorded 12.11.00) MDRG.

Chapter 7

Sorry Seems to be the Hardest Word

More legal action by Sir Elton John resulted from Pell's raids of John Reid's rubbish. The star decided to sue PricewaterhouseCoopers, his former accountants, and Andrew Haydon, the ex-managing director of John Reid Enterprises (JRE), for £14m. The case was the fall out from the stories in *The Mirror* about Elton John's 'cash crisis'. He hired the solicitors' firm, Eversheds, to prepare his case against PricewaterhouseCoopers and Haydon. Elton John wanted £14m of touring expenses back, claiming that the accountants and Haydon were negligent in allowing JRE to charge him overseas tour expenses. He claimed that they should have been met by JRE under a management agreement; Elton John accepted around £3.4m from Reid in settlement of claims against him[i].

Pell was amazed that the two sides argued in the High Court about whether certain of Elton John's financial details should be disclosed to the court[ii], saying: 'Darling, it was in the papers three years ago. I mean the cat's out the bag – literally out of the bag, the black bag outside John Reid's office.'

However, the singer lost his case against the accountants and Haydon in a ruling in 2001 that cleared them of claims of negligence and exonerated Reid. Elton John appealed the ruling in relation to the accountants, but it was upheld in 2002 in the Court of Appeal[iii].

Nonetheless, Pell told one interviewer that he took the credit for the fact that Elton John had received a large sum from Reid[iv]: 'I'm not asking Elton to give me a cut of the money or write a song about me, but I'd like a bit of acknowledgement.'

Brick Court chambers, one of the leading sets of barristers' chambers in the UK, was to become embroiled in yet another development in Pell's Elton John saga. And despite the legal trouble for Pell and his associates over his earlier Elton John stories, and despite the imminent exposure of what he regarded as an attempt to pervert the course of justice in the Neil Hamilton-v-Mohammed Al Fayed case, an unrepentant Benji the Binman clashed tiaras with the singer and targeted legally privileged documents.

Brick Court chambers would also feature when it emerged that Pell obtained confidential Bloody Sunday inquiry documents from its rubbish. Mark Hollingsworth, the journalist middle man who sold Hamilton's libel documents to Fayed , again acted as Pell's go-between. Pell says that two days before the *Mail on Sunday* broke the Fayed story in 2000, he was still dealing with Hollingsworth[v]. 'At the same time, we're doing the Elton John story together, the one that ends up getting injuncted.'

While preparing Elton John's case in 2000, Eversheds asked counsel, at Brick Court chambers, to advise on whether it had a conflict of interests over the firm's past links with parties in the case, preventing it from acting for the singer. Pell found in the rubbish outside Brick Court chambers a draft advice prepared by junior counsel, Neil Calver, with notes written on it by leading counsel, Jonathan Hirst QC, a former Bar Council chairman, suggesting that Eversheds should not act for Elton John because it had a conflict of interests[vi]. As in the case of the Hamilton libel papers, Pell had found a document subject to legal privilege. Although the leak came from Brick Court chambers rather than Eversheds, Pell dubbed the solicitors 'Nevershreds'.

He said: 'I have given Hollingsworth this document from Elton's new barristers… telling Eversheds that they can no longer act for Elton. It's an amazing splash. I give that one to Hollingsworth. Hollingsworth gives it to *The Express*; they love it, they love it, they love it. "The story's going in this week." Thursday morning, Hollingsworth rings me up… "Benjamin, I've got bad news for you. They've been injuncted."'

'What?'

'Yes. Don't worry, though, your name hasn't come up. Nobody suspects anything.

I said, 'Wh- wh- wh- wh- why have they been injuncted?'

The following day, Hollingsworth rings me up and says, 'I've now managed to get the truth out of the *Express*. Unfortunately, they made it obvious when they rang up Elton's lawyer that they had documentation.'

I said, 'I've always said to you, Mark, you shouldn't allow...'

'Oh, I'm so sorry. It won't happen again. Don't worry, we've had a result. I've got you another story in this weekend's Sunday Times.'

I said, 'Oh no, but what about the Express?'

'There's always another day, don't worry.'

Although Hollingsworth was not responsible the triggering the injunction, a furious Pell told his media-barrister Richard Murray: 'Everything he touches turns to sand.' He said that this problem with the *Daily Express* helped make his decision to 'do the dirty' on Hollingsworth and Fayed. 'He went to the well once too often,' says Pell.

Later, Pell gave McVicar a different version of this story[vii]:

Pell: He rings up the Express...

McVicar: Do they know it's a Benji story?

Pell: Well, it's obvious – it's a bloody confidential document. Anyway, Wednesday night, I ring him up, 'How's it going?'

'Oh Benjamin, I've got bad news for you.'

I said, 'What?'

He said, 'They've been injuncted.'

'Injuncted! What the hell has happened?'

'Don't worry, Benjamin, you're name has never come up. They don't know there are any documents, and I think they've done the best they could do.'

A reporter on the *Daily Express*, Rachel Baird, was told to make telephone calls to check out this latest Elton John story. Eversheds successfully applied for a High Court injunction to stop the contents of the memo being revealed, and demanded that the *Daily Express* reveal the identity of its source. Baird and the *Daily Express*' then editor Rosie Boycott were resolute in not revealing a confidential source. Eversheds went back to the High Court to seek an order for the newspaper, Boycott and Baird to reveal the source.

In March 2000, Mr Justice Morland ordered Boycott and Baird to disclose the source. He ruled[viii]:

It is a matter of speculation who it was that obtained the draft advice or a photostat of it. In the absence of any evidence that there has been a leak of confidential information before or since this incident, it is unlikely that the culprit is in-house. It is more likely to have been an employee of the cleaning firm, the outside waste disposal company or possibly a scavenger on a waste dump. Whoever it was, I consider that it is unlikely that the person would have passed the draft advice direct to Ms Baird. The probabilities are that the culprit passed on the draft advice for financial reward to a professional hawker to the media of confidential information about celebrities.

So that journalists can effectively discharge their right, indeed their duty, to expose wrongdoing, abuse, corruption and incompetence in all aspects of central and local government and of business, industry, the professions and all aspects of society, they have to receive information including confidential information from a variety of sources, including seedy sources and disloyal sources.

No court may require a person to disclose, nor is any person guilty of contempt of court for refusing to disclose, the source of information contained in a publication for which he is responsible, unless it be established to the satisfaction of the court that disclosure is necessary in the interest of justice or national security or for the prevention of disorder or crime.

Clearly if there is a person or there are persons who search for and select confidential information subject to legal professional privilege and hawk it around for passage to the media, the achievement of justice will be endangered. Clients will lose faith in their lawyers. Solicitors will lose faith in barristers. Members of chambers and their staff will lose faith in each other. Suspicion and mistrust will abound... Such a source presents a very real and continuing danger to the interests of justice threatening the confidentiality of legal professional privilege, a cornerstone in the achievement of justice. Balancing the competing interests of justice and of investigative journalism in the exercise of my discretion, in my judgement, I do not consider it disproportionate to order, and do so order, the defendants to disclose the identity of the source.

A sensible approach that would protect legally privileged documents without compromising the confidentiality that journalists must give sources is to make lawyers responsible in law to protect sensertive documents – drafts or otherwise. They can do this by taking two simple steps in particular: first, buy a shredder; second, use it.

Mr Justice Morland delivered his judgement in the afternoon of Friday March 3rd. In the morning of the same day, he granted Hamilton a stay on paying £500,000 towards Fayed's legal costs following the ex-MP's unsuccessful libel action[ix]. The suspension of payment followed the *Mail on Sunday* article published just over a fortnight earlier. As *Private Eye* suggested: 'Mr Justice Morland must have experienced a sense of déjà vu on the afternoon of Friday March 3rd.'

The judge gave the journalists until noon the following Wednesday to disclose the source – high noon, indeed. The judge gave Express Newspapers and its journalists permission to appeal.

Private Eye reported:

Mr Justice Morland oversaw the drafting of an undertaking by the Express reporter to identify the person or persons from whom she had obtained the documents in the event that the appeal court uphold the disclosure order. He described a theoretical situation to stem lengthy legal discussion over the chain of sources:

Mr X might be a journalist who might have said, "I got it from Mr Y who is closely connected to Brick Court chambers," or, "I got it from Mr Z who emptied the bins," or, "I do not know what his name was, but he says he is the man who emptied the bins."'

One binman who has caused Sir Elton considerable trouble in the past is of course Benji Pell.

And amongst the contributors to *Private Eye* at the time was Mark Hollingsworth, the freelance journalist and middle man who supplied to the *Daily Express* the Elton John legal document obtained from the rubbish by Pell.

As Pell later observed with regards to the Eversheds case[x]: 'My name was the... devil that dare not speak its name. Who was the judge in this case? Justice Morland. Who was the judge in the case of... Hamilton and Fayed? Justice Morland. Who did Benjamin Pell give the Elton John document to? Mark Hollingsworth. Who did Benjamin Pell do the deal with Fayed with? Hollingsworth.'

However, the following month, Express Newspapers and its journalists won their appeal before Lord Woolf, then the Master of the Rolls and later the Lord Chief Justice, Lord Justice Pill and Lord Justice May. According to the judgement given by Lord Woolf on behalf of the court, Baird obtained the draft advice on Tuesday, February 2nd, and tried to telephone the relevant partner at Eversheds but did not reach him until the following day[xi]...

> It was obvious from this telephone call that Ms Baird was aware of the contents of the draft advice. It is also reasonably clear that the document which had come into her possession was either the original or a copy of the draft which had originated in chambers...
>
> Prior to the hearing of the appeal, someone – it is not suggested that person had any connection with the parties to this appeal – placed the contents of the advice on the internet. On the day of the hearing of this appeal, the claimants, having become aware of this, obtained an injunction to prevent further publication. The person who was responsible for this action has so far not been identified.

Pell identifies himself, in his taped interviews with McVicar, as the culprit for placing the contents of the advice on the internet[xii]. He posted them on a website called Forum Exchange run by a London socialite. Pell says: 'She had a message board on there. One day, she wakes up, and there's a message on there, saying, "Sir Elton John should sack his lawyers because we've just discovered a document regarding his lawyers and the fact they can no longer act for him."'Immediately, Elton John's lawyers Eversheds injuncted her and closed the website down. She was personally in court but Pell contributed nothing towards her costs. He says he only found out about the legal action against the website after reading a short story about it in *The News of the World*[xiii].

Pell claims falsely that he helped draft the legal documents replying to Elton John's action against the website, despite the fact that he could not go to court[xiv]. He says that he wrote in a 14-page letter: 'What we have here, in fact, is an arrogant abuse of the British system of justice... This elevates Sir Elton John's private business dealings to the level of a state secret.'

In fact, Pell had nothing to do with drafting the letter: it was done by an American lawyer. He also lied to the woman, telling her that he was not responsible for putting it on the website in the first place. Nonetheless, he took it upon himself to spite Eversheds. 'How did I ultimately get my own back on them? So, I thought to myself, "Okay, darlings, if you're going to get the bloody... website closed down, what is Benjamin Pell going to do?" This is one of my favourite things ever. How is Benjamin Pell going to react? I went on to every single Elton John website, and I put a message on, saying, "Elton should be made aware of the fact that his lawyers, Eversheds, have been informed by leading counsel that they are no longer able to act for him in the litigation with John Reid. Having negligently allowed this memorandum to fall into the hands of the Press… surely highly trained ex-public school boys can not be so stupid. They are continuing to pursue fruitless actions in the courts. Elton, you took on [the socialite] and lost…" And that was on 57 Elton John websites… And then an anonymous 'phone call was made to the Eversheds press office the following morning, saying, "I think I should alert you to the fact that there are 57 websites out there all dedicated to Elton John, all will have to close down."

Lord Woolf continued in his judgement[xv]: 'There had been no previous incident of this sort involving the chambers. Since the matters came to light, the chambers have reviewed their security and have introduced precautions, which should make it more difficult for there to be a repetition of what has occurred. No system, however, can be entirely foolproof.'

He noted that Brick Court chambers had 'made no attempt themselves to trace who was responsible for stealing the advice'. Indeed, Mr Justice Morland had concluded that any inquiry conducted within chambers was likely to be 'utterly impracticable'. However, Lord Woolf disagreed: 'Before the courts require journalists to break what journalists regard as a most important professional obligation to protect a source, the minimum requirement is that other avenues should be explored.'

He concluded:

Although there has now been a publication on the internet of the contents of the advice, which suggests that there is an individual at some stage of the chain who is motivated to cause mischief to the claimants, this is still a one-off infringement of professional legal confidentiality which does not justify making an inroad on the other privilege, the privilege of the journalist. The judge thought that there could be within the chambers a sense of mistrust if the perpetrator was not detected. This is unlikely. It may be regrettable that this should be necessary, but the fact is that if the chambers had taken the precautionary measures, which they have now taken, the leak would probably have been avoided. Now that the danger has been brought home and the necessary steps have been taken, there is no reason to think that clients will lose faith in their lawyers because of this single incident in the chambers.

In fact, unknown to the original judge and the Court of Appeal, there had been a previous example of legal papers being taken by Pell from Brick Court chambers, but it had not by this stage come to light (see chapters 14 to 16 about the Bloody Sunday inquiry security breach), as well as many further examples of legally privileged documents being taken from other lawyers offices (the Hamilton's libel documents for one. Others: see chapters 8 and 9 on All Saints and various other celebrities, and chapter 10 on Jonathan Aitken).

Pell outed himself as the source of the Elton John document in his taped interviews with McVicar, as detailed earlier in this chapter. He also gave this account in a statement[xvi]:

My best known story involving the Daily Express was the story about the opinion given in the Elton John litigation against Price Waterhouse. I found the opinion given by Jonathan Hirst and Neil Calver, outside Brick Court chambers, which dealt with whether Eversheds had a conflict of interest in continuing to act for Elton John. That opinion found its way to Rachel Baird of the Daily Express, firstly through Mark Hollingsworth, another freelancer, who passed it to… Paul Halloran. Most of the senior executives of the Daily Express knew where the document had come from.

Although Pell was not named by the *Daily Express* or any of its journalists as the source, the Fleet Street grapevine – and, in turn, *Private Eye* – identified him. In addition to its story of March 10th cited earlier, the *Eye* ran another after the appeal, saying[xvii]:

As the retrieval of confidential legal documents from dustbins in return for wads of money is a Pell speciality, he must be tremendously relieved that the legal protection granted to the journalist also extends to the guttersnipe.

Pell was becoming infamous as a result of retrieving confidential Elton John documents from the rubbish of the singer's manager and his lawyers. And he became tarred with an appalling reputation in the legal profession, as he told Jones[xviii]: 'I was looking for somebody to do my debt-collection work, and so I found this firm called Theodore Goddard. They are quite a large City firm. "My name is Mr Bell." You know, I never say my real name when I 'phone up people. And then when he took my calls, and I said, "Fine, thank you very much," he seemed interested.

'"So can I have your name again please?"

'"Oh, it's Benjamin Pell."

'He said, "Benjamin Pell? Is that the same Benjamin Pell who was involved in the John Reid case?"

'I said, "Well, as a matter of fact it was; does that make any difference to you doing debt-collection work for me?"

'He said, "We would never want to be associated with somebody like you."'

Although Reid had succeeded in tracking the source of the leaks, he had nonetheless lost Elton John as a client. Pell, reading an unidentified article to Jones, claims to have telephoned Reid to tell him that Elton John had sacked him:

> Basically, they've reported this thing about how he got the news about how he'd been sacked. 'Within a- (laughs) within an hour, the word had spread, and reporters and photographers had gathered outside Reid's St John's Wood mansion. "It's news to me," he said, "I don't know if I've been sacked." But...' and this is the coup de grace from Benjamin Pell, 'before he went out to dinner that evening, his 'phone rang again. A gay-sounding male voice he did not recognise asked in a triumphant tone, "John, have you heard, you've been sacked?"' (cackles) That was me. (more cackling, hysterical laughter). He obviously remembers it.

Pell crowed about bring Reid down: 'Unfortunately for John Reid Enterprises, because of me, last year, he had to actually put his property up for sale. I even managed to make money out of this story, because... I actually got a copy of this and got that into *Punch*, that he was trying to sell his building and he made a million-pound loss on his building because he had to sell it last year cos he was desperate to get rid of it.' Pell says that Reid had to lay off staff and moved to offices no more than a quarter the size. 'All because of me.' Pell gleefully referred to Reid as, 'The ex-manager of Elton John: the one who I got the sack.'

He told another interviewer[xix]: 'I was spending six days a week, going round in a van, throughout the night; coming back with 80, 100 bags; going through them; going out again that same night. No one has ever done that before. And no one has ever had the effect of getting people like Elton John to sack a manager.'

Reid said in 2001 that because of the events of 1998, he folded his company, saying[xx]: 'I had 24 staff and the impact on their lives was quite serious: the wreckage it caused...'

Elton John later told Larry King, the American talk-show host[xxi]: I've had my fair share in Britain of battling the tabloids... It's been a national pastime for me in England. [King asked him how well he dealt with it emotionally.] It still hurts. I have a much better relationship with the Press than I did, I think because I stood my ground. They respected for that and because I've been successful. And I think, you know, I think, as you get older you mature a little bit... I don't mind people's opinions of you. You know, that's fair game. You're a public figure. People can have an opinion. They have a right to write what they think... I can deal with that. It's when they write something that's completely untrue. And if you're a journalist, surely the thing that you should be writing is the truth, or at least checking your facts. And that's what drives me crazy.

What really stung Elton John about those stories in *The Mirror* that originated from Benji the Binman was that they were all too truthful, based as they were on genuine confidential documents.

The Queen of Rock also told the King of the Chat Shows:
I always liked spending my money, even when I was a kid, when I had a paper round – or paper route, as they call it over here. I used to get my money at the end of the week, buy my mum something, or buy a record, and that was it. I'm a very wealthy man. I have a lot of money stashed away, but I do live my life from day to day. And I think, with Jonny [Gianni Versace] being murdered and seeing so many things happen in the last few years- yeah, I have homes in Atlanta, London, Windsor, and Nice, and now in Venice in Italy. And I love collecting art. I've got a great collection of photography. I spend my money but I don't, you know, I do- I'm a lavish kind of

guy, and that's the way I am.

King then queried him about the reports that he was in financial trouble.

There were some- yeah, that was some reports, when I left- parted company with my ex-manager, Mr John Reid, and it led to a lawsuit against Price Waterhouse in England, which is still going on. It's gone to the Court of Appeal and it will be heard in June [but he lost, as detailed above]. There were reports that, you know, that I was short of cash and blah, blah, blah. And there was a- you know, having gone through the books and looked at what was happening, my instincts were right. I called my lawyer in and said, 'I don't know, the money's not going where it should be.'

And we were proved right. And consequently we parted ways. I have a new management team. I have my own office now. I kind of run my own affairs. And there was a- you know, there was a scare. It was like, where has all this money gone? And, you know, I'm not- I've only been interested in the artistic side of life. And I trusted someone to look after me on the business side of life. And that went on for 27 years. And it went on for 27 years too long without me taking an interest... And that was one of the biggest blows to me, when that parting happened, because, you know, when someone's been with you for 27 years, it's hard to say good-bye. But it-- you know, it was a necessity.

King asked him if it was painful too. Elton replied:

It's very painful. It's upsetting.

Elton John and John Reid, like Hamilton and Fayed, had been 'Pelaxed'. And, as Reid told the Channel 4 documentary[xxii]: 'He (Pell) subsequently targeted another manager who I know quite well, John Benson, and I think that led to the break up of his relationship with his group.'

That group was All Saints: the next chapter of the life of the 'scavenger' of dumped waste.

The Fleet Street Sewer Rat

References

[i] Nick Craven, 'Bitter end of my 26 years with Elton. Former manager tells how star began to lose trust in him,' *Daily Mail* (05.12.00); Lewis Smith, 'Sir Elton's former lover tells of hurt at Palace snub,' *The Times* (05.12.00); Cathy Gordon, John Aston and Cathy Mayer, 'I WANTED TO STAY FRIENDS WITH SIR ELTON, SAYS SACKED EX-MANAGER,' *Press Association* (04.12.00); Sean O'Neill, 'Elton "kept lover from investiture,"' *The Daily Telegraph* (05.12.00).

[ii] McVicar audio tape (recorded 12.11.00) MDRG.

[iii] Stephen Howard, 'ELTON LOSES £14m TOUR COSTS APPEAL' *Press Association* (24.06.02).

[iv] Frances Welch, 'Rubbish is fine – except on the Sabbath,' *Sunday Telegraph* (04.02.01).

[v] McVicar audio tape (recorded 30.12.00) MDRI.

[vi] McVicar audio tape (recorded 30.12.00) MDRI.

[vii] McVicar video tape (filmed 14.01.01) DVRG.

[viii] Mr Justice Morland, 'John and others -v- Express Newspapers plc and others,' (03.03.00).

[ix] *Private Eye* No 997 (10.03.00).

[x] McVicar audio tape (recorded 12.11.00) MDRG.

[xi] Lord Woolf, 'John and others -v- Express Newspapers plc and others,' Court of Appeal, Civil Division (19.04.00).

[xii] McVicar audio tape (recorded 12.11.00) MDRG.

[xiii] 'Elton's web suit,' *The News of the World* (23.04.00).

[xiv] McVicar audio tape (recorded 12.11.00) MDRG.

[xv] Lord Woolf, 'John and others -v- Express Newspapers plc and others,' Court of Appeal, Civil Division (19.04.00).

[xvi] Benjamin Pell witness statement, Benjamin Pell -v- Express Newspapers and Mark Watts (08.04.03).

[xvii] *Private Eye* No 1001 (05.05.00).

[xviii] "3½-hour rushes," Moving Perspective (filmed 1999).

[xix] David Thomas, 'The binman lifts his lid. For years, he made a living raiding famous people's rubbish bins for confidential documents. But Benjamin Pell, who begins a new career on television this week, is unrepentant: "There's no excuse for not shredding,"' *Sunday Telegraph* (21.04.02).

[xx] Valerie Grove, 'Elton chose to just cut me off. I had seen him do it to others in the past,' *The Times* (21.04.01).

[xxi] 'Larry King Weekend,' CNN (02.03.02).

[xxii] 'Scandal in the Bins,' Channel 4 (first shown 11.01.01).

Chapter 8

Saints and Sinners:
All Saints

All Saints entered the charts with 'Never Ever' and, unfortunately for the band, it attracted Pell's attention. The group of four Londoners, Shaznay Lewis, the band's main song-writer, Melanie Blatt, and the sisters, Natalie and Nicole Appleton, first broke into the charts at number 4 in August 1997 with 'I Know Where It's At'. The second single, 'Never Ever', entered at number 3. Pell told the Channel 4 documentary[i]: 'The first time I heard that was September, and I was completely blown away. It's an unbelievable track, a beautiful track. A mixture of hallelujah, of Amazing Grace.'

> The spooky thing is it all coalesces: it all comes together. The 31st of August, the day Diana died, All Saints entered the charts at number 4. So, then I started ringing up the record company to find out more about All Saints. 'Who are All Saints?' etc, etc. And then I bought the record, bought the label, and I saw 'John Benson Music Management'. So I became obsessed then with finding John Benson.

John Benson was the manager of All Saints, a rival to the Spice Girls and signed to London Records. Pell tells Jones[ii]: 'I needed to know who had written this song, I thought this was an absolute classic of the nineties. Being an absolute anorak... I rang up London Records... They had obviously been told not to give anything away. These record executives are complete idiots – absolute tossers.'

Pell was alerted to existence of the All Saints, when he read an article in August '97's *Music Week* how they were set to supplant the Spice Girls. Pell '...didn't like the Spice Girls, for a variety of reasons. I just thought they were manufactured group, and music wasn't very good.' All Saints brings out, besides Pell's vindictiveness, his racism. 'So, anything I could get on the Spice Girls- anti-Spice Girls, I was interested in. So when I read this article in *Music Week* about this group to rival the Spice Girls I thought, however bad their music is, I am going to use this group... to get at the Spice Girls. As it turns out, they were four beauti- well three beautiful girls and one black girl: three absolute beauties plus the black girl, Shaznay Lewis.'

Pell told the Channel 4 documentary[iii]: 'I was looking everywhere to find John Benson. I thought, "How can I get him to notice me?" So, end of November, I went to All Saints Road, and I nicked all the road signs off All Saints Road. I mean, which for me was absolutely crazy. I mean, somebody like me doing something illegal like that. I bought a crowbar from a, er, er, one of these HSS's. I remember the exact one. It's in Kentish Town Road. I've still got the receipt at home. It cost me £24 for one night. You've got All Saints Road, this druggie- all the druggies are there at 4 o'clock in the morning, so everyone was seeing what I was doing. Everyone thought I was completely mad. So, that evening I came home with four road signs from All Saints Road, and I thought, "Now, now this will give me a chance. Now what I can do is ring up London Records." I biked it over to them the following morning and... typical record company, and they were complete arses. They just didn't realise. Here was this fanatic – he's obviously a nutter, but he really genuinely wants to help with All Saints.'

Pell's attention on All Saints coincided approximately with his targeting of Elton John; at this point, he was yet to break his first story on the row between the singer and Branson. Pell told McVicar that he tried to persuade Ally Ross of *The Sun* to run a story about the removal of the All Saints Road signs by a fan, and, as part of that attempt, he also offered the correspondence between Elton John and Branson[iv].

Pell told Jones how he hit upon the idea of nicking the road signs[v]. '...The famous thing about the Beatles was that you couldn't go into Abbey Road... in London NW8 without noticing that the road signs were always being nicked... Why don't I nick... these road signs, and then at least I can get them some publicity. Maybe then they'll start returning my calls.

'Rang up... London Records, said, "Do you realise what I did last night?"' The receptionist was miffed but Pell told her: 'I said, "I stole the road signs from All Saints Road. Isn't that a great story?"' She didn't believe him, so he drove over to the offices in Hammersmith '...got them there, she was in hysterics, this lady, "Excellent, really. Well done." I then hardly spoke to her again, completely mad woman, anyway. So I thought at least now, now at least, I said to her, "At least, I can get John Benson to ring me."

'"Oh yes, don't worry, now he will ring you." And obviously, the amusing thing was, he didn't ring me.'

Having been rebuffed by London Records, Pell targeted the rubbish of the solicitor to All Saints[vi], Helen Searles and her eponymous firm. Pell told Jones[vii]: "Having done Elton of course, having seen how valuable the stuff from John Reid's rubbish was, I then started doing the rubbish of Searles."

He found the home address in London of Shaznay Lewis, and went there, using an alias[viii]. There he did '...my normal Benjamin Pell routine, or Peter Jeffrey as I'm known then... for about half an hour, and, you know, in the end she just closes the door and thinks, "What a fucking arsehole."'

Pell discovered that two Americans who had written 'Never Ever' were suing over the All Saints version and he telephoned one of them[x]. 'The wife said to me, "We're actually injuncting the girls, and they can't appear at the Brits [Brit Awards] because we're putting an injunction on them." I got that into *The Sun*, and I was the headline in their 'Bizarre' column.'

In fact, All Saints won two Brit awards in 1998, one for 'Never Ever' and another for the accompanying video; the litigation was eventually settled.

Meanwhile, Pell was plundering whatever rubbish he could from Searles he quickly hit the jackpot. He showed Jones his find on camera[xi] '....this is their band agreement, and this was able to give me and the press the knowledge of who was getting all the money. And that was a revelation cos look, Shaznay, the black girl, was getting 55%, Mel was getting 20%, and those two other girls were only getting 12.5%, so you can imagine Fleet Street made a lot of that.'

Pell, still using an alias, finally contacted Benson just before the Brit

Awards in 1998[xii]. He had got his number from Searles' binbags. 'I now had Benson's mobile number. I got hold of him about half-past eleven. I said: "Hello, John. It's Peter Jeffrey here."

'He said: "Oh, the name's familiar."

'"Do you know the girls have won two Brit Awards?"

'And he said: "You're the Peter Jeffrey- you- do you know how much trouble you've caused? You went round to Shaznay Lewis's house last night, didn't you?"

'I said: "I know."

'He said: "You- do you know how much trouble you've caused? I've had her mother in tears all morning, and you've caused so- she's been in crying. What have you done? Well, what- what do you want? Who are you exactly?' And then he seemed to calm down a second, may- maybe the drugs were wearing off.

'He said: "But I've heard about you, Peter Jeffrey. I think we can do business together. Why don't we meet up?"'

Benson had his own agenda for Peel aka Peter Jeffrey. He had picked up the lie put about by Pell that he was a hacker and he wanted him to target Searles. Benson had run into contractual problems with All Saints, and Searles were acting for them in their attempt to dump his as their manager. When this proposition was put to him, Pell did not tell Benson that he was already raiding the firm's bins. Instead he played Benson along, pretending he was a computer hacker:

He's a really nice guy, funnily enough. You know, he sees I'm a complete fanatic when it comes to All Saints. I know everything about them. I know more than he does. Well, not surprising considering he's a complete arsehole.

'We know about you hacking into Elton John and John Reid.'

"I said: 'Fuck.'

And he said: 'We know all about you,' and we got talking and stuff."

Pell gave a similar account to Jones, saying[xiii] which he filmed outside London Records: 'Benson said to me, "Yes, I've heard all about you, Peter Jeffrey; we know you've infiltrated our building and Polygram in Chancellor's Road in W6. We all know you've infiltrated the computer system in this building, we've had to change our computer codes all because of you."

'"I will arrange to meet you in two days time at my local pub... the Clifton Arms in Clifton Road in Maida Vale. Maybe we can decide whether we can do something together. I know everything about you, Peter Jeffrey. I know about you and Elton John. I know you were behind the Elton John story."

'So, basically, already by then, my name was reasonably well known in the small circles in the music industry.

'For the next four months, he actually employed me, mainly actually, as it turns out, to go through the rubbish of, erm, of Searles.' But the relationship was rocky: the first disruption came when the *Evening Standard* broke a story in March 1998 about his targeting of Elton John's rubbish[xiv]. But he was also feeding into the press whatever he was picking up about All Saints.

Pell told the Channel 4 documentary[xv]: 'Next, I'm now getting stories from Benson. So now I've had at least six 'Bizarre' headline stories. 'Girls to appear with Bill Clinton,' 'Girls to do a Levis advert.' I mean, Benson was telling me things in confidence, heaven knows what he thought – but they were appearing in press the following day.'

Pell told McVicar that after Benson mentioned to him that Nicole had tea with the actor, Brad Pitt, he gave an exaggerated version of the story to *The Sun*[xvi]. 'I ring him up that weekend in America, and he tells me, "You wouldn't believe it, Nicole had tea with Brad Pitt yesterday." So... that was my first actually made-up story. I said to the "Bizarre" column, "Brad Pitt and Nicole are going out together." Cos, by now, they trust me, they had that as their headline, "Brad Pitt and Nicole in love scene," or something.' In fact, according to Nicole, she had never even met Brad Pitt[xvii].

Benson began to realise that he had took a viper into his nest and his relationship with Pell took a fractious turn. Pell knew that his time was up[xviii]: 'The following day I ring up *The Sun*, and I said, "Look, I think this guy- I don't want to have any dealings with this guy any more. I've got a great story, though, before I finish off with this guy which will really fuck him off. You know, the girls are going to be doing 'White Christmas' for their Christmas single. Isn't that crazy?"' It went into the next day's edition.

'So basically we have a big fall out, and Benson said the

following day, "I don't want any more dealings with him. He's really-he's upset the girls. The girls can no longer do 'White Christmas' any more as their Christmas single. He's completely ruined it.'"

The final straw for Benson, however, was after Pell found an explosive document that was a transcript of a tape recorded meeting between him and the band in the presence of their solicitor. Pell began hawking it around to possible buyers. The transcript would shatter the band's "girl power" image of being four young women in control of their lives. It showed that Nicole had an abortion following pressure from the band management. The father was Robbie Williams. None of this was known at the time. The extent of public knowledge then was that Nicole and Robbie had recently been engaged, although they soon parted and she eventually had a son with Liam Gallagher of Oasis. In addition, the memo detailed how Mel Blatt had come under similar pressure, although she defied it to have her baby after falling pregnant to Stuart Zender, former bass player with Jamiroquai, whom she later married.

Pell started offering to Fleet Street details from the document. The *Daily Star* ran a front-page splash, saying[xx]:

> All Saints star Melanie Blatt's joy at being pregnant has sparked a furious bust-up in the babe band... Furious Shaznay Lewis... stormed, 'You're wrecking my dream.'

At this stage, Benson was still unaware of Pell's role in selling to the Press lurid details of the private lives of members of the band , which he had retrieved from rubbish. Indeed, he had suggested that Pell help the band's official biographer prepare a book on All Saints[xxi]. The biographer, who also knew Pell as Peter Jeffrey, '...had mentioned to me that she'd had dinner with the group about a day before, and she'd noticed that they were depressed or something. "Do you know what's up?"

"'Now because I was trying to impress her, as I always do try and impress people, I said, "Well I can tell you exactly what's up. They had a meeting last week, and Nicky, er, had an abortion because the record company said they'd sue her unless she aborted."

"'What?" She was absolutely gobsmacked.

'I said, "I'll fax it over to you. But, obviously, you do realise that this is totally confidential, and you must never tell anyone."

'"Oh, don't worry… Don't worry, Peter." So I faxed it over to her. "Thank you so much for that, Peter." Outrageous, really.

'So I ring up *The Sun*. I tell them, "Well, I've got a good way now of pissing off the record company. Did you realise that Nicky Appleton had an abortion because the record company said- and that's probably why she's rushing into this engagement with Robbie Williams; she probably feels guilty about it." Anyway, I fax over the memo to *The Sun*. They ring up John Benson.'

He was with the band's biographer who picked up the gist of the *The Sun*'s inquiry. According to Pell, the biographer said to Benson that she knew who gave them the story – Peter Jeffrey aka the binman. 'And so obviously, you know, the shit hit the fan,' related the gleeful Pell.

All Saints secured an injunction against Pell preventing the publication of the document's contents. The *Evening Standard* reported[xxii]:

> All Saints have become the latest victims of a celebrity-obsessed stalker who previously rifled through Sir Elton John's dustbins.
>
> Benjamin Pell, who was the subject of a High Court injunction by Sir Elton in March, managed to get hold of a confidential memo detailing All Saints's meeting with their management. The girls' solicitors issued a High Court writ against Pell to prevent him from going public with the document.
>
> Pell has been ordered to hand back the papers, destroy any copies he has made, and pay costs and damages which, it is believed, may run into thousands of pounds.
>
> Although Pell – who has given his occupation as trainee solicitor in the past – has previously claimed that he does promotional work for the band, he is not known to have worked for the girls' management company, John Benson Music Management. It remains a mystery as to how he got hold of the papers.

Pell told the Channel 4 documentary that because of this betrayal Benson arranged for him to receive what it called 'a no-nonsense warning' outside his home in Hendon[xxiii].

Pell said: 'And that's the beating, okay?'

'The purpose of the attack was to scare me; was to silence me; to assassinate me. I just don't know what- But, as you know, they didn't do a very good job anyway, and, as you said to me, if they really wanted to do a good job they would've got better- you know, more professional people involved. So if they did want to scare me, they did scare me. I was shitting myself that day.'

Watching a preview of this documentary at home, Pell laughs at his suggestion on the programme that the attack was an attempt to assassinate him[xxiv].

Benson denied having anything to do with the attack on Pell, pointing out that a lot of people had more cause than him to take out Pell[xxv]. In fact, as McVicar later discovered from one of Pell's hirelings, he instigated the attack himself to make it appear that he was the victim not the victimiser.

Pell retained a new solicitor to defend the All Saints legal action[xxvi]. However, Pell fell out with him after sending him documents retrieved from the rubbish of barristers retained by the solicitor's firm. The solicitor warned both his senior partner and the various barristers' chambers they use.

Pell told Jones that he asked the solicitor about the progress on a specific case[xxvii]. 'He said: "Benjamin, how do you know about that?"

'"Oh I got that from 5 Raymond Buildings bins." I just told him that cos I thought, you know, he's my lawyer, I can tell... he knows what I'm like.

'"Oh Benjamin, you know, I didn't know you were doing 5 Raymond Buildings."

'So I laughed, and said, "Well, is there a problem?"

'He said, "Well, you know, y- I've got to tell them."

'I said, "What do you mean you've got to tell them? You're my lawyer. You know, what I'm telling you is in confidence."

'And he said, "No, no, no, no. I mean, this is different though cos, you know, I'm dealing with them." Oh, basically what he meant was to say, "I don't want to be seen in a year's time when your story comes out to have hidden the fact that I knew you and knew your activity."

'Accordingly, I had a brainwave in the middle of the meeting, and

I say to him, "I'll make a promise. I won't tell- I won't do them anymore, but you mustn't tell them."

'He said, "Okay then."

'It was a Benjamin Pell promise, of course, which I wouldn't keep... Of course I went back there the following day. I mean, I'm not going to take any fucking threats from bloody lawyers – 'specially my own lawyer.'

He complains that the solicitor nonetheless 'betrayed' him. '...what happens? He comes back from holiday... "By the way, Benjamin, I'm really sorry, but the day before you left I had to raise the matter with my head of department."

'"What? You promised me you wouldn't."

'"Oh Benjamin, I'm afraid, at the end of the day, I had to weigh up- I've got a duty to my profession, I've got a duty..."

'"But... you knew what the position was." Bastard, but all of that is on tape. That guy is shafted; he should never work again.'

Speaking to the camera, in his usual style, he gave the solicitor the following message:

> I've got a letter for you. I'm going to be writing you a letter in the next two or three days, saying I'm not paying any of your bills, and if you have any problem with that I advise you to write to the Law Society... Cos I'm telling you this: this guy has done me a lot of damage. Even if he doesn't think he has, he has. And I'm going to do him damage in return.

Pell gives a similar, albeit shorter, account to McVicar[xxviii] in which he reported the solicitor saying: 'It's in the interests of justice that you- that what you're doing is exposed.'

Music Week branded Pell as 'Public Enemy Number 1' in an article that reported on his arrest for taking documents from Aitken's solicitors some months earlier [see chapter 10][xxix]. It said:

> It is understood that the individual has previously been linked with a stream of press exposes about the activities of stars such as Sir Elton John, George Michael, All Saints and The Verve as well as industry figures including managers John Reid, John Benson and Jazz Summers.

A number of entertainment law firms have previously brought proceedings against [Pell].

'Everyone has to be on their guard against him because he operates on the fringes of the law, and he's very cunning,' says one leading music business lawyer who became embroiled in a legal tussle with the individual after his company's confidential documents were splashed across national newspapers. 'I can't stress how important it is to shred all documents – he even went through my bins at home.'

Over the past year, the individual has even offered stories to MW [Music Week] – offers that were declined. However, when MW visited him at his home in north London last week, he refused to be interviewed.

Two leading London entertainment law firms are known to have previously injuncted the man, obtaining 'search-and-seize' orders which led to raids on the north London house which acts as the nerve centre for his activities. They both retrieved hundreds of pages of documents and subsequently won proceedings against him. A partner at one of the firms involved says, 'If he starts his activities against us again, he'll go straight to jail because he will be in contempt of court, it's as simple as that.'

The chairman of a leading independent UK record label claims his company was also targeted by the man.

'We tried to reason with him but that didn't work, so I hired private detectives, but the problem was that we couldn't catch him in the act. It's about time the police got involved because somebody has to put a stop to this interference in our private affairs.'

Meanwhile, All Saints split from their erstwhile manager John Benson, although he was later obtain a knockdown settlement from their record company. Benson hates Pell with a vengeance and threatened him one evening in Soho's Groucho night club. 'He's a sewer rat that should be just exterminated,' he said bitterly as the shaking binman scuttled away still clutching one of his black rubbish bags.

Pell's favourite memory of his havoc he wreaked on the All Saints is a reference to him that Shaznay and Natalie made in an interview that the band gave in 1998[xix]. They were asked if they'd had any stalker.

Natalie said, 'I am reading a book about serial killers, about how they haunt you and start sending you pictures, and the next thing you know they're cutting your head off. We have had one – sort of. He became obsessed with us.'

Shaznay took up the story: 'He's a very talented guy, actually. He came to my house in January; I thought he was the paper-boy because he had loads of papers with him. He had Melody Maker actually; he had copies of all these magazines we were in for my mum... I answered the door and said, "Thank you." But he started asking me hundreds of questions about the band.'

She was asked if she was frightened: 'Yes. I just wanted to shut the door. My mate behind the door was freaking out. But, if he'd been talking bullshit, maybe I would have shut the door. But he's very intelligent and clued up. I answered all his questions, and then, after 40 minutes, my mater realised he was taking the piss, and that was it. Phew!'

Pell told Jones: 'Those four girls remembered my appearance at her door. But she was clever enough to realise – even a stupid black woman as that – was clever enough to realise that I was a reasonably clever bloke and cunning.'

The Fleet Street Sewer Rat

References

[i] 'Scandal in the Bins,' Channel 4 (first shown 11.01.01).

[ii] "3½-hour rushes," Moving Perspective (filmed 1999).

[iii] 'Scandal in the Bins,' Channel 4 (first shown 11.01.01).

[iv] McVicar audio tape (recorded 1999) MDRV.

[v] "3½-hour rushes," Moving Perspective (filmed 1999).

[vi] 'Scandal in the Bins,' Channel 4 (first shown 11.01.01).

[vii] "3½-hour rushes," Moving Perspective (filmed 1999).

[viii] 'Scandal in the Bins,' Channel 4 (first shown 11.01.01).

[ix] McVicar audio tape (recorded 1999) MDOR.

[x] 'Scandal in the Bins,' Channel 4 (first shown 11.01.01).

[xi] "3½-hour rushes," Moving Perspective (filmed 1999).

[xii] 'Scandal in the Bins,' Channel 4 (first shown 11.01.01).

[xiii] "3½-hour rushes," Moving Perspective (filmed 1999).

[xiv] John Sturgis and Sandra Laville, 'ELTON SUES OVER "STOLEN" SECRETS. STAR ACCUSES "HACKER" OF SELLING DETAILS OF CREDIT CARD SPENDING SPREE,' *Evening Standard* (13.03.98).

[xv] 'Scandal in the Bins,' Channel 4 (first shown 11.01.01).

[xvi] McVicar audio tape (recorded January 1999) MDOI.

[xvii] Lindsay Baker, 'HANGING TOUGH: All Saints have spent more of the past two years in the tabloids' gossip columns than in the studio. But when Shaznay Lewis finished writing their new album, they all agreed it was time to grow up,' *The Guardian* (30.09.00).

[xviii] 'Scandal in the Bins,' Channel 4 (first shown 11.01.01).

[xix] "3½-hour rushes," Moving Perspective (filmed 1999).

[xx] Lee Harpin, 'BRAT'S YER LOT: All Saints baby bust-up,' *Daily Star* (18.04.98).

[xxi] "3½-hour rushes," Moving Perspective (filmed 1999).

[xxii] Saba Salman, 'All Saints gag Elton's stalker,' *Evening Standard* (26.06.98).

[xxiii] 'Scandal in the Bins,' Channel 4 (first shown 11.01.01).

[xxiv] McVicar audio tape (recorded 12.11.00) MDRG.

[xxv] John McVicar, 'ALL THESE STARS ARE BEING TARGETED BY ONE MAN: who'll be the next victim on the hitlist of Benjamin Pell?' *Punch* (01.08.98).

[xxvi] McVicar video tape (filmed 08.02.01) DVOO.

[xxvii] "3½-hour rushes," Moving Perspective (filmed 1999).

[xxviii] McVicar video tape (filmed 08.02.01) DVOO.

[xxix] Paul Gorman, 'Police arrest "Public Enemy No 1,"' *Music Week* (14.08.99).

Chapter 9

Let Me Entertain You:
Robbie, Nicole and other celebs

All Saints tried to keep secret a story that can only be told now because the Appleton sisters have since chosen to tell it[i]. The band had injuncted Pell to prevent its revelation after he found out about it from the rubbish. 'I want people to know what happened,' said Nicole. The Appletons published a double-biography two years after the break-up of the band, which was serialised in the *Mail on Sunday*[ii] (and *Daily Mail*), that revealed the 'harrowing story' of how Nicole was 'forced to abort a baby fathered by Robbie Williams that she desperately wanted to keep'. It was 'a devastating indictment of the music industry and the cynical way it manipulates the lives of its vulnerable young stars'.

Nicole said that, four months into the pregnancy, she was pressured to have a 'quickie' abortion, which left her feeling suicidal. 'I was horrified, violated by what I felt was the power of an industry that leads a woman to sacrifice her child to keep a band together,' she said. The operation was physically and mentally traumatic for her, but she felt isolated. 'No one mentioned it,' she said. 'It was as if nothing had happened,' adding, 'What mattered was our success and ability to make money. I felt powerless.' She said that Robbie had been 'really happy' to hear in March 1998 that she was pregnant. 'Rob put his hands on my belly, and said, "This baby is saving my life." It was an answer for him, a reason for his life.' She said that the abortion contributed to her break up with Robbie.

According to Nicole, when she and Mel broke the news of their pregnancies to the band's other members and Benson, Shaznay was furious. 'I thought she was going to hit me,' Nicole said. Nicole initially decided that she was going to have the baby, but recalled her mother telling her: "The record company telephoned. They told me you are making a big mistake, and that Rob is bad news. They want me to help you change your mind, help you think about the repercussions on you and Natalie."' Nicole said that Benson insisted that the future of the band depended on her and Mel having abortions.

Nicole told how she was called to a meeting with her record company in New York in April 1998. 'They wanted to talk to me about my pregnancy, and the meeting ended with the record company asking me: did I want them to organise an abortion for me? They said that, if so, they could organise it for the very next day, and that it would be quick and easy; I would be out of the clinic the same day. I was speechless. Even the record company had an interest in my private life. After the weeks of pressure I had been under, I was so battered. I felt weak. The fight went out of me, and I just gave in.'

Mel remembered it differently, saying[iii]: "Nic's abortion story doesn't make sense. It was very traumatising for her... but nobody can terminate a child's life except the mother. In this case, there was family pressure to abort, but in the book it was supposedly other influences.'

Nonetheless, Nicole's account shed light on her relationship with Robbie. When they parted, the *Daily Mail* reported that she had 'dumped' her fiancé, Robbie, after she became the 'target of an obsessed fan'[iv]. It continued:

The break up followed the revelation that a memo containing 'highly personal' information about All Saints was being hawked around the Sunday tabloids by Benjamin Pell, who has boasted of making money by rifling through the dustbins of the famous. The group were forced to issue a High Court writ against Pell to prevent him from going public with the memo, which detailed a meeting between the band and its management. Miss Appleton is said to have told a friend this week, 'The engagement is off. Robbie and I are no longer an item. Things just haven't worked out. We are still trying to stay friends and talk a lot on the phone. I don't bear him any bad feelings, and I know we will always be close. But at the moment we just can't be together.' The couple, who are two of pop's hottest properties, had been together for just six months.

According to close friends, the incident put unbearable stress on the couple's fragile relationship. 'Nicole became very uneasy about the whole incident, and this in turn started to affect things with Robbie,' one said last night. 'She felt as if she was being stalked, and became very nervous. Somehow things changed between them, and they started rowing.'

Thus Pell could add other celebrity scalps to his growing collection – he had contributed to the break up of Nicole and Robbie.

Jones filmed Pell as he read an article from the *Daily Mail*[v]:

This is a very, very important article in my life. I was going to threaten to take... the, erm, *Daily Mail* to court. They are going, basically, over the story about All Saints and how they were cracking up at that stage... 'Tensions arose because of legal problems.' You're telling me, legal problems? Your lawyers are throwing away your abortions. 'The original manager took the band to court... Such problems could have been dealt with. What caused real damage was the deterioration of Nicole's relationship with Benson, once Nicole's great friend. Matters reached a head when a sinister and unscrupulous character called Benjamin Pell became involved.'

My name was being banded around as some nutter following these pop stars to their house, like Shaznay Lewis, or breaking up engagements, so heaven knows what the public are thinking about me.

That's what was written about me in the *Daily Mail*. This is why I wanted to sue them for libel... 'Pell has earned notoriety by uncovering secret documents relating to stars in their rubbish, and selling them to down-market tabloids.' They were claiming, on the one hand, that I sold stories to down-market tabloids, without mentioning the fact that many of my stories actually end up in their own paper.

Pell instructed a solicitor to sue, but there was a problem. 'Of course, being a lawyer, two weeks after this, she writes to me saying: "Oh Benjamin Pell, I've decided I can't represent you; there could be a conflict of interest."

'I said: "What do you mean you say a conflict of interest?"

'She said: "I can't discuss with you what the conflict could be."

'I said: "Oh I know what it is, it's cos you're representing Stephen Pearson [former commercial director of football's Premier League]."

'She said: "How the hell do you know that?"

'I said: "Look, I know everything about your firm. You're not gonna represent me then, fine, goodbye," and that was it. So, I never heard from her again. She charged me 150 quid for this one letter. And of course I didn't take action against the *Daily Mail* because nobody would represent me.'

Asked what legal action Searles took against him, Pell replied: 'Breach of confidence and breach of copyright.' And the verdict? 'Breach of both: everything, basically.'

Filmed outside the Searles office, he said:

Searles injuncted me: Searles, the company who I eventually ruined when their main client, in fact their only client, All Saints, sacked them. Searles, it was an absolutely amazing turn of events, actually injuncted me and took action against me, well not only me, but against Benjamin Pell also known as Peter Jeffrey, Alan Slater and Alan Field. And they got an injunction... restraining the defendant from appropriating or attempting to appropriate documents and papers from the plaintiff's rubbish bins, copying or attempting to copy any such documents. So, by taking those bags, if these were truly Searles bags, I would be in contempt of court and could go to jail for a period of up to 25 years.

Pell then proceeded to show to camera the Searles' documents that he had kept:

Minutes of meetings, meeting, photographer's meeting, publishing. Just get this all on film. Attendance note 6th November 1997; sample clearance 20th November 1997; meeting [?] on merchandising All Saints, cc to John Benson. I always felt that when they were doing a cc, they should put cc B. Pell. Sample clearance 16th December 1997; 10th February 1998; 'Attending John Benson telephone,' 20th January 1998; 20th February. Don't forget by showing you all of this, I'm committing a criminal offence because I've sworn an oath saying that I've given all of this back. 17th November 1997; 24th November 1997; 7th November. I've kept everything basically, as you can see.

Jones then asked if he has stolen their rubbish since the injunction? Pell replied

Of course, I mean I- funny enough, for three or four months, I didn't bother. But what I did was, about two weeks ago I was just- I was driving down a bank holiday weekend, I thought, 'Fuck it.' I'd been in Music Week the week before, so I thought, 'Look I'm getting sick of this. Cos I knew that one of the comments made in Music Week came from [a Searles solicitor], and he said in Music Week... 'If he ever goes near our rubbish again, he goes straight to prison.'

So, I thought, 'Fuck you, for a laugh.' So, as I was doing the bins, I said, 'I'm off to jail, I'm off to jail.' And within that bag, I got some shredded stuff regarding Jamiroquai which ended [with] me getting a £600-worth story in The Sun about a dispute they had, where literally all I needed to do was piece together five horizontal shredded notes... I mean, of all the firms who have ever started on me, Searles are the worse. Well, all I know is that I got the satisfaction of Searles being sacked by All Saints, so. I got the satisfaction of doing their rubbish again. The fact that it is a criminal offence of course makes it a bit more exciting... I'm still doing Searles, but obvi- obviously only on an intermittent basis.

This is Searles. Okay now, we've got to be fair to Searles. You obviously know that Searles are shredding 90% of their stuff; and, obviously, 'til I came on the scene, they weren't shredding a thing. Now, it would be a criminal offence for me to be seen with this because, basically, I've sworn an affidavit, in August of the last year, that every single Searles document, I've handed back to them. Now, I did actually give them 250 documents back at the time of the case, which obviously I'd photocopied and hidden here. So, as far as they're concerned, none of this is in my possession any more, and as you can see I kept everything.

Filmed at a 'safe house', Pell said:

This is some more Searles stuff, okay. We've got a- Searles, Searles, Searles. Okay, we've got to find the main documents here. Look, I've even taken- I've even kept employment records of- of their staff. I mean, I kept everything, basically. As you can see, this is- this is basically the best sort of proof you can have that anything I've ever taken from any firm of lawyers has been kept. Because if you think my house is bad, you should see what I've got hidden here. I'm lucky that none of the staff here are remotely interested in... pop music. So when my story comes to be told... they'll get an unpleasant surprise when they see they've been harbouring stolen property for the last year and a half.

Jones asked how bags were in there and Pell replied: '70... But the chances of them ever discovering this safe house are- well, they're literally impossible.' Pell later told the Mappin trial that his confession to Jones of committing these crimes were further examples of his 'developing story-lines'.

Pell reads out to Jones an affidavit signed by a Searles solicitor:

'Mr Pell has shown himself to be thoroughly untrustworthy. I am concerned that Mr Pell will seek to sell his story elsewhere.'

Pell continued: 'Here was the original injunction against me from, funnily enough, Justice Bell. Friday 12th June [1998]... The four members of All Saints versus Benjamin Pell also known as Peter Jeffrey, Alan Slater, Alan Steel. And that was the injunction. Can you see that? "The defendant must not communicate to, or disclose to, any third party, or make known the information,' cos that's why it is such an important in- injunction. And i- it says in this order, if I don't keep to this order, it's a criminal offence."'

Before the Appleton sisters broke the story themselves, Pell took Jones to the office of one of his cleaning clients where he had hidden the document, and even bumps into one of his cleaners there. Pell says: 'So this is a very important safe house; you're lucky I haven't blindfolded you [laughs]. If I ever take hostages, this is where I'm going to keep them. But let me explain to you why I've come here.'

'Now, basically, this is one of my favourite- well this is *the* favourite safe house."

The cleaner says to Pell: 'You can't be filming in some people's premises.'

Pell: 'Why?'

Cleaner: '"Why?"!'

Pell: 'What do you mean? Ridiculous- er, we clean here.'

Cleaner: 'Yeah, I clean here-'

Pell: 'At night, this is our premises; during the day, they rent it off us.'

Cleaner: 'When you come and clean, you don't have to come in and clean this late.'

Pell: 'I do. I want to make sure you're doing a proper job.'

Cleaner: 'Yeah, that's not right.'

Pell commented to Jones: 'I'm sorry [about the] smell, by the way. This is a safe house to end all the safe houses. You want to see abortions, you've got to fucking well work for your living, darling (cackles). Such a safe house, all my most sensitive documents are in here (another cackle). Basically, to get into there you have to move this cupboard out (more cackling). I had all this stuff in here ever since- basically when Russells [a firm of solicitors representing various pop stars] injuncted me, that night, everything went into bags and were hidden in here. The night Searles injucted me, everything got hidden in here. The night that John Reid injuncted me, everything was in here. It's the only building I have in the whole of London with a [unintelligible]; that fucking Paki accountant they've got is so stingy. They've got a store-room here (they don't even know it exists) with this cupboard in front of it, this stuff has been in here, literally, for over a year. It absolutely stinks in here... I can tell you this, every thing in here is highly, highly confidential.'

Pell then shows the injuncted document to the camera so that it can be read. 'Here we have the first version of the memo. It minutes a heated discussion between the four All Saints members, Benson, Helen Searles and the band's accountant, amongst others, at a meeting at 5pm on 20th May 1998 at the management's office. Pell reads it out to camera. The memo makes clear that Nicole let rip into Benson over the pressure that she says he put on her and Mel to have abortions.

Of course, this book has already covered how Pell targeted Elton John and All Saints but there is the space to include all of the taped material in which Pell talks about his other celebrity victims.

Besides finding documents about Robbie Williams while targeting All Saints, Pell also trawled the rubbish of advisors to the former Take That star. Jones films Pell outside an office, saying: 'This is the office occupied by Robbie Williams' management company... I can tell you plenty of stories about him.' Pell says that he found documents that raised questions about whether Robbie was bisexual. He says that he also sold a story claiming that Robbie was treated for 'sex addiction'. And, just as he found Elton John's financial records, he discovered that Coutts bank had cut off Robbie's credit card. Pell was also behind a false story suggesting that Robbie had a serious gambling addiction (see epilogue).

Pell says that he stole papers on the Spice Girls that raised questions about Mel C's sexuality. And he retrieved a copy of the £1m wedding contract between OK magazine and Victoria Adams, Posh Spice in the Spice Girls, and footballer David Beckham; he says that he sold it via Max Clifford to Neil Wallis, then editor of The People[vi].

Another celebrity target was the former Rolling Stone, Mick Jagger. Pell tells Jones that he found stories about Jagger not giving his staff a pay rise for five years, and Jagger's divorce settlement[vii]. Pell admits that he also falsified a document that he found in the rubbish to make it seem that Jagger was suffering from sex addiction[viii], which ran as a front-page splash and which raises doubts about the story of Robbie's supposed sex addiction.

Pell says that he duped Lee Harpin, then of the *Sunday People* [who later wrote the false story about Robbie's gambling addiction for *The News of the World*][ix]: 'When Mick Jagger was sending his child to see a dyslexic counsellor, I obviously Tipp-Exed out the bits referring to the dyslexia. I'm actually quite good now at Tipp-Exing out relevant bits... I Tipp-Exed out the bits relating to the... dyslexic counsellor, and I just put in the name of the doctor. I said to Harpin, "Oh, this is Mick and Jerry Hall seeing a doctor, must be the sex therapist." He believed it, and it ended up on the front page.'

Pell says that he raided the bins of Simons Muirhead, solicitors representing various celebrities, including Oasis, the pop group, and the late Paula Yates. Pell says that he found out about Oasis's legal troubles and even a blackmail threat against Liam Gallagher. He tells McVicar[x]: 'You just ask Paula Yates. I ruined her life when she was alive; the bloody day she died, her lawyer goes on television and says, "Allow her her privacy."'

The following Pell says that he obtained her will from rubbish. Asked who used it, Pell replied: 'The *Daily Mirror*, they splashed on it,' adding that he was promised £1,000 for it.

Another solicitors' firm targeted by Pell was Russells, which also represents several celebrities, including George Michael, the singer, the Verve, another pop group, and Linford Christie, the athlete. Pell reads to Jones one headline in *The Sun*[xi]: '"George cops a writ." My friend, George Michael is back again with my favourite lady by-line, Victoria Newton. And that was the story in April of 1998.'

'George Michael, I don't think, takes too kindly to the fact that his new residence in Regent's Park Road ended up as a double-page spread... I don't think... with *The Sun* having the headline, "George Michael moves to a house which is twelve minutes from five public toilets."'

Jones asked him why Russells injuncted him and he answered: The straw which broke the camel's back – there'd been a proliferation of stories emanating from their offices for weeks and months before – but the story which broke the camel's back was the one about the Verve leaving Virgin. The headline was, 'Verve on the verge of leaving Virgin,' and they wanted £20m. This ultimately led to the Verve breaking up because of my story. The Sun and the *Daily Star* within two days were injuncted. And for a week afterwards they were being pressed by Russells to disclose who their source was, who had passed on these minutes of meetings with Queen's Counsel, with barristers and with solicitors.

He says that a friend, Anne Pounds, told him: 'Benjamin, you are in deep shit. I am in terrible trouble. We could all go to jail for this. Everyone is after you. Get everything out of the house.'

'And within a day, she was handing over thousands of documents to her lawyers... All those documents from Russells, including my hand-written note saying, "This is the story which appeared in *The Sun* last month." So... my so-called best friend of four years, was allowing Russells within three hours to be able to get a court order against me cos they had in my own hand writing the fact that all of these stories had come from me.' For years Pell had been faxing Anne Pounds confidential documents in order to impress her.

As a consequences Russells also obtained an anton pillar order against him. Pell read to Jones the supervising solicitor's report:

I rang the doorbell on two more occasions and he attended [?] at the door... At 4.55, Mrs Pell returned to her car, walked up to the front door. I asked her whether her son had returned.

Look at my mother. 'I showed Mrs Pell the relevant paragraphs of the order. Mrs Pell informed me, yes, she understood the order as, "We'd already had one."

'I said to Mrs Pell I did not believe that she genuinely understood the seriousness of the matter... Did she understand if she didn't comply, she would be in breach of the court order for which she could be imprisoned for contempt?'

'Mrs Pell replied, "Well, you'll have to send me to prison then," and then shut the door.'

Pell continued his yarn: 'I'm there in the house, hiding from anyone... I'm praying for 5.30 cos 5.30 is the cut off point. I'm groping to the front door. It's a wonder the fuckers didn't see me. My mother said [unintelligible as Pell is hysterical] the house. By then, they could hear me. And they're knocking on the door, "Let us in, let us in."

'And then I said to my mother, "We've only got another 14 minutes to go, 13 minutes to go." I remember distinctly 'phoning up David Leigh, and I'm saying to him. "David, what do I do?"

'And he said, "Benjamin, one thing you shouldn't do is, don't let him in the house."

'So I thought, "Fine, they are not getting in this house tonight; no way are they going to get in this house. Whatever it takes. I'm either going to have to throw another tantrum; we are not having those in the house."'

Pell returned to reading from the solicitor's report:

'At approximately 5.28, an elderly man drove into the driveway in a van. I introduced myself to him; he confirmed he was Benjamin Pell's father. I informed him that his son and Mrs Pell were inside the premises, but wouldn't open the door to us. Mr Pell said to me he didn't want me to explain the order to him, and that I couldn't come in as he wasn't prepared for anyone to invade his house. I explained to him that he... could go to prison for contempt of court. Mr Pell informed me that he would take his chance.'

'And basically we didn't let them in the whole of that day. And, of course, what did I do that evening? Hid all the Russells documents, and actually took them [?] that night to... the safe, safe house. The very, very safe house, where they have been ever since.'

He claimed that he appeared in the High Court in September 1998 and told the judge that Russells was 'in great fear of losing clients as a result of my activities'. He continued: 'And then, of course, being Benjamin Pell, I added, "Just like John Reid was sacked by Elton John."

'Judge Moses turns round to Barbara Dohmann, one of the top QCs in Britain... "Is this true? Did Mr Pell's activities lead to Elton John sacking John Reid?"

'And so Barbara Dohmann said, "Yes, I think you will find, your honour, that... it's true what Mr Pell is saying."

'Justice Moses turns round, and he says, "Mr Pell, you are an outrage. Your activities are absolutely disgraceful."

'I said, "I'm- I'm really sorry, what do you mean?"'

'He said, "I was in practice for 45 years before becoming a judge. What do you expect lawyers to do? Eat their rubbish? Burn their rubbish? Put the rubbish down the toilet? You are a disgrace."'

'And I fully expected him to take the black cap, and say, "I now sentence you to death by hanging."'

Pell told McVicar a similar story[xii]: 'Talk about a sledgehammer to crack a nut. I mean, there they were, all battalions out there: ... Barbara Dohmann, the bloody chairperson of the [Commercial] Bar [Association], David Pannick, Jonathan Hirst... they're the top people in the bloody country. And here I am, the rejected lawyer, managed to do it to them.'

Pell described to Jones the farce he made of the court orders[xiii]. He was ordered to return all the papers and documents that he had stolen but he returned only photostats. Pell pretended that after photostating them had returned the originals to where he found them. It seems that the court could no longer contend with Pell as he described Justice Moses looking dolefully at Barbara Dohmann and saying: "'I suppose that will have to do."' She answered, according to Pell, 'But, er, we want an assurance from Mr Pell that... if he ever dumped this stuff, the originals in his house, he will immediately forward them to us.'

Pell replied '"Of course, I have no hesitation, my dear honour, of course," (to much cackling, he added) Idiot.' On film, he then proceeds to show Jones all the stuff that he'd sworn on an affidavit that he'd returned. He makes the point that Russells, Searles and solicitors for John Reid had all been in his parents house '...little did they realise of course there was never a time I- even if I was about to hand over to them all my keys, they wouldn't even have known where to start looking. Do you think they can go up to one of my [cleaning] clients and say we have reason to believe that documents... are being hidden in your office? The clients will tell them to piss off.'

Pell then gives Jones a roll call of the celebrities he had hit and the sums he had obtained from Fleet Street for the information '...£5,000 from *The News of the World*; I got really good money for that, that was a front-page story in October of last year: Emma Bunton to play Sleeping Beauty... Here is an invoice from Lee Harpin....; Nicole snubs Benson (that's Nicole Kidman), £100; Jerry's settlement (that's Jerry Hall), £100...Paula (that's Paula Yates)... £350; Jagger woos Jerry with film, £600; Jagger's sex therapy session, £2,000.'

A newspaper diary item reported that Pell also sold stories to the Mirror Group on Clive Anderson, Leslie Ash, Geri Halliwell and Rik Mayall[xiv]. Another newspaper reported that Pell had also gone through the rubbish of Andrew Lloyd-Webber and Lionel Ritchie[xv]. Other victims include Ben Elton, Harry Enfield, Michael Flatley, Uri Geller, Ian Hislop, Jools Holland, Griff Rhys Jones, Vinnie Jones, Stanley Kubrick, Paul McCartney and his late wife Linda...Trigger Happy TV[xvi]. But not only were celebs on Pell's hit list...

References

[i] Natalie and Nicole Appleton, 'Together,' *Michael Joseph* (2002).

[ii] Katie Nicholl, 'The pressure that forced me to abort Robbie's baby,' *Mail on Sunday* (22.09.02).

[iii] Caroline Sullivan, 'I'VE KEPT MY INNOCENCE,' *The Guardian* (25.07.03).

[iv] Rick Hewett, 'Pressures that drove Robbie and his Saint apart; couple argued over "obsessed fan",' *Daily Mail* (01.08.98).

[v] "3½-hour rushes," Moving Perspective (filmed 1999).

[vi] Benjamin Pell second witness statement, Benjamin Pell -v- Express Newspapers and Mark Watts (08.04.03); Amanda Perthen, 'BECKHAM AND POSH SIGN THEIR LIVES AWAY IN AMAZING £1M WEDDING DEAL. DAVID BECKHAM AND VICTORIA ADAMS SIGN WEDDING DEAL WITH *OK* MAGAZINE,' *Sunday People* (05.07.98).

[vii] "3½-hour rushes," Moving Perspective (filmed 1999).

[viii] Lee Harpin, 'JAGGERS GET SEX THERAPY. MICK'S LAST BID TO SAVE MARRIAGE,' *Sunday People* (16.05.99).

[ix] "3½-hour rushes," Moving Perspective (filmed 1999).

[x] McVicar video tape (filmed 08.02.01) DVOO.

[xi] "3½-hour rushes," Moving Perspective (filmed 1999).

[xii] McVicar video tape (filmed January 2001) DVRV.

[xiii] "3½-hour rushes," Moving Perspective (filmed 1999).

[xiv] 'Media: diary,' *The Guardian* (31.07.00).

[xv] 'Picking through trash of the rich and famous,' *The Daily Telegraph* (16.03.98).

[xvi] "3½-hour rushes," Moving Perspective (filmed 1999); Benjamin Pell second witness statement, Benjamin Pell -v- Express Newspapers and Mark Watts (08.04.03)

Chapter 10

Born to Run:
Jonathan Aitken

Never was Pell happier than when a new target was suggested to him. He claims that a former employee at one of Britain's biggest solicitors' firm, Denton Hall, told him that his old firm would make a good target. According to Pell, the former employee said that while he worked there confidential documents were not always properly shredded. So, in 1998, Pell started taking the rubbish of Denton Hall.

Pell told the Channel 4 documentary[i]: 'Within about two weeks after doing… Denton Hall for the first time, I'm going through it, it's all- it was very interesting stuff: very interesting stuff about Amnesty [International], very interesting stuff about, er, Capital Radio, about the football Premier League. I mean, they did huge clients. Suddenly I'm picking up… "I, Said Ayas, state the following. I am friendly with Jonathan Aitken. Jonathan Aitken was helping me and MI6..." and there's pages and pages about "Jonathan Aitken was helping MI6". I thought, "Fucking hell."'

Pell had found a statement by Said Ayas, who was a long-time friend and business associate of Aitken's and an erstwhile financial advisor to Prince Mohammed, the eldest son of King Fahd of Saudi Arabia. Denton Hall was representing Ayas in legal action brought by the prince, who claimed that his former aide had stolen $230m from him[ii].

Aitken, now 61, was at the time preparing to be interviewed by police over the perjury he committed during his libel trial against Granada Television, the makers of *World in Action*, and *The Guardian*. The trial collapsed in 1997 when it emerged that Aitken had spun an elaborate and false story about how he had paid for a stay in 1993 at the Ritz hotel in Paris, which is owned by Mohammed Al Fayed. In evidence in 1995 to what was then called the House of

Commons privileges committee, Fayed revealed that Ayas paid the bill, but Parliament suppressed his testimony only for it to emerge in a newspaper article published just before the libel trial began[iii]. The article revealed that Prince Mohammed, heir to the throne in Saudi Arabia, ultimately paid the bill via Ayas, meaning that Aitken broke Parliament's rules by failing to declare the gift in the House of Commons register of members' interests. In fact, as the police would subsequently discover, a personal assistant to Ayas actually paid the bill[iv].

Aitken was permitted to drop his case against Granada and *The Guardian* after promising to pay their legal costs. He was later sentenced to 18 months in jail for perjury and attempting to pervert the course of justice in the libel case, and served seven. The judge described it as 'calculated perjury pursued over a long period of time'[v].

I helped make the second of two *World in Action* programmes[vi] about Aitken, in particular finding several confidential documents, including a letter written by Aitken that exposed the former Tory minister's role in promoting the sale of British defence equipment to Iraq when he was a backbench MP. This was at a time when the Government's policy – later announced to Parliament – was supposed to ban exports that would significantly enhance Iraq's military capability. In case of any doubt, I obtained the documents from well-placed sources: none came from rubbish.

I worked with David Leigh, who was the producer of both *World in Action* programmes and who went on to work on *The Guardian*. And I was working for a television company on an expose of a senior establishment figure who was already suing the broadcaster for libel over a previous programme, which created an unusual atmosphere in which to work. *The Guardian* was sued over articles[vii] reporting the revelations in each of the *World in Action* programmes. Aitken had resigned his cabinet job as chief secretary to the Treasury to launch his libel case.

Aitken brought several other libel actions, including two against me personally and newspapers for which I wrote: one for an article published in *The Sunday Telegraph*[viii] and another in *The Independent on Sunday*[ix]. The former settled with Aitken before his libel trial debacle; the latter never heard any more from Aitken following that trial. On the eve of the collapse of the case, Aitken and his wife announced that they were to divorce. After it ended, they went into hiding: he fled to California and she went to Switzerland.

Pell says that he initially offered the Ayas statement to *The Independent*, but it did not run the story. However, *The Daily Telegraph* ran a front-page story saying that Aitken was forced to lie in the libel case about his stay at the Paris Ritz because he was there on a secret intelligence operation[x]. It said that Aitken could finally reveal his role as a secret government intermediary passing on British intelligence about Iran to Saudi Arabia because Ayas had described the link in a draft witness statement. It quoted the draft statement as saying: 'I recall Mr Aitken saying the British Government would keep the promise made by John Major to supply the King (Fahd) with special intelligence on Iranian threats. I recall Prince Mohammed saying that Mr Aitken should pass this intelligence directly to King Fahd (through) Prince Mohammed, with myself (as) the link.'

That story was planted in *The Daily Telegraph* by Aitken, as the newspaper accidentally revealed when it faxed an advance copy of it to Alan Rusbridger, editor of *The Guardian*, seeking his comment[xi]. The copy included a note to sub-editors saying: 'This comes directly from Aitken but cannot be sourced to him.' Aitken had beaten Benji the Binman at his own game. Aitken arranged for the story to be planted just before it emerged that he was being charged. But he was urged by intelligence contacts to retract the claim because of fears that he would bring attention to MI6's role in securing Britain's multi-billion pound defence contract with Saudi Arabia, Al Yamamah[xii]. He duly denied *The Daily Telegraph* story within 24 hours of its being published.

Because Pell had tried to sell the draft Ayas statement to others, the heat was turning up on him. A diary article in the *Sunday Mirror* suggested a link between him and leaks about Aitken[xiii], reporting: 'In an ironic twist of fate, the man who discovered documents in a waste bin revealing Elton John's lavish expenditure earlier this year is likely to be called as a witness if and when Jonathan Aitken goes on trial for perjury. The Bagman... has for weeks been flaunting the statement by Arab go-between Said Ayas.' It added: 'Aware that this time round he is dealing with matters more dangerous than tantrums and tiaras, the Bagman has gone to ground."

Pell then thought that the newspaper that would be most interested in the material he had found would be *The Guardian*. On the Channel 4 documentary, Pell recalled telephoning the newspaper[xiv]: "'Can I speak to Alan Rusbridger?'

"'Oh, he's busy.'

"'Can you put me through to someone, so- it's to do with Jonathan Aitken.'" So they put me through to the [deletion sound]. It's the first time I'd ever spoken to [deletion sound] and I said to him: 'You know, you wouldn't believe what I've got,' and I faxed it over to him.

'And he said, "It's unbelievable."

Channel 4 bleeped out from Pell's contribution to the programme the name of the journalist to whom he had spoken at *The Guardian*. It was, of course, David Leigh. At this stage Leigh did not know that Pell's information came from the bins, however it was so explosive the journalist for obvious reasons cultivated Pell.

'[Deletion sound] said to me, "We can never give you any money. We can give you a hundred quid for this story, but why don't you get in touch with *The Sunday Times*." And I got hold of [deletion sound], whatever, I sold him the story instead, and obviously now I was able to sell all my other broadsheet stories.' Pell developed a relationship with *The Sunday Times*.

Channel 4 also bleeped out the name of the journalist at *The Sunday Times* whom Pell mentioned: David Leppard. When Pell watched a preview of the documentary, he reacted:[xv]: 'That is pathetic… I hope you're going mad… I can name Denton Hall, but I can't say that David Leigh told me to [target lawyers' rubbish for Aitken documents]? Pathetic, pathetic, I've got no other word for it.'

'What is the problem with saying "David Leigh"? I've got the tapes, I can prove it.'

McVicar told him, 'The problem is Channel 4 are terrified of *The Guardian*.'

Granada and *The Guardian* had, by this stage, won the libel case brought against them by Aitken, but they had run up legal costs of an estimated £2.2m in total. Aitken was liable for their costs bill, but soon after the case collapsed he claimed that he did not have the money to pay[xviii]. He later declared himself insolvent, claiming to have debts of £8.5m, and offered to pay 6.5p in the pound. But after various leads and articles – not all of them based on documents taken from binbags – he admitted that he had exaggerated the debts by £6m, and offered to pay a third of the other side's legal costs[xix].

Given Aitken's track record for lying, Granada and *The Guardian* were convinced that his original offer did not reflect his true assets. Their frustration undoubtedly explains why Leigh turned to Pell. When Aitken switched solicitors to Harkavys, Leigh suspected that Pell might be able to uncover the truth. Pell told Jones that Leigh called and told him[xx]: 'I've got a new target for you.' Leigh pointed Pell towards Aitken's new lawyers, Harkavys. The Channel 4 documentary played the tape with Leigh's name deleted.

However, when Pell was cross-examined by Adam Wolanski about this during his High Court case against Mappin, he lied and lied again about this[xxi]. He said that he had been 'doing the rubbish at Harkavys for three months before David Leigh told me about them'. Unfortunately for Mappin, his counsel did not have the benefit of the McVicar tapes to nail Pell's perjury.

Harkavys was a bonanza for Pell[xxv]:
> Within the first day of going there, I was finding affidavits, instructions to counsel, questions about where the money had gone, estimates of where the assets were, every one of his policies at Battersea Life Aitken Hume pension... where Lolicia was hiding. With- within about a month, we were able to build up a to- to- total picture of where this man's assets were disappearing to. I mean, there are too many documents to show you, but they're just totally remarkable, including confidential letters from Jonathan Aitken to his lawyers, to the other side's lawyers, to other people... His bail application was in the rubbish, everything was: letters from lawyers to him, from him to the lawyers. And most damaging, of call- of course, was the fact that The Guardian and Granada were always able to be a step ahead of the other side: they always knew what his response was going to be.

Pell tried to sell the Lolicia story through two people[xxvi]. 'The first Aitken story – the one where we found Lolicia – was a Clifford story... I double-dipped. I gave it to Max Clifford at the same time I gave it to Mark Hollingsworth... Two days later, the *Mail on Sunday* are approached by both of them individually, with the same story.' But he claims he got £5,000 for this story via Clifford.

He also said that he sold a second story to the *Mail on Sunday* about Aitken – via Hollingsworth. Within about two weeks of targeting Harkavys, Pell found documents showing that Aitken, contrary to his claims to his creditors, had significant assets[xxvii]. This enabled lawyers for *The Guardian* to freeze Aitken's assets. The *Mail on Sunday* reported[xxviii]:

> Disgraced former Tory Cabinet minister Jonathan Aitken risks being jailed this week if he fails to disclose the full extent of his wealth in the High Court... Lawyers for the newspaper and TV company discovered the former Treasury Chief Secretary was about to transfer his major remaining assets to his wife as part of a Swiss divorce settlement. Aitken... is believed to have agreed to settle with Lolicia by handing her his elegant 18th Century mansion in Lord North Street, Westminster, valued at $2 million, a parcel of land in Australia and a small sum of cash...
>
> His solicitor was actually in Australia arranging the transfer of the land to Lolicia when it was halted by the Guardian injunction.

Speaking on the day of publication, Pell said that he sold the story for £17,000[xxix]. 'Last night, I found, basically, his new affidavit which he's swearing by Tuesday of next week, and that gives 32 pages of all of his assets. And David Leigh, after I handed it over to David, immediately this morning, said, 'Complete rubbish. All nonsense.'

Pell told Jones[xxx]:

> When you're acting in court with Aitken against you and I'm able to give you instructions to counsel three or four days before the case, I'm actually able to give you a list of where all of the assets have been hidden. So, there you have *The Guardian* and Granada Television, who have been faced with legal costs because Aitken committed perjury... here he is, trying to hide his money. Michael Coleman [Aitken's solicitor] goes off to Australia in September, and I was able to leak to David Leigh the letters from Coleman to Aitken, telling him what he was doing with his land, where he was hiding his assets, the land in Saudi Arabia, the land in Australia, the land in this country, Lolicia pisses of to Switzerland, and we're able to discover her in the *Mail on Sunday* because I find the documents.

After the first story appeared in the *Mail on Sunday*... 'Aitken faces jail as assets are frozen' and they discovered where Lolicia had been hiding – something which the newspapers had been trying to find for two years – they said to the court the following day, 'This is absolutely outrageous, you know, these leaks could only have emanated from *The Guardian* newspaper or from Granada.' And of course *The Guardian*... knew exactly where they'd leaked from – they had leaked from me.'

Pell said that he stole from Harkavys' rubbish the solicitor's instructions to Aitken's counsel. Pell betrayed his mercenary nature as he noted: 'Look at the quantity of it. Look. I don't have any particular axe to grind against Jonathan Aitken... I'm not in favour of him, not against him. Of course, I don't mind people hiding their money. I'm a past master at hiding my own money. But, at the end of the day, I'm just reporting to you what is quite clearly, here, an attempt by Jonathan Aitken – and all power to him – to hide his money from *The Guardian*. I would do it; anybody would do that. But, of course, the worse thing here about this is the fact that all of the- these methods of hiding his money were being brought to the attention of *The Guardian* and their lawyers.'

Aitken ultimately reached a settlement with his creditors in 2001, releasing him from bankruptcy, reportedly paying half of around £2.8m he owed, which included an estimated £2.2m in legal costs run up by Granada and *The Guardian* and more than £300,000 tax claimed by the Inland Revenue[xxxi].

Pell said that he also trawled rubbish from 3 Raymond Buildings, the chambers where Aitken's defence barrister for the perjury charge, Sir John Nutting QC, was based[xxxii]. 'They're the chambers where I got the Aitken stuff, amongst others, apart from the Harkavys stuff.'

Nutting has also prosecuted in several high-profile cases such as IRA bombers and Anthony Sawoniuk, the retired British Rail ticket collector who was the first person to be convicted in the UK of Nazi war crimes. In 1999, he was as given two life sentences for murdering Jews in German-occupied Belorussia (now Belarus) during World War II[xxxiii]. Nutting was also retained, as a Treasury Solicitors, by the Security Service, better known as MI5, for work on various cases.

One intelligence source confirmed to me that Nutting knew, and liaised with, the then director-general of the Security Service, Sir Stephen Lander. Pell obtained some of Nutting's confidential documents, such as fee notes to clients, including one to the Security Service at PO Box 1084 in London. It showed that Nutting invoiced the Security Service £2,800 excluding VAT for 14 hours of advice in 1998. Pell also obtained fee notes for work on the Sawoniuk case, showing that he was charging the Crown Prosecution Service £120 an hour just for travelling.

One source close to Pell at the time said that the binman approached *The Mirror* with his material on Nutting. The source said that *The Mirror* put questions about it to Nutting, who 'went ballistic'. *The Mirror* duly ran a story in February 1999. It began[xxxiv]:

> The lawyer leading the prosecution in Britain's first war crimes trial is charging tax-payers £120 an hour to travel to and from work. QC John Nutting is also claiming £3,243 for visiting Belarus this week as part of the case against ex-railman Anthony Sawoniuk."
> Last night, the fees charged by £350,000-a-year Mr Nutting were slammed by both the Crown Prosecution Service and Labour MP Martin Brinton. A CPS source said, 'The fees just for his travelling are incredible. This is a hugely expensive gravy train. No one would argue Mr Nutting is not one of Britain's finest lawyers. However, the bills for his services are astronomical.'

An interviewer who later asked Nutting about the story in *The Mirror* reported that the barrister was 'clearly riled'[xxxv]. Nutting said: '*The Mirror* got a totally false story about a dispute between the CPS and myself over the fees,' saying that the fees were laid down by the then head of the CPS, Dame Barbara Mills QC, three years previous when another war crimes trial was anticipated. But it was another Pell coup.

Michael Coleman, senior partner at Harkavys, told the Channel 4 documentary[xxxvi]: 'Mr Pell was a gentleman unknown to us, and if he had any sense he wouldn't have targeted my firm.'

As Pell watched this, he cackled and said[xxxix]: 'If you had any sense, darling, you wouldn't be on this programme, you stupid man! I've ruined the reputation of your firm, if only you realised it.'

Nonetheless, although he didn't admit it, Coleman realised that an article about two of his clients, the wealthy St George brothers, had eminated from a leak in his office[xliv]: 'That story had been invented in this office, and that coming back to me indicated that someone... had access to our confidential information. Certainly, hacking was an immediate consideration. One of the first things we looked at was to see whether we were being looked at through our computers as opposed to through the garbage. It was two or three weeks later that we'd worked out that it was in the- at the garbage level.'

At this point, Pell interjected[xlv]: 'Oh yes. Bit like your firm.'

He continued: 'He's just come from nowhere, Michael Coleman. The only trouble is he's risen without a trace; he's going to sink without a trace as well, thanks to me... Revenge is a- is a nice, nice thing to do... He is going to be absolutely up shit creek without a paddle, and he doesn't know the quarter of it. He doesn't know what a nutter I am. He doesn't know what a vindictive d- vindictive bastard I am.'

Jones recorded Pell on the telephone to his solicitor, saying: 'You wouldn't believe, Paul, the stuff I've found. I've got stuff about Coleman's divorce, about his legal action (he's trying to acquire this house). I have got so much on Coleman; you would not believe it.' Pell claimed, under cross-examination by Wolanski, that this was another 'false story-line'[xlvii].

Wolanski put to Pell: 'The truth is that you derive great pleasure in ruining other people's lives.'

Pell replied: 'I do not. I'm an extremely easy person to deal with.'

Coleman told the documentary[xlviii]: 'It was then [in February 1999] that we set up a very involved series of... minute cameras to find out who the culprit was. I was rather sceptical that we could use cameras the size of cigarette butts in the dark to get photographs of someone crawling around amongst our garbage.'

Pell interjects[xlix]: 'But wouldn't it have been cheaper to buy a shredding machine?'

Coleman[l]: 'On the- I think the first, or the second night that we used the system, we actually got a close-up, full facial of- of this chap.'

The documentary's narrator, Victor Lewis-Smith, who was also its executive producer, said: 'With the police ready and waiting, Pell set out on his usual nightly routine unaware of what was in store.'

Our bin scavenger was annoyed even by his (then) friend's commentary, Pell commented[li]: 'Oh, well, he's the only person to catch me out in three years, so don't be so arrogant, Victor, okay.'

Coleman[lii]: 'My security team set about identifying him and finding out information about him, because we were naturally concerned that it might be a secret service operation because I was handling, at the time, other sensitive matters. So before calling the police in we wanted as much information about this person as we could obtain. And it was shortly after we'd identified him as an independent who was raiding and selling information to newspapers that we called the police in.'

Pell interjects[liii]: 'Yeah, but why did you call the police in? Why waste police money- why waste tax-payers' money because you can't be bothered to buy a shredding machine?'

Coleman[liv]: 'In the room where you're filming this interview, the police sat themselves down in the dark, much as they would on a movie. And they also set up plain-clothes police at each end of Harley Street... waiting to make an arrest.'

Pell interjects[lv]: 'Oh, he talks about me as if I'm sort of spy or something, coming in from the cold. I mean, it's- it's just ridiculous. Talk about a sledgehammer to crack a nut.' The irony of such an apposite image was lost on Pell.

Pell gave his account to the documentary[lvi]: "Drive along, parked at the bottom of, erm, er, Wigmore Street, or the junction of Wigmore Street where it meets Harley Street. And to go downstairs, take the four bags out, as full as ever...'

Coleman recalled: 'And I think it was about 3 o'clock in the morning, whilst they were sitting in this room, that- looking through the window, Mr Pell came down the stairs and was nabbed.'

Pell: 'At the bottom of, erm, Harley Street about a five-foot-four man in plain clothes, obviously plain clothes, I didn't think he was a policeman, coming towards me. My first reaction was, "Harkavys, dodgy lawyers." You know, people like Aitken on their books. "They've probably got a hit man out to kill me." I thought it was going to be another Benson scenario... I put the bags down, and started going towards the car. "Excuse me, sir, can you come towards me?" Anyway he comes there, and he says...shows me his thing, is CID, police.

'So I thought, "Fuck," you know, I can see, now, exactly what's gone on here.

'"Erm, can I have your name, please?"

'"Benjamin Pell."

'"What are you doing here?"

'"Erm, I'm a cleaner."'

Pell says while watching this at home[lix]: 'Yeah, I did try and blag it for two minutes, "I'm a cleaner."

Pell continued on the documentary[lx]: 'He said, "What are you doing with those four bags?"

'"Oh," I said, "I'm just, erm, you know, trying to get rid of some of my... I did my normal little play which is always to say, "I'm getting rid of my rubbish. I can't get rid of it in Westminster, so wherever..." As soon as I said, "I'm swapping over my..." He said, "Benjamin Pell, I'm hereby arresting you for theft of confidential information. You do not have to say anything," and he gave me the caution.'

Pell was taken to Marylebone police station. 'Yeah, I get up to the station. They say, "We've got a great train robber here. You won't believe what we've got here."

The police provided Pell with a duty solicitor. Pell tells Jones[lxiv]. 'The guy I had was some dick-head... who, funnily enough, knew my family from synagogue. And he sat down with me in the, er, prison cell. He looked at me, probably dressed like this, if not worse, and said, "Benjamin, how do you make your money?"

'So I said, "No, no, this is how I make my money... I said, "I make my money by going through rubbish."

'He said, "Well, yes, but how do you make your real money?"

'I said, "Well, I actually make money out of this."

'He just could not understand it... he just couldn't believe that I was actually able to make any sort of money out of doing what I do.'

Two detectives later accompanied Pell to his home to search for stolen documents. Pell recounted to the documentary how the police attempted[lxv] to 'recover anything relating to Harkavys, dignitaries and sensitive information'. He gave one officer some old documents...

...I use the dining room as my faxing room and my photocopying room, so one of the clever CID officers, if that… isn't a contradiction in terms, said, 'Oh, what- what have- what- you have a computer in there. What do you have in there?'

I said, 'Well, I just use that for the internet.' And he walks in there, and he sees all my stuff from that week. So he gets all of my Oasis stuff; he gets two or three of my- and he's getting good stuff in there, and he also gets my stuff relating to West Yorkshire Police. I thought, 'Let's be clever here. Let's try and get them out of this room because otherwise they're going to take every pile out of here, and they're going to find everyone. Let's get them in the shed,' because I knew once people are in the shed, they'll give up.

Coleman explained the significance of the shed: 'As I understand from the police, at the moment, he has at his home, or has had at his home, subject to a destruction order now, something in the order of two million documents.'

Another of Pell's traits is he cannot throw anything away.

Pell continued: 'So as soon as they opened the shed door, everything comes crashing down on poor Lee Clements [one of the detectives], he's only about five foot three in the first place. He said, "What the hell have you got in here?"

'I said, "Well, I told you, I keep all of the really sensitive stuff in here as well. You know, the really sensitive stuff."

'He said, "Well, there's no way we can go through all of this." So he said, "Fine. It's okay," and so he closed the door again.'

On the documentary, Pell then said to them[lxvii]: 'By the way, I say to them, you know, "I mean, I know you think it's a bit crazy, but I am actually certifiable and stuff, and I can get- you know, I've had- you know, I'm mad, basically."

'And he said, "Believe me… you don't need to tell us that. We can see that." And then, suddenly, this letter drops out of this pile…'

Victor Lewis-Smith' voice-over explains: 'The letter, from a doctor, showed that Pell had been prescribed medication for an "obsessional compulsive mental condition. The letter's diagnosis allowed the police to treat Pell as a nutcase collector not a peddler of information. He was charged with stealing documentary waste. The more serious half of his criminal enterprise, his trade with Fleet Street, was not investigated.'

Pell's nutter act had won the day again.

Watching this at home, Pell put everything in a nutshell[lxviii]: 'Well that of course was the biggest scandal of all cos otherwise the whole of fucking Fleet Street would have had to be in the dock with me, and I don't think there's enough room.'

To vent his anger over being arrested at Coleman of Harkavys, Pell sold some Aitken documents to *The Sunday Times,* he had had for 'months and months'[lxix]. The newspaper ran a story based on Aitken's letters to his solicitors[lxx]:

> The disgraced former cabinet minister, Jonathan Aitken, who is facing a lengthy prison sentence and financial ruin after being convicted of perjury, has instructed his lawyers to compare his plight to that of Charles I walking to the scaffold. In letters to his legal advisers, Aitken has proposed that he should assume the mantle of the doomed monarch, who went to his execution in Whitehall 350 years ago with his head held high...
>
> In one recent letter to his solicitor, he says, 'I share your view that in this situation I should be seen to be playing the white man. I would like my stance to be worthy of the lines written by [the 17th-century poet] Andrew Marvell about Charles as he walked towards the scaffold, 'He nothing little [sic] did or mean, upon that memorable scene.'

The newspaper reported that Aitken thought that Nutting, his barrister, could gain sympathy from the judge because of his divorce and impending bankruptcy. It quoted from one his letters:

> So I think my position is not that of someone seeking to do sinister manoeuvres with assets. It should be that of a man already strapped for cash who now finds himself caught between a rock and a hard place in regard to the ownership of 8 Lord North Street. With a Swiss divorce court judgement registered on me by Lolicia's lawyers and an injunction from *The Guardian*, I think I am already in a situation which might well merit a paragraph of purple prose.

The Scandal in the Bins programme featured a News International remittance slip showing that *The Sunday Times* paid Pell £3,375 for material for three stories, including one on Aitken.

Nutting duly did use some of the suggested lines in his submissions to the judge on Aitken's behalf, saying[lxxii]:

> Not since the days of Oscar Wilde has a public figure who told lies in a libel case suffered such humiliation and public vilification and personal vindictiveness at the hands of some members of the Press. The fall from grace has been complete, his marriage has broken down, he has lost his home, he is one of only three people this century forced to resign from the privy council, he is bankrupt and his health has suffered. His public humiliation has been absolute. These are real and considerable punishments.

Aitken also sought public sympathy before he was sentenced by letting it be known, for example, that bankruptcy officers had seized his Rolex watch to help raise money for his creditors. However, Aitken had concealed from the public the fact that he was given a series of expensive watches by the Saudi royal family, and, in contravention of House of Commons rules, failed to declare these gifts[lxxiii].

Pell was angry about what he said were shortfalls in payments from *The Sunday Times*. Jones recorded Pell threatening Leppard in a telephone call over a £9,000 invoice being cut by £6,000: 'I mean, that's just ridiculous. I mean, that Aitken story – do you want me to ring up Michael Coleman and tell him you knew that those letters I gave you were stolen property. Do you want me, do you want me to do that? No, it's not, no, I haven't...I wouldn't call that blackmail.'

However, Pell says that he plans to threaten various journalists in order to secure what he claims are thousands of pounds of debts: 'All I know is I'm owed £25,000 by these fuckers. And, at the end of the day, if I go down, they all go down with me. And I'm going to be using it as a weapon. In fact, tomorrow, when you come to my house, you're going to have me on tape 'phoning up all of the people who owe me money, saying, "I'm in terribly, terrible trouble. As you know, I'm in court at the moment. I've got no money. Can you please pay me?"'

Meanwhile, Pell was coming under scrutiny not only from the police but also by the Security Service. It began investigating Pell after he sold confidential documents from Nutting, Aitken's barrister, to *The Mirror* in February. Given that Nutting represented the Security Service and was a friend of its then head, Stephen Lander, it seems likely that the barrister alerted them to this apparent security breach. In any event, Lander mentioned at a meeting with journalists from *The Guardian* that the Security Service was investigating Pell. I telephoned Lander to ask him about Pell. 'Benji the Binman,' he said, but he would make no comment, saying that the Security Service was no longer his 'locus'.

While being filmed near 3 Raymond Buildings, Pell said: 'In here, apparently, that I started an MI5 inquiry into my activities because these two bags which I'm holding contain rubbish emanating from the chambers of somebody called John Nutting, who used to be Aitken's QC and apparently works for MI5.'

Despite having been arrested for taking documents from outside the office of a solicitors' firm, and despite triggering an MI5 investigation after he trawled the rubbish of a barristers' chambers, Pell continued trawling lawyers' rubbish. And Pell found more confidential documents in the High Court battle between Prince Mohammed and his erstwhile aide, Ayas. Pell says[lxxv]: 'I find the box... Denton Hall... I find a box outside-' breaking into laughter before continuing, 'Now this will shock David Leigh. David Leigh has always thought that I found that box outside Denton Hall's office. I didn't, I lied to you, David Leigh. I found the box outside Essex Court chambers... at 24 Lincolns Inn Fields. This was a box of literally every single document from the Said Ayas/Prince Mohammed court case. Now, you remember, that is the same court case which gave me the Aitken affidavit, saying he was doing it for King and country... it gave me story after story about the Saudi royal family, this was the ultimate though.

'When I gave Leigh the box, this was a huge box, really huge, he was salivating. He said, "Oh, this proves that what Aitken said- this proves this arms deal." He said, "There are at least 20 stories in here, Benjamin. Let me have- keep this box." And you know what I'm like: I never give anybody anything.

'I said, "No, I'll photocopy it for you… and I'll bring it over to you tonight."

'He said, "You can't photocopy a thousand pages."

'I'm Benjamin Pell, I did. The following morning… I ring him up, saying, "David, did you get that? Yeah?" I left it at *The Guardian*. So, I mean, *The Guardian* doorman will know me cos I used to go there every three or four days leaving parcels for David… So, I was up for- well, I was up all night anyway, it took me about four hours to photocopy.'

The Guardian ran several well-informed articles based on documents from the Ayas litigation[lxxvii]. It cited, for example, a document drawn up by Ayas for his lawyers, as well as 'testimony to his lawyers' given during meetings at Denton Hall, in which he set out how he had earned more than $150m in commission – and Prince Mohammed $1bn – on defence deals. *The Sunday Times* chimed in with further details about Prince Mohammed's finances[lxxviii].

Pell even showed Jones where he photocopied the huge volume of Ayas legal papers – at the office of one of his cleaning clients. Showing Jones's camera the photocopier in question, he said[lxxix]: 'So I was here all night… It is the fastest photocopier in London. I photocopied all the Ayas stuff here, for example, all photocopied using this machine.'

> The amazing thing is here [pulling Ayas documents from a box], of course, it gives you not only the story about the court case with Prince Mohammed, but it gives you all of these allegations regarding Prince Mohammed's lifestyle and everything. And so, these are possibly the most sensitive documents you can ever find anywhere in a rubbish dump or anywhere else. And, er, and I'll show you the best bits here if you can get this on camera. Here, for example, I mean this is so fantastic. Every single cash payment made by the prince to Ayas… every single payment is here.

> Ayas will definitely not laugh this off. Look at this, 'Check to HRH Prince Mohammed BFBAAS Banque Orient… Check to Said Ayas – cash. Check to Said Ayas…' You have literally got every single transaction that Said Ayas did in his time for Prince Mohammed. Look, these are cheques from HRH Prince Mohammed bin Fahd bin Abdul Aziz al Saud, the son of the fucking King Fahd, for goodness sake. What the hell are these cheques doing in the rubbish?

He [Ayas] would never have thought in a million years that all of this would end up in the hands of some nutter. Fortunately for Ayas, though, in the hands of a nutter who knows what these are worth... and thought about the best way. And the best way to use these documents is not to fuck Ayas, is not to fuck Prince Mohammed, is to fuck Denton Hall. I mean, I've never photocopied so much in my life. I did this last week, and, er, look at this, every single cheque. He will- he will have a heart attack when he sees this, he will have a heart attack. Affidavits, every single affidavit on the case, Philip Raphael, Daniele Ayas, you even get his poor wife, who thought she was going to be murdered... Some of her affidavit is hilarious, 'I was walking in Sainsbury's, these three Arab-looking gentlemen came up to me, attempted to murder me at the check-out counter,' ... Here, all the affidavits from the other side as well... his villa, Ayas's escape, because, don't forget, Ayas thought he was going to be murdered... so he escaped from Saudi Arabia. Here, documents reviewed on 25th March by the committee of investigation and public prosecution in... Saudi Arabia...

Ayas estimated he has made in his own name $160 million. I mean, if Ayas knew that I had all of this stuff, 'Ayas estimated the prince had spent well over 200 million in gambling.' I mean, Prince Mohammed's lifestyle, 'The prince was not a diligent businessman; he would come to the office at around 7 o'clock in the evening. He showed no interest in meeting clientele or visitors... The prince was more interested in talking to his girlfriends or playing poker.' Actually, this is one of my favourite bits cos, here, it talks about how stupid he is... And they also said, at one point, that he's just waiting for his father to die or something, so um. Here, here, look at this, look, look, 'Jealousy exists between the two sides of the Saudi royal family and in particular between Prince Abdul Aziz and Prince Mohammed and his brother, Prince Faisal. King Fahd recently had a stroke; his sons are now looking for his wealth. Apparently he has created a bank in Geneva with the assistance of the Greek tycoon, [the late John] Latsis.
"

Pell gleefully reads to Jones a memo he found that had been drawn up by another Denton Hall solicitor and which is unrelated to Aitken or Ayas. 'I am a solicitor who's been employed from 6th September 1999 by Messrs Denton Hall.'

'On Friday 3rd September, myself and another solicitor left the employment of Messrs Edge Ellison and joined Denton Hall. We had a farewell party at the Carlisle public house. We arrived at approximately 5:30. I believe that, some time between 7 o'clock and 7:30 that evening, I observed a group of people, whom I did not recognise, joining our farewell party. Although they did not all arrive together, they all arrived within a short space of time. By 7:50, there were 27 of them. Very soon, they started talking to my colleague. I therefore presumed that all of them, or some of them at least, must have been known to many of my guests. During the course of the evening, until around 9:30, none of their group made any attempt to talk directly to me. At approximately 9:30, I was crossing diagonally across the room towards the bar, when one member of the group took a step towards me. He said, "Hello, you must be [name deleted]." He'd been asked to come along and have a word with me. He indicated that he knew I did drug-trafficking cases. He explained that he represents a family by the name of Adams [the notorious north London crime family]. He went on to say that they ran a business in the East End, and he expressly referred to drugs. He said that should I find any evidence, I shouldn't get involved. He said to me, 'It's good, [name deleted], that you don't have a wife or kids, otherwise things could get pretty bad.'"

Pell shrieks with laughter, and says: 'He goes on for a few pages on this. This poor guy, he's going to Denton Hall, when in two days he has the most dangerous family in Europe threatening to murder him. But to make matters worse, this story will now find its way into the papers, "Leading drug lawyer in death threat by Adams family." He's now definitely going to get killed. Cos there's one thing- he didn't want this to happen, is this ending up in the papers.'

Meanwhile, Prince Mohammed and Ayas settled their case in May 1999[lxxxiii,] then the following month Aitken was sentenced. Pell boasts to Jones[lxxxiv]: 'And isn't it sad, if you look at all the people I've hit: Elton John's ended up with a heart attack; Jonathan Aitken's ended up in jail; I mean, who's going to be next?'

In November 1999, Pell appeared in Blackfriars crown court and pleaded guilty to a charge of theft. As the Channel 4 documentary reported[lxxxv], the judge deferred sentencing until the following month, and, in the meantime, imposed on Pell a curfew order under which he had to remain at home between 8pm and 8am. Judge Hordern told him that if he were found on the streets between those times he would be liable to arrest... The judge also told Pell that before sentencing he must rid his home of all the waste he had collected[lxxxvii]. 'This offence is far more serious than it appears on the surface,' he added ominously.

However, even this couldn't keep Pell away from the bins. Lewis-Smith's voice-over intoned: 'We decided to see whether Benji would obey the curfew. He soon emerged unrepentant from his house; pulled on the rubber Marigold gloves, and drove away on his nightly round. No judge's order could override a Pell obsession.'

As he watches this, Pell said[lxxxviii]: 'Oh you, you bastards, you bast... Are you sure I can't get done for this? Are you sure, Really? It's not like, okay, ah not, but it's breaking the...'

Lewis-Smith[lxxxix]: 'When he realised that we were filming him, he feared that we might expose his curfew breaking to the judge.' On film, when confronted by McVicar while breaking his curfew, Pell blustered[xci]: 'Do you want me to continue being able to do what I do?' He judges – correctly, so it turns out – that no journalists, in this case the Channel 4 team, would send him to prison for plundering rubbish bags for newsworthy information. When McVicar pointed out that he was breaking his curfew, Pell replied: 'Well, don't get all moralistic on me. Okay? Because they don't – they don't give a fuck. I'm just shitting myself that next Monday this man is going to send me to prison. Look, I'm worried that next Monday I'm going to be in Pentonville. Okay?'

In the Mappin case, Wolanski put it to Pell that he broke the curfew order on the very day it was made[xcii].

Pell: 'That is absolute nonsense.'

Wolanski: 'And you confessed as much on the Channel 4 documentary filmed by Mr McVicar. Correct?'

Pell: 'I did not confess at all. First of all, it was two days later so you've got the wrong date for a start, and, second of all, it wasn't a break of a curfew, there was a 15-minute delay because my car had trouble. If you ask Mr McVicar, he'll confirm that I ran out of petrol. That was not a breach of a curfew.'

When Wolanski put to him that was a very clear breach of the curfew Pell replied: 'What, 15 minutes late?'

Pell, of course, was not only lying again but also getting away with again. Wolanski could not nail him despite the fact that, in an interview filmed before the Mappin trial, Pell told McVicar[xciii]:

> You were fully entitled to break- tell the police I'd broken my curfew.
> McVicar: Yeah, but I didn't do that.
> Pell: I know. Well, what if- would they have arrested me, or what would have happened?
> McVicar: Well, yeah. You'd have had to have been arrested.
> Pell: Shit.
> McVicar: Because you would have been arrested straight away.
> Pell: Would I have gone to prison?
> McVicar: Yeah, you'd have had to.
> Pell: Shit... So, in other words, really, seriously... had you rung up the police and said, 'I'm holding on to him here' I would have been arrested? Fuck.
> McVicar: Well yeah, you were breaking your curfew.
> Pell: Shit, I know, I know. To this day, John, I've never told Paul [Graham, his then solicitor]... I've always lied to him..

Pell is as slippery as...well...a sewer rat. But despite all his blatant lies on oath, his nutter act enables him to escape the force of the law.

References

[i] 'Scandal in the Bins,' Channel 4 (first shown 11.01.01).
[ii] Luke Harding, Owen Bowcott, David Pallister, Jamie Wilson, Clare Longrigg and Christopher Elliott, 'Saudi scandal: on the trail of a prince's missing millions,' *The Guardian* (10.01.98).
[iii] Mark Watts and Kevin Cahill, 'Commons gagged Fayed,' *Sunday Business* (01.06.97).
[iv] Luke Harding, David Leigh and David Pallister, 'Arms and the man of straw. The final chapter: from secret weapons deals to deceit over his finances, his lies persisted to the very end,' *The Guardian* (09.06.99).
[v] Mark Watts, 'Revealed: the truth behind Aitken's Rolex watch gifts,' *Sunday Business* (13.06.99).
[vi] 'The LISI File,' *World in Action*, ITV (the second programme on Aitken first shown 11.12.95); 'Jonathan of Arabia,' *World in Action*, ITV (the first programme on Aitken first shown 10.04.95).
[vii] David Pallister, 'Aitken tried to arrange girls for Saudi friends,' and, 'Aitken connection to second

arms dealer disclosed,' *The Guardian* (10.04.95); David Pallister and Richard Norton-Taylor, 'NEW CLAIM OVER AITKEN ARMS TO IRAQ LINK: letter reveals offer to bring in orders for firm from Middle East,' *The Guardian* (12.12.95).

viii Mark Watts, 'Aitken firm in Iraq gun deal,' *The Sunday Telegraph* (18.02.96).

ix Mark Watts, 'Aitken cleared over Iran arms. New BMARC inquiry planned,' *The Independent on Sunday* (02.06.96).

x Rachel Sylvester and Jon Hibbs, 'I lied for my country, says Aitken,' *The Daily Telegraph* (21.05.98).

xi Matthew Norman, Diary, *The Guardian* (22.05.98).

xii Mark Watts, 'Revealed: the truth behind Aitken's Rolex watch gifts,' *Sunday Business* (13.06.99).

xiii Chris Hutchins, 'CONFIDENTIALLY SPEAKING,' *Sunday Mirror* (24.05.98).

xiv 'Scandal in the Bins,' Channel 4 (first shown 11.01.01).

xv McVicar audio tape (recorded 12.11.00) MDRG.

xvi Transcript of evidence of Benjamin Pell, Benjamin Pell -v- John Mappin and Story Master Ltd, (12.03.02).

xvii "3½-hour rushes," Moving Perspective (filmed 1999).

xviii David Leigh, 'Aitken: how a tangled web was woven,' *The Guardian* (03.06.99).

xix For example: Mark Watts and Lucinda Kemeny, 'Secret Aitken fund revealed,' *Sunday Business* (19.12.99); Andrew Woodcock, 'Accountants probe Aitken's "secret bank account" claims,' *Press Association* (13.05.00).

xx "3½-hour rushes," Moving Perspective (filmed 1999).

xxi Transcript of evidence of Benjamin Pell, Benjamin Pell -v- John Mappin and Story Master Ltd, (12.03.02).

xxii McVicar audio tape (recorded 12.11.00) MDRG.

xxiii 'Scandal in the Bins,' Channel 4 (first shown 11.01.01).

xxiv McVicar audio tape (recorded 04.10.98) MDRO.

xxv "3½-hour rushes," Moving Perspective (filmed 1999).

xxvi McVicar video tape (filmed 08.02.01) DVOO.

xxvii McVicar audio tape (recorded 04.10.98) MDRO.

xxviii Nick Fielding, 'Aitken faces jail as assets are frozen,' *Mail on Sunday* (04.10.98).

xxix McVicar audio tape (recorded 04.10.98) MDRO.

xxx "3½-hour rushes," Moving Perspective (filmed 1999).

xxxi 'Aitken bankruptcy deal to halve £2.8m debts,' *The Guardian* (29.10.01).

xxxii "3½-hour rushes," Moving Perspective (filmed 1999).

xxxiii Robert Mendick. 'Historic case signals end of war-crime trials,' *The Lawyer* (05.04.99); 'Lords reject war criminal's appeal bid,' *Press Association* (19.06.00).

xxxiv Gary Jones, 'WAR-CRIMES LAWYER SLAMMED OVER FEES,' *The Mirror* (19.02.99).

xxxv Robert Mendick, 'Historic case signals end of war-crime trials,' *The Lawyer* (05.04.99).

xxxvi 'Scandal in the Bins,' Channel 4 (first shown 11.01.01).

xxxvii McVicar audio tape (recorded 12.11.00) MDRG.

xxxviii 'Scandal in the Bins,' Channel 4 (first shown 11.01.01).

xxxix McVicar audio tape (recorded 12.11.00) MDRG.

xl 'Scandal in the Bins,' Channel 4 (first shown 11.01.01).

xli McVicar audio tape (recorded 12.11.00) MDRG.

xlii 'Scandal in the Bins,' Channel 4 (first shown 11.01.01).

xliii McVicar audio tape (recorded 12.11.00) MDRG.

xliv 'Scandal in the Bins,' Channel 4 (first shown 11.01.01).

xlv McVicar audio tape (recorded 12.11.00) MDRG.

xlvi "3½-hour rushes," Moving Perspective (filmed 1999).

xlvii Transcript of evidence of Benjamin Pell, Benjamin Pell -v- John Mappin and Story Master Ltd, (12.03.02).

xlviii 'Scandal in the Bins,' Channel 4 (first shown 11.01.01).

xlix McVicar audio tape (recorded 12.11.00) MDRG.

l 'Scandal in the Bins,' Channel 4 (first shown 11.01.01).

li McVicar audio tape (recorded 12.11.00) MDRG.

lii 'Scandal in the Bins,' Channel 4 (first shown 11.01.01).

liii McVicar audio tape (recorded 12.11.00) MDRG.

liv 'Scandal in the Bins,' Channel 4 (first shown 11.01.01).

lv McVicar audio tape (recorded 12.11.00) MDRG.

lvi 'Scandal in the Bins,' Channel 4 (first shown 11.01.01).

lvii McVicar audio tape (recorded 12.11.00) MDRG.

lviii 'Scandal in the Bins,' Channel 4 (first shown 11.01.01).

lix McVicar audio tape (recorded 12.11.00) MDRG.

lx 'Scandal in the Bins,' Channel 4 (first shown 11.01.01).

lxi McVicar audio tape (recorded 12.11.00) MDRG.

lxii 'Scandal in the Bins,' Channel 4 (first shown 11.01.01).

lxiii McVicar audio tape (recorded 12.11.00) MDRG.

lxiv "3½-hour rushes," Moving Perspective (filmed 1999).

lxv 'Scandal in the Bins,' Channel 4 (first shown 11.01.01).

lxvi McVicar audio tape (recorded 12.11.00) MDRG.

lxvii 'Scandal in the Bins,' Channel 4 (first shown 11.01.01).

lxviii McVicar audio tape (recorded 12.11.00) MDRG.

lxix "3½-hour rushes," Moving Perspective (filmed 1999).

lxx David Leppard and Chris Hastings, 'Aitken plans to meet his fate like Charles I,' *The Sunday Times* (07.03.99).

lxxi Luke Harding, David Leigh and David Pallister, 'Arms and the man of straw. The final chapter: from secret weapons deals to deceit over his finances, his lies persisted to the very end,' *The Guardian* (09.06.99).

lxxii David Pallister and Jamie Wilson, 'Ex-minister jailed for 'web of deceit' *The Guardian* (20.06.99).

lxxiii Mark Watts, 'Revealed: the truth behind Aitken's Rolex watch gifts,' *Sunday Business* (13.06.99).

lxxiv "3½-hour rushes," Moving Perspective (filmed 1999).

lxxv McVicar video tape (filmed January 2001) DVRV.

lxxvi "3½-hour rushes," Moving Perspective (filmed 1999).

lxxvii For example: Luke Harding, Owen Bowcott, David Pallister, Jamie Wilson, Clare Longrigg and Christopher Elliott, 'Saudi scandal: on the trail of a prince's missing millions,' *The Guardian* (10.01.98); 'Aitken, the fixer and the secret multi-million pound arms deals,' *The Guardian* (05.03.99); David Pallister, 'Arms dealing Saudi settles with prince,' *The Guardian* (21.05.99); Luke Harding, David Leigh and David Pallister, 'Arms and the man of straw. The final chapter: from secret weapons deals to deceit over his finances, his lies persisted to the very end,' *The Guardian* (09.06.99).

lxxviii Chris Hastings, David Leppard, Jonathon Carr-Brown and Wayne Bodkin, 'The prince who blew a billion,' *The Sunday Times* (05.07.98).

lxxix "3½-hour rushes," Moving Perspective (filmed 1999).

lxxx McVicar video tape (filmed January 2001) DVRV.

lxxxi Transcript of evidence of Benjamin Pell, Benjamin Pell -v- John Mappin and Story Master Ltd, (12.03.02); Mr Justice Gray, judgement in Benjamin Pell -v- John Mappin and Story Master Ltd (19.03.02).

lxxxii McVicar video tape (filmed January 2001) DVRV.

lxxxiii David Pallister, 'Arms dealing Saudi settles with prince,' *The Guardian* (21.05.99).

lxxxiv "3½-hour rushes," Moving Perspective (filmed 1999).

lxxxv 'Scandal in the Bins,' Channel 4 (first shown 11.01.01).

lxxxvi McVicar audio tape (recorded 12.11.00) MDRG.

lxxxvii 'Scandal in the Bins,' Channel 4 (first shown 11.01.01).

lxxxviii McVicar audio tape (recorded 12.11.00) MDRG.

lxxxix 'Scandal in the Bins,' Channel 4 (first shown 11.01.01).

xc McVicar audio tape (recorded 12.11.00) MDRG.

xci 'Scandal in the Bins,' Channel 4 (first shown 11.01.01).

xcii Transcript of evidence of Benjamin Pell, Benjamin Pell -v- John Mappin and Story Master Ltd, (12.03.02).

xciii McVicar audio tape (recorded 09.11.00) MDRY.

Chapter 11

Mad for It:
carry on bin raiding

Pell thought that it was time to see a psychiatrist. But there was indeed method in his madness. He wanted a psychiatrist's report for the court to consider before deciding what action to take over his theft of documents from Harkavys, Aitken's solicitors.

With Bible in hand, Pell told Jones[i]:

I'm the first one to admit that I am completely mad. But at the end of the day, to be mad is a very, very good thing, as the Bible showed us. This is first Samuel, the story of David... he'd been escaping from Saul, who was trying to kill him, and he flew- he fled to a place called Gath... And it says in here, 'And David laid up these words in his heart, and was afraid of Achish, the king of Gath,' cos he didn't really want him to be there.' So what did David do? Clever king, 'He changed his demeanour before them, and he feigned himself mad in their hands, he scrabbled on the doors of the gate, and he let his spittle fall down upon his beard.'

Well, I don't have a beard, but you've seen me spit a few times, as your lens is testimony too. Then Achish says to the servant, 'Lo, when you see a man that is mad, why do you bring him to me? Do I like madmen that you have bought this fellow to play the madman in my presence? Shall this fellow come into my house?' And look at the way our faith has interpreted it, 'There are many examples in Arabic and Persian stories of the use of this stratagem, which is all the more likely to succeed because of the special dread in which lunatics were held as men possessed by a powerful spirit.'

Jones asks him: 'So now you're going to call your psychiatrist?'

Pell added: 'I'm going to call my psychiatrist to confirm that, like King David, I am mad.'

Laurie Taylor, professor of sociology at the University of York, told the Channel 4 documentary[ii]: "Yeah, I met him once... I was in the

Groucho Club, and suddenly this figure scuttled into range and stopped briefly in the corridor. And I suddenly saw someone else [John Benson, former All Saints manager] lurching towards him and saying, "You not dead yet?" And I suddenly saw this little wizened, dirty figure clutching himself. I thought, you know, some sort of-some lunatic.'

However, having watched some of the McVicar video tapes, Taylor said: 'You suddenly see the fearsome, convoluted, but nevertheless, logic which exists within those tapes. I mean, this isn't someone who's off his head at all.

'Not mad; seeming mad. He's only got to really gear it up one more- one more stroke and everybody's falling away, and they think, "Well, yes, we are dealing with a mad person."

'It is an extraordinary act. It almost plays up every worst facet of his character. I mean, the clothes and even some of the mannerisms, the constant scratching, you know, as though he's in need of a bath; as though he's dirty; as though he's infested...

'Some of the people he's getting back at seem to be people that formally he loved: the Elton John story. And yet there are other people he's getting back at, the solicitors where you might say, "Well, okay, there are good reasons for him to get back at the solicitors because he wanted to be a solicitor."

'Good reasons perhaps to get back at newspaper editors insofar as among his various obsessions there's an obsession with newspapers. In a way, in relation to the newspapers, he's making the headlines. In relation to the solicitors, he's showing them. He's stealing their documents. He's upsetting them. He's disrupting their business. He is in control of these people. He's in control of solicitors. He's in control of the newspaper editors. He's in control of pop stars. All these people he had a fascination with, in some cases hated, and in some cases loved, are let into his world. They're jumping when he calls.

'It's very clever. It's very ingenious. He gets away with it.'

And in confirmation of Taylor's assessment of Pell as 'not mad; seeming mad,' Pell talks to an interviewer from an Israeli newspaper about feigning madness[iii], saying that the psalms 'taught him: if you're in trouble, you go mad'.

However, perhaps by playing the madman so much he has driven himself mad. He refers to 'my ethos in life', saying: 'I am the only normal one in the whole country, but outwardly, of course, I appear mad.' Asked how he feels about other people's discussing whether he is mad, he says: 'I love it, I love it. I mean, Laurie Taylor, the professor, saw right through it. Fortunately, he was the only one. Laurie Taylor immediately analysed this: this isn't someone who's nuts at all, it's all put on.' Of course, it is not all put on, but when it matters it is.

And Pell tells McVicar that telling lies is justifiable for Jews[iv].

Lying has always been okay. The Jews have always had to use a bit of- we've had to be- use a bit of duplicitous, we've had to use a bit of mendacity sometimes to get- to get our way. The Bible justifies lying 'if it is for a good purpose'.

Pell showed Jones how he set about duping a psychiatrist into preparing a report that would persuade the court to treat him leniently, not by declaring him mad but, nonetheless, to say that he has a mental condition[v]. Before seeing the psychiatrist, he told Jones:

Me, see a psychiatrist? Yeah, I'm seeing Dr Arsen tomorrow, or 'Dr Arse', at 12 o'clock, why? For only one simple reason, the lawyers have told me that psychiatric evidence could be absolutely crucial in getting the whole thing turned out- er, thrown out immediately. So that's why I'm seeing him tomorrow.

I mean, obviously my parents have been asking me to see a psychiatrist for the last- well, as you know, I've been seeing somebody... since I was 16, on and off. But this is the first time I've actually willingly allowed myself to see someone. I actually begged of him, I wrote him a letter three weeks ago, and I said, 'Please, I'd like to meet you.'

And it's perfect. I mean, these people have got nothing- ... I don't believe in psychiatry anyway; I think it's absolute nonsense; I think they need more therapy normally than their patients. As long as he doesn't prescribe Prozac or amphetamines or any other form of drugs, I'm fine. All I want is a letter from him to the court saying, 'Benjamin Pell is in a serious condition. He's suffering terribly from kleptomania, and you have to treat him with the clemency he deserves.'

Pell took Jones to film his consultation with the psychiatrist at the Maudsley hospital in south London. Pell begins by explaining to the psychiatrist why he is there...

Pell: It is advisable that I get all of my medical problems documented at this stage.
Doctor: Yeah.
Pell: I've been arrested now for stealing rubbish.
Doctor: Really? From whom?
Pell: Does that matter"
Doctor: No [unintelligible].
Pell: It's Jonathan Aitken's lawyers.
Doctor: Right, okay, right.
Pell: And I was in court yesterday, and there were about 15 members of the Press outside the building trying to get pictures of me.
Doctor: Hm, em-
Pell: Well, I had a moustache on, so they didn't recognise me. I mean, they still took pictures, but they haven't used them.
Doctor: Hmm, okay. Look, I haven't seen you for a little while, right, so I'd just like to know- cos when you rang me, I thought, I was surprised to hear from you.
Pell: Well, I wrote to you.
Doctor: I thought- yeah, I know, you wrote and then, you know- but I thought you might be in trouble somehow.
Pell: Well, I am.
Doctor: Right. So... tell me, how can I help? ... Cos in the past, you said I couldn't help.
Pell: Yeah, well, cos my parents were pushing me, you know. Every time I didn't come here, they knew about it, or they could guess. They were practically following me around the world, you know, just to see if I was talking to you. But my obsession has got much, much worse now.
Doctor: Hm mm, which obsession is that?
Pell: Keeping everything. I mean, you've been in my- you were in my house in February, weren't you, same time as the [unintelligible: both talking] situation, yeah. And it's much, much worse. I've now extended into another shed, I've got the whole of the back of the garden, I'm now in the dining room as well, we've now got a computer, which we keep in the dining room during the week, and it's driving my parents mad.
Doctor: Hm mm. So, who needs the help? You or your parents?

Pell: Well, I think they do. I think, at the end of the day, you know, it's not interfering with their well being, it's only a bit of paper. But it drives them completely bonkers. They're always going on about it. If I ever tidy any part of the house or anything, they'll always go on about the bits which aren't tidy. So, I can tidy up the dining room, they'll go on about the stairs, or upstairs, or go on about the shed. There's no part of the house which they will not complain about at any point.

Doctor: Hm mmm, hm mmm.

Doctor says to the cameraman: Can I ask you, do you know Benji, somehow, for a long time, or-?

Cameraman: Little bit.

Doctor: Little bit. You know the set up as well as home, or you've been to the house with him?

Cameraman: Hmm.

Doctor: You would agree that the excess of his... drive to collect or obsession, whatever, Benji- Benjamin.

Pell: Benjamin. I'm a Benjamin, yeah, yeah, yeah.

Doctor: They call you Benjamin?

Pell: Yeah, Benjamin, yeah, yeah, yeah... And I certainly don't like Ben.

Doctor: Hm mm.

Doctor to cameraman: What's your view?

Cameraman: I'll just let Benji talk right now.

Doctor: Okay.

Pell: I mean, anybody who's come in to the house- lawyers have been in my house, and people just say- journalists come into my house all the time, and they just think it's weird. I don't think it is.

Doctor: But they come into the house in order to, what, interview you?

Pell: No, no, I'm giving them stories.

Doctor: Okay.

Pell: And I deal with the Press on a regular basis, and I, er- and I'll get, you know, I get the stuff from the rubbish, and I give it to the Press. And I've been doing that successfully for, er, a year and a half now.

Doctor: Hm mmm. Now, let me come back to you. Again, you don't think you need particular help? If anyone needs help, it's your parents who put up with having a son who... collects endless things.

Pell: I mean, they've got to realise that if I do have a problem, it's a problem of obsess- obsessionality. But I'm the first person ever to have that problem, which is why I've been, in inverted commas, so successful. I mean, there've never been stories like my stories emanating from these sources. I mean, it's unbelievable. All the journalists tell me that what I've done is unique, and, er, my name will go down in history. So, you know, eccentric people have to be, I think, er tolerated in society.

Doctor: Hm mmm. Is that cos your parents can't tolerate you?

Pell: Yes, they don't realise what I'm doing.

Doctor: So, are you saying that the real work that should be done is for me to help your parents accept...

Pell: Both of them, they should be proud of me. They should know that in five years' time, people will say to them, 'My goodness me, you have that genius of a son working in your house all those years... what a clever man.'

Doctor: Hm. I think they realise that you're clever.

Pell: No, no...

Doctor: They needn't think you're a genius, but they're just fed up walking, er, over your papers when they go to the bathroom.

Pell: They don't need to. It's not as bad as that in the hall. The hall is actually quite clear now. The hall is clear; my room is obviously a mess and the...

Doctor: But that's your room?

Pell: That's my- well...

Doctor: But then in your brother's room was something else at all...

Pell: But it's not as big a mess as it was. I mean, the dining room is always a mess, the kit- the outside is a mess, and the area between the kitchen and the garden is a mess because that's where I keep my bags. I have usually about 100 bags surrounding the house. That drives them mad.

Doctor: Surrounding it?

Pell: Yeah. And every week, they phone up a man, get him to remove them... Sometimes, it's like murder there. I mean, two months ago, he came and I- my- I was, literally, kicking my father. He was taking away any bags at random and just dumping them onto the van. I mean, the man must have thought he was going into a madhouse.

Doctor: Hm. Do you think that, um, if a compromise was being found with your, as you see it, er, parents' inability to see your genius...

Pell: No, of course... They've got to realise what I'm doing. What I'm doing is unique. I mean, it's amazing that nobody else has done what I've done. But what I'm doing is totally unique, and, therefore, they've got to put up with it. They have no choice. I can't stop doing what I'm doing. It's impossible. I've gone too far down that road now.

Doctor: Hm mmm. And, of course, if you lived somewhere else, we've discussed this, and it wouldn't be an issue.

Pell: No, of course, it wouldn't be an issue, but the problem is they'd come round there and start cleaning that place up.

Doctor: Why would they want to do that?

Pell: Well... They drove my brother to America. So er, that's- that's what they're like. They will start getting involved in my own- obviously, it won't be to the same extent. But I think it's just an excuse to have a go at me. Cos, at the end of the day, it doesn't affect them at all in any way. Just cos there's a bag outside the kitchen, or maybe 20 bags outside the kitchen, so what? So what? My mother comes down at 7 o'clock in the morning, and the kitchen smells because I've been going through rubbish throughout the night. So what? You know, I open the window.

Doctor: "m. So, I mean, you're- I take it you're quite fond of your parents, aren't you?

Pell: Well, yes, I mean, sort of.

Doctor: Hm hm. Could you, I mean, do you make enough money to have your independ- an independent living?

Pell: I can't live by myself.

Doctor: The reason being?

Pell: I was attacked outside my house a year ago, you know, very badly attacked, and I can't, I'm too scared. I mean, every time I come home...

Doctor: Who can- who can protect you in your house: your father or your mother?

Pell: No, at least, when you're coming home, psychologically, you know that there's somebody in the house. If I was living alone, I'd be paranoid. Every time I came in to the door, I'd be worried there was somebody upstairs – waiting for me.

Doctor: But your parents are not in a state, or physically able to...

Pell: No, it's psychological. I wear a hard hat now whenever I go out.

Doctor: You have what?

Pell: A hard hat, a white, hard hat in case somebody attacks me.

Doctor: Hm. Do you have baseball things to put on your head or what?

Pell: No, no. Hard hat.

Doctor: And who- who hit you before? Someone...

Pell: I don't know who hit me. I was outside the house, coming home in April- in, er, June of last year, and I was physically attacked. I mean, my glasses were broken; my jaw was, er, beaten; and, er, it's horrible – really scary. It was the night before giving evidence in a- in a court case.

Doctor: On the other hand, your parents say they need to lead their lives. They're elderly people, and they want to... have their own routine. What would happen if they kicked you out?

Pell: Well, they'd never do that. Where are they going to kick me out to, Hendon Park?

Doctor: Hm, well, it could- I mean, financially, you could survive, couldn't you?

Pell: What, in Hendon Park?

Doctor: No, not in Hendon Park. Outside your parents' house, wherever that might be.

Pell: Yeah, of course, I mean, I could live in a warehouse. I mean, ba- and in order to transfer all of my stuff anywhere else would be impossible. I mean, people say I should get premises, but, y- you know, not to live there, but to keep- but even there, I'd be paranoid about somebody breaking into... I mean, if it's under my- if it's in my hall, that's fine, I can live with that. If it's in my house, that's fine. I can't have it too far away.

[Cut in footage.]

Doctor: So, why did you come today? Just because your parents sent you?

Pell: Yes, I mean...

Doctor: To keep them quiet?

Pell: Yeah, yeah, I mean, two weeks ago, my father... he was just going mad about some rubbish or something, I don't know.

Doctor: See... the only job that I think I could do for you would be to help you to live with each other, er, more harmoniously, you know, really, rather than to change...

Pell: You don't actually- you don't think I'm obsessed with rubbish?

Doctor: Yeah, you said yourself, of course you are. But you make a living out of it...

Pell: "Yeah, but- but you don't think that's a problem?"

Doctor: Well, it's not a problem to me personally, because I don't live there, but if I lived there it might be a problem to me. Being obsessed with rubbish doesn't appear to be a problem for you.

Pell: Cos when I first saw [another doctor], and when I first saw psychotherapists, then I was obsessed with keeping text books, and keeping notes and stuff, and newspapers. It's now progressed since then.

Doctor: With all these things... whether you call it obsessions or not, with all these things is that if you can with it and if you don't bother anyone else, well, of course, there are lots of eccentrics who live and no one bothers them.

Pell: Yeah.

Doctor: But, em, your obsession is clear to impinge in a major way on your parents' lifestyle, so they say.

Pell: Because they let it.

Doctor: Well.

Pell: They let it affect them. I mean, I don't- you know, there's no stuff in there...

Doctor: Yeah, I- I know, but they can't help it.

Pell: Yeah, I know.

Doctor: I've seen them. It's unlikely that they'll change, isn't it?

Pell: No, that's true, definitely.

Doctor: And it's unlikely that you will change, in a funny sort of way, isn't it? Er, because particularly you make a living out of it.

Pell: Well, I can't- I mean, as you know, I can't stop. You know, every time I get a new target, I can't then not do them again.

Doctor: Yeah.

Pell: So, when I first started, I had one target...

Doctor: Yeah.

Pell: ...and now I have about 115.

Doctor: Yeah, yeah.

Pell: I had to buy a new van last- two months ago to cope.

[Cut in footage.]

Pell: But the CPS don't seem to find it funny because they're going to the expense of, er, taking me to court. And the firm of solicitors who caught me in the act went to the trouble of having me on camera for five consecutive weeks, taking their rubbish. And I had seven police officers waiting for me that morning, and I missed the Sabbath that weekend because of my arrest because they had to keep me in custody for eight hours. So, it was horrible. Can you imagine how my mother reacted when, at 7:15 in the morning, she gets a knock on the door from seven police officers, saying we've come to your house to inspect- to search for documents? I mean, the good thing is, cos the house is in- well, the house is always in a mess...

Doctor: They couldn't find anything?

Pell: Well, they couldn't find a thing. And when they went into the shed, everything fell on top of them, and he just- he just laughed and went- he said, 'Fine,' he said, 'We've done enough.' And he came in there with three vans ready to take away every document in my house, and they ended up taking about that much [gesturing to signal a small pile of papers].

Doctor: Hmm.

Pell: So.

Doctor: Is it likely that you'll ask me to write a psychiatric report for court purposes?

Pell: Probably, yeah, yeah. I'm not going to plead insanity because I'm not insane, but...

Doctor: No, no, no, no, no. No, I am sure you're not, you know...

Pell: I mean, the only other... similar thing in my life was in 1989 when I was arrested at Charing Cross station for fare evasion. And I managed to get off on that charge because, at that stage, I was seeing someone at Charing Cross Hospital, and I- I've always been obsessive about money. So, I am obsessive, and the courts like hearing about obsessive people, it gives them an excuse to deal with them, you know, reasonably sympathetically, but...

Doctor: So, you've got something invested in coming to see me so that I can, at least, write a report and say...

Pell: No, no, no, I mean, no, no, no...

Doctor: ..can I do some straight talking?

Pell: Well, my solicitor said to me, 'Are you currently seeing someone?' And I said, 'Well, I've been, on and off, seeing people over the last-' well, since I've been 16, I've been seeing people. I mean, my father brought me to see this horrible doctor... when I was 16 for about two years, you know. So, em, I've always been seeing people. But, no, no, I'm not seeing you today because of parental pressure or because of pressure from my solicitor, I'm just seeing you today because...

Doctor: You want to have a document that will prove that you've seen me?

[Cut in footage.]

Pell: If I get a criminal conviction, it means I can never practice as a solicitor. That'll be it, all because of me stealing five bags of rubbish. I mean...

Doctor: Hm mmm. They've only charged you with five bags of rubbish?

Pell: Yeah, on five separate occasions of taking rubbish. Theft of confidential waste, they call it.

Doctor: Confidential waste?

Pell: Mm, I know.

Doctor: That sounds like a contradiction in terms, doesn't it?

Pell: "That's good. I shall tell my lawyer that. I mean, you should read it. If somebody was taking your rubbish, then obviously everything in here- I mean, you should see the stuff I get from lawyers' offices, I mean...

Doctor: No, you told me- told me that, yeah.

Pell: No, this is- I know, I'm going to tell you about this. Last week, one of the top barristers in this country, he was seen by somebody at Guy's Hospital cos he was on Prozac, and he was arrested by the police and bound over cos he was- He's one of the top five barristers in his field, and he is obviously not well. It's very sad. But that: to be left in the rubbish? I mean, it's just outrageous. It is a national- it is an international scandal. I mean, I've only discovered the scandal-well actually- I've discovered the London scandal, but this is a scandal of international proportions. And the stories I discover affect people throughout the world. I mean, three weeks ago, I had a knock on the door on a Saturday morning from a detective agency from Warner Brothers, the movie company, and I was involved in the Stanley Kubrick situation. So, there- there're not many people in the world- I mean, Bill Clinton is one of the few people who aren't in some way affected by my activities. Seriously, I'm not just saying that in a boastful way; it's true. Prince Charles, the Diana Memorial Trust, Richard Branson, some of the top names in the media/entertainment world have been affected by me.

Doctor: What's the likely sentence you're going to get do you reckon for that crime.

Pell: I mean, you can go to prison for theft. If they consider it to be important enough, yes. I mean, don't forget I was going through the rubbish of Jonathan Aitken's solicitor; I was finding all the documents regarding Jonathan Aitken's affairs. His wife, Lolicia, was tracked down to Switzerland because of me. She'd been hiding from the Press for three years. Because of me... she ends up on the front page of the Mail on Sunday. See, it's a frightful business. So, they may want to make an example of me. I mean, Jonathan Aitken is a very powerful man. I wouldn't be surprised if he's behind this arrest. I don't know. But he can't be, though, because he can't be aware of what I do. So, the whole thing is baffling to me. See, I don't know how these people would react if they found out what I'd been doing. That's one thing I've never- I know that Elton John, when he found out what I'd been doing, he sacked his manager. And that's what I'd do. All Saints, when they found out what I'd been doing, sacked their- their solicitors. But, and that's it, really they're the only two solicitors' firm who were fully aware of my activities, and it- it became public knowledge. Since then, I've reasonably kept a low profile – fortunately. I mean, I'm in the papers every so often. I was in The Times two weeks ago, but I can live with that.

Doctor: Must give you quite a kick, doesn't it? The papers...

Pell: Ah no, I used to get a kick out of it, being in the Press. I hate it now. No, no, no, I don't- don't want any publicity at all. I hate that. Fortunately, my parents don't know anything about it. They know nothing. They don't e- obviously, they know about the arrests, but it's so easy to pull the wool over their eyes, I just said to my mother, 'I was arrested, but they're not charging me.' And that was it.

Doctor: Hm. So, let's see, you can tell your solicitor... If they ask, and say am I prepared to write a report about you, I would, yeah?

Pell: Okay.

Doctor: The answer is... I would, and- a psychiatric report. Em, to do that, er, if that's- if that's what your solicitor thinks, just to write...

Pell: Well, obviously, he- he's not clutching at straws. On the face of it, I have committed the offence of theft.

Doctor: But if he thinks it helps... your case to have a psychiatric report on you, I am quite...

Pell: All I know is that I'm- I don't think I'm mad.

Doctor: No, no, no.

Pell: I think the world is mad.

Doctor: No, no, no.

Pell: Maybe that makes me mad... But I don't think I'm mad. I think what I'm doing is quite normal because I've discovered a huge loophole in confidentiality. It's an amazing loophole. And any other journalist finding this loophole would do what I'm doing. But I'm admitting to the fact that I'm now obsessed with it. Yes, admit that.

Doctor: But... I wouldn't say that you're mad, but I would say that you've got what psychiatrists call... you may disagree... an illness, which is called obsessional...

Pell: Why do you call it an illness?

Doctor: Psychiatrists call it an illness, I said. But I'm not saying that- I don't want to get into a sort of a philosophical debate with you... I think, you know, I have an open mind about it.

Pell: Well, if you thought the house was mad in February of last year, you ain't seen nothing. It's got much, much worse.

Doctor to cameraman: You would agree with that? Yeah. Um, you've seen the house in different stages as well, yeah?

Pell: You see, I don't think it's mad to have discovered all of these loopholes, and therefore to fill the house. I think it's mad for my parents to react in the way they do... too ashamed even to talk about me when visitors come over...

Doctor: Right, hang on.

Pell: ...which is pathetic.

Doctor: Two issues, right?

Pell: They should be proud of me.

Doctor: Right, hang on.

Pell: Okay.

Doctor: Two issues. Your solicitor is one issue. If your solicitor thinks it would help your case to have a psychiatric report prepared on you, yes, then I'm prepared to do that, but the solicitor has to write me a letter.

Pell: Got it.

Doctor: "Okay? Instruct me to do that. Right, okay? Um, if I do that, I will have to meet with you once or twice to go through... a formal discussion about bits and pieces I can put into the report. Yeah? But my diagnosis, in inverted commas, I would say that you have what psychiatrists call an obsessive-compulsive disorder...

Pell: Well, that's what [another doctor] wrote... a year ago.

Doctor: ...where you can't, er, control, um, er, some of the actions which then take the form of, er, compulsive prying into other people's garbage, basically. Right?

Pell: Yeah, yeah."

Doctor: And I'll say there's no known cure for it, basically.

Pell: Ha, ha.

Doctor: You're likely to... it's what you do.

Pell: It will continue forever, until people start to...

Doctor: That's issue number one, but I'll- I'll...

Pell: Okay.

Doctor: If your solicitor instructed me, I would, um, er, formally meet with you, yes? We spend, maybe on two occasions, one hour for me to just go through bits and pieces I don't know about. Okay? Er, then I would write that report. Okay? That's number one. Point two is how to make the living situation for you and your parents more bearable.

Pell: Mmm.

Doctor: It's another issue. I don't think I could do that here, but if

you come and see me here... But then, if I come to your house, I would ask you not to be on the internet or telephone during that time.
Pell: Well, I wasn't on the internet, in fact.
Doctor: No, wherever you were. Well anyway, you were not there. It was difficult to address issues in the family...
Pell: Cos I don't like meeting with you and my parents at the same time. Cos I'm not gonna be honest with you in front of my parents.
Doctor: Well, you don't have to be honest with me, but I...
Pell: Well, you don't want me to lie to you either.
Doctor: But, there's a difference between that cos there's also a way of, let's say...
Pell: My mother started crying, getting emotional, then my father starts...
Doctor: Well, well, the issue is that, you know, your parents find it increasingly more unbearable to live in the same house with you when you have these kinds of, um, collecting habits.
Pell: Yeah.
Doctor: Okay?
Pell: I accept that.
Doctor: Alright? And you find it quite difficult to live with them when they keep criticising you all the time.
Pell: Exactly. If they didn't criticise me, I'd have no problem with them.
Doctor: But the only thing I could say is that I could see whether I could help...
Pell: Yeah.
Doctor: ...the three of you to find a somewhat less unbearable...
Pell: Cos you- you solved the problem of the hall. When you were there in February, the hall, d'you remember that? The hall was literally cluttered.
Doctor: Yeah, yeah.
Pell: Now the hall is empty, really, apart from my coat and a few things. So, I've done the hall and my other office upstairs.
Doctor: What I'm saying is that I'm prepared to meet with you and your parents not to address your own personal issues, which may or may not need to be addressed anyway, but to address the issues of living together possibly in a slightly less erm...
Pell: Fraught atmosphere?
Doctor: Fraught atmosphere. Right? So, I'm prepared to do that.
Pell: Okay.
Doctor: But, you would have to be there.

Pell: Okay, yeah I would- yeah, yeah.

Doctor: Okay? So- so, I could arrange a time with you and your-your parents now. I can arrange a time when I come to the house to address that issue.

Pell: Okay.

Doctor: As far as the psychiatric...

Pell: You won't take sides?

Doctor: No, I've got nothing invested. I'm prepared...

Pell: You won't go in there and say, 'You are right, Mr and Mrs Pell, you know, if he doesn't get rid of that stuff within a week, get rid of him.'

Doctor: Get rid of him?

Pell: Yeah.

Doctor: No... I don't think I'd give silly advice like that. I'd just say, 'I'm getting the three of you to consider-'

Pell: You're not a social worker?

Doctor: Me? No, definitely not.

Pell: Exactly. So. And, see, a lot of social workers do...

Doctor: No, no, I- I would see, if I come to your house, I see my role as helping you to have a slightly...

Pell: "Can you explain to them, though, that it is an obsession?

Doctor: Hm mmm. They know that.

Pell: Yeah, no, no.

Doctor: They also think it's an obsession that...

Pell: But they- but they are not sympathetic about it. They don't realise that. And I don't think- if they realised it was an obsession and illness, they wouldn't criticise me so much, you know.

Doctor: Hm mmm. What is the- um, any day is fine for me.

Pell: No, I'm home all day. I'm home all day. I never go- I don't go out much.

Doctor: Same goes for your parents?

Pell: Yeah. I mean, my father should always be home, and my mother's always home, unless she's shopping.

Doctor: Right. Um, how- how urgent is it that I come round if only to keep your parents quiet, as you see it probably?

Pell: Oh, we've got the Jewish holidays coming up."

Doctor: Yeah, I know.

Pell: But they're on Saturdays- Saturdays and Sundays this year, so there's no problem, so.

Doctor: So, let's say, week starting 20th September, that's a Monday.

Pell: Yuh.

Doctor: Erm, if I came to your house, something like, what 4:30?
Pell: That'll be fine.
Doctor: Yeah?
Pell: Yeah.
Doctor: You gonna have the cameras there, or-?
Pell: No, no, no, no.
Doctor: Can I bring my own camera?
Pell: No, no, I don't need- I don't need the proof of my visit when you're there. Cos my parents will be there, so that's fine. Okay.
Doctor: Okay, if you point the camera at me now, your cameraman. I hereby certify that I'm the real Dr Arsen, who's been seeing Benji for the past, um, 23 minutes.
Pell: And I didn't come here under duress. I came here willingly.
Doctor: Okay, fine, great. Thanks for coming.
Pell: Okay, thank you, doctor, that's very kind of you. Thanks. My lawyer's name is Paul Graham in case he writes to you.
Doctor: Yes, okay.
Pell: Okay, see you then.
Doctor: Okay bye.

[As Pell leaves the session with the psychiatrist, he told Jones] We're now exiting after having performed exactly what I needed to, pulling the wool over his eyes.
Oh, would you like me to write to your lawyer?
Mmm, do you want to? Ha, ha, ha.

My belief, based on the footage of the session, is that Pell is wrong to think that he succeeded in duping the psychiatrist. The psychiatrist indicated in his remarks that he understood why Pell had chosen to see him at that time.

Nonetheless, Pell clearly intended to dupe the psychiatrist and thinks that he did so. 'I mean, I thought I was brilliant. And that's exactly how I'll be in court, you see, which is bad. Imagine if he was the court, and I was being so open with the court. Exactly what I needed to achieve, completely pulled the wool over his eyes.'

Jones filmed Pell at home speaking on the telephone his solicitor, Paul Graham saying: 'And by the way, I've spoken to my doctor, Dr Arsen, and he's willing to do anything you want.'

Pell was back in court in December 1999 for sentencing for his theft of documents from Harkavys. The Channel 4 documentary re-played the judge's words[xii]: 'Mr. Pell, you are well aware now that what people throw away still belongs to someone, and that when they put discarded paper among their rubbish that still belongs to them.'

But Pell is annoyed by this passage in the documentary, saying[xiii]: 'I don't like that bit, but anyway.'

The documentary said that the judge added[xiv]: 'I don't think I need say anything further.'

To which, Pell, watching this at home, says[xv]: 'Exactly, just continue doing what you're doing for the next two years, and we'll be okay.'

Then the sentence was awarded, the documentary reported[xvi]. 'You will be fined £20 to be paid at £10 per week. First payment 8th January next year.'

Lewis-Smith's voice-over observed sardonically: 'The tender-hearted payment plan was tailored to Benjamin's claim in court that he lived off a £10-a-week handout from his father; no mention was made of his annual estimated income of £100,000 a year.'

Pell says that the judge was misled into thinking that he earned only £10 per week from his father[xvii]. Pell says that his barrister had told the judge this, but it was a misunderstanding, "So I never said it; I was never in the witness box. So was never...I never had a chance. So, it's not my lie, or it's not my misunderstanding." However, this was to catch up with him when he sought help from the police after he was defrauded by Mappin.

Pell also had to pay £200 prosecution costs over the Harkavys theft[xviii].

During his High Court case against Mappin, Pell was cross-examined by Adam Wolanski about the session with the psychiatrist[vi]. Wolanski attempted to nail Pell for tricking the psychiatrist, using the transcript of the footage that Jones had shot. Pell is as evasive and duplicitous as ever. Wolanski, referring to Pell's Biblical parallels, put to him that he played the fool in order to get an advantage over other people?

Pell replied: 'No, I don't. That's a piece of Biblical interpretation and I read it out to the camera because I think it's, once again, something we could develop, but it doesn't mean that I actually intend being mad for the rest of my life, and that I'm like King David. I mean this is too absurd even to consider.' The delight he expressed to Jones about pulling the wool over the psychiatrist's eyes was merely another example of his 'developing story-lines' for Hollywood writers[vii].

Nonetheless, Pell makes similar admissions to McVicar[viii]. He spoke about the report that Arsen wrote for the court. 'I would like you to see it,' he said. 'You've got to see what Arsen wrote, "Benjamin's got delusions of grandeur. He thinks he's going to be famous one day… He thinks that his bloody function in life [is] to expose these lawyers' negligence. I can't comment on that. All I know is that he's beyond therapy… and if he's incarcerated, I've got good reason to believe he'll go mad."'

McVicar asked Pell why Arsen said he was beyond therapy and Pell replied:

Cos he wanted to make sure the court realised that if they decided, for example, to put me in prison and punish me that they're punishing here an ill man. And they can't be seen to do that: I'm ill. In other words, there's nothing they can- there is no treatment for me. Isn't that funny?

I just said that to Arsen to paint this picture. Arsen said to me, 'Are you obsessional?'

I said, 'Obsessional? I'm obsessional. I look at the letterbox twice after I've posted a letter, all bollocks, of course; I clean the phone every time I've used it, all bollocks, I never- I'm obsessional about, yes, facts and keeping stuff, but never about that, would never have done that, letter- letterbox maybe, but… Basically, Arsen wrote everything I wanted him to write. It's five pages of absolute bollocks.

Pell makes a similar point to an interviewer from an Israeli newspaper, after first telling him how he lied to another psychiatrist whom he saw many years previous after his father became concerned about Pell's obsessive collecting of newspapers[xi].

The psychologist was making me… ha, I was lying to him of course, he was saying to me, 'Look, Benjamin, you've got to try and, every day, start throwing things away, and- 'Ooh, very good progress, Benjamin.'

Cos I was thinking, yes- 'Five- ooh, very good, oh ten bags this week! Benjamin, you're making excellent progress.'

And, of course, I was lying to him.

[When the interviewer asks about the diagnosis of his being an 'obsessive compulsive'] That's not true at all: cracks in the pavements, absolute nonsense. I sat down in the Maudsley clinic; the professor said to me, 'What would you like me to write?'

I said, 'Really, is it as simple as that?'

He said, 'Yeah.'

References

[i] "3½-hour rushes," Moving Perspective (filmed 1999).

[ii] 'Scandal in the Bins,' Channel 4 (first shown 11.01.01).

[iii] McVicar video tape (filmed 24.01.01) DVOR.

[iv] McVicar video tape (filmed 08.02.01) DVOO.

[v] "3½-hour rushes," Moving Perspective (filmed 1999).

[vi] Transcript of evidence of Benjamin Pell, Benjamin Pell -v- John Mappin and Story Master Ltd, (11.03.02).

[vii] Transcript of evidence of Benjamin Pell, Benjamin Pell -v- John Mappin and Story Master Ltd, (12.03.02).

[viii] McVicar video tape (filmed January 2001) DVRV.

[ix] Kevin Maguire, 'Muckraker who feeds off bins of the famous,' *The Guardian* (27.07.00).

[x] McVicar video tape (filmed January 2001) DVRV.

[xi] McVicar video tape (filmed 24.01.01) DVOR.

[xii] 'Scandal in the Bins,' Channel 4 (first shown 11.01.01).

[xiii] McVicar audio tape (recorded 12.11.00) MDRG.

[xiv] 'Scandal in the Bins,' Channel 4 (first shown 11.01.01).

[xv] McVicar audio tape (recorded 12.11.00) MDRG.

[xvi] 'Scandal in the Bins,' Channel 4 (first shown 11.01.01).

[xvii] McVicar video tape (filmed 17.01.01) DVRB.

[xviii] Certificate of conviction, Benjamin Gerald Pell, The Crown Court at Blackfriars (22.11.99).

[xix] "3½-hour rushes," Moving Perspective (filmed 1999).

[xx] 'Benji the binman fined,' *The Barnet & Whetstone Press* (09.11.00).

[xxi] Certificate of conviction, Benjamin Gerald Pell, The Crown Court at Blackfriars (07.11.00).

Chapter 12

10 Downing Street and other heavyweight victims

David Leigh of *The Guardian*, encouraged to Pell set his sights on more political targets other than Hamilton and Aitken. In mid-1998, Pell told Jones[i]:

> Within two weeks of meeting David Leigh, he [Hollingsworth] gave me a list of all the top lobbyists in the country. And he actually numbered them for me, the top one being [Lord] Tim Bell, who I did for about nine months, 'til I got bored with it; Burson-Marsteller... They're people, basically, who are paid by businessmen to put pressure on government to try and find out what policy is going to be, and, even better than that, not only to find out what the policy is going to be, but to change policy as well. They're obviously worth targeting because they are aware months and months in advance of what's going to be happening.
>
> This is why David Leigh and Mark Hollingsworth gave me pages and pages of people to target. Look, how naïve Hollingsworth was, he even asked me to target Lady Thatcher, and he can't deny, this is on his typeface because this is his typewriter; Labour Party HQ; Conservative- this was the list- this was the hit list which I was given within two weeks of meeting Mark Hollingsworth in July of last year. Here, Mishcon's are one of my solicitors he asked me to target. These are all the lawyers he asked me to target. Look, this is how I first targeted Simon Muirhead, Schilling & Lom, Richards Butler, Oswald Hickson, these are the original names which I was asked to target. 'I hope this is useful and helpful. Please call me if you would like to discuss any of the above.' Yes, Mr Hollingsworth, I'd like to discuss this when I've passed this on to the police...
>
> It was Mark Hollingsworth who said to me, 'Benjamin, there are two target areas you're missing out on. It's very good you're doing All Saints; you're doing all of that music stuff. You should be doing other firms of lawyers; it's good that you're doing Denton Hall. Why don't you do firms like Simon Muirhead, Schilling & Lom? Also, you

should be doing the lobbying companies, and you should be doing firms like Freud [the PR company].'

Of course, just because Pell targeted an organisation, it does not necessarily mean that he succeeded in obtaining confidential documents from its rubbish. But, Pell claims, he did have success at 10 Downing Street. Three newspaper articles published on the same day in July 2000 about a spate of leaked documents from Number 10 increased the heat on Pell. *Sunday Business* reported the fear among Labour party insiders that someone was targeting Tony Blair and his closest advisors by raiding rubbish[ii]. It reported that Special Branch officers had been drafted in to investigate the leak of memos to and from Blair. The suspicion inside the party was that the homes of one or more of the recipients of the memos had been targeted.

The *Mail on Sunday* named the 'shambling, unkempt, grubby-looking' Pell as the 'prime suspect' who was the 'focus of a huge security inquiry rocking the Government'[iii]. And the *Sunday Mirror* reported that two intelligence agencies, the Security Service (MI5) and GCHQ, were helping with the investigation[iv].

The leaks began when *The Sunday Times* splashed a confidential memo written by Philip Gould, Blair's pollster, saying that Labour faces losing support among voters to the Conservatives because the Prime Minister was believed to be failing to deliver key election promises[v]. The memo was sent to Blair and his then press secretary, Alastair Campbell.

Two weeks later, the same newspaper published a four-page memo by Gould to Campbell warning in advance that the prime minister's speech to the Women's Institute in June 2000 would fail: he was indeed slow handclapped[vi]. Gould wrote a toned-down version of the memo for Blair. He predicted that the speech would backfire because it was 'condescending', with Blair 'once again pandering' to his audience and opined that 'voters regarded Blair as out of touch'.

Towards the end of the same month, *The Sunday Times* published details of the tax return of Lord Levy, Blair's chief fund raiser and a former chairman of the charity, Jewish Care[vii]. Levy sought an injunction against the newspaper – unsuccessfully – because, he said, it had obtained his tax details 'unlawfully'.

Its sister newspapers, *The Times* and *The Sun*, the following month published a memo written by Blair and sent to a small number of close advisors and ministers, admitting that he and the Government were regarded as 'out of touch with gut British instincts' over asylum, crime and defence[viii]. Two days later, another Gould memo to Blair, warning that the 'New Labour brand' had been 'badly contaminated' and was 'the object of constant criticism, and even worse, ridicule', appeared in *The Times* and *The Sun*[ix]. And a further Blair memo, together with details from a 'bizarre dossier' compiled by Gould, was published a week later in *The Sun*[x], which claimed that it showed that Blair had decided to 'ditch the pound' and 'force Britain into the euro.'

Following reports in three Sunday newspapers about the source of the leaks, *The Sun*, a recipient of many of the leaks, said that it had emerged that a 'snooper' had 'raided dustbins belonging to Cabinet big guns Gordon Brown and David Blunkett[xi]. *The Guardian* said that Pell had retrieved the Number 10 documents from rubbish and had sold them to newspapers through Max Clifford[xii]. It reported that Special Branch detectives discovered that a Gould memo referring to the 'New Labour brand' being 'badly contaminated' and published in *The Times* and *The Sun* a week earlier was a first draft ripped up into small pieces and left by him in a black plastic bin bag outside his home in north London. It also said that a source outside News International had earlier that year asked to target the home addresses of Gould and Levy, although *The Guardian* did not name that person. Pell, as set out later in this chapter, named Hollingsworth as the person who asked him to target Levy and Gould. What the paper didn't know is that a speciality of Pell's is to painstakingly piece together ripped or even shredded memos.

Clifford, however, told interviewers that he had nothing to do with the political leaks[xiii]. On the BBC's *Today* programme, its presenter, John Humphries, asked him whether *The Guardian* had 'got him bang to rights'.

Clifford laughed it off, replying: 'No, no, not at all. It's a great story, but, unfortunately, it's got nothing to do with reality.'

Denis MacShane, then a backbench MP who went on to become foreign minister with responsibility for Europe, and a former BBC reporter and president of the National Union of Journalists, said: 'It's not a laughing matter this, this is about a newspaper organisation paying out large sums of money to Mr Pell.'

Humphriess: 'Do you think they're doing that, Mr Clifford?'

Clifford: 'Well, more than likely, I mean, that's the way the game works these days.'

Humphries then asked Trevor Kavanagh, political editor of *The Sun*, and the reporter who wrote that newspaper's articles based on the Number 10 leaks, whether he was 'guilty as charged'.

Kavanagh replied: 'The suggestion by Denis MacShane that we are repeatedly handing over large cheques to Mr Pell, in this case, is absolutely wrong; not a penny has changed hands.'

Humphries: 'So, I have to ask you where you got the documents.'

Kavanagh: 'Of course you do.'

Humphries: 'And you won't tell me.'

Kavanagh: I won't.'

Pell that night also publicly denied being behind the stories, telling the Press Association[xiv]: 'I must… make it clear that I was not involved in any way whatsoever with any of the political leaks of the last few weeks. That includes Lord Levy's tax affairs and the memos from Messrs Gould and Blair.' However, *The Guardian* stood by its story, saying it was based on more than one source with 'intimate knowledge of the memos and their handling', adding: 'We do not expect him [Pell] to confess any association in something that has triggered an inquiry involving Special Branch.'

Pell's public position was undermined by what he was saying privately: he was boasting that he had obtained the Number 10 documents and Levy's tax details. For example, he tells one Israeli interviewer, while being filmed by McVicar, that raiding rubbish is a 'dirty business', but that the results are good[xv]. 'You ask Tony Blair whether he thinks it's a good idea or not.' Asked what his biggest story was, Pell answered: 'Depends. If you're a politician, I suppose it's Lord Levy.' And asked what story was the biggest 'politically', Pell says: 'The Gould memo and the Levy one… that's the one about Lord Levy… that was his bank account details which ended up in *The Sunday Times*… Those are the biggest politically.'

However, Pell sows confusion because, while at some points he tells McVicar that he was responsible for these political stories, at others he denies any role.

On another occasion, he says[xix]: 'And who gave me this list of people to target? Mark Hollingsworth… A list of people to target: Michael Levy, Philip Gould, the political lobbyists. That was given to me by Mark Hollingsworth.

Another of Pell's targets was Cherie Booth, 49, the prime minister's wife. Filmed at night, Pell tells Jones: 'We're now off to the chambers of the wife of the prime minister, Cherie Blair.' Her chambers was then in Gray's Inn Square.

After returning home, he shows one document he found. 'This comes from her chambers: her home address, her mobile number, her nanny's mobile number, Tony Blair's number.'

'I found a letter regarding the wife of the prime minister and a dispute over legal bills. Then, it ends up on the front page of *The Sunday Times*, the biggest selling broadsheet in Europe. "Cherie Booth tries to stop her legal fees being cut."'

The article was published in July 1999[xxi]. 'A story which I assume made some pillow talk in the Blair household that evening,' says Pell. 'So, it's just a sort of sense of power you get when the most powerful man in this country has to talk about one of my stories, that is quite exciting.'

Pell's public denial of being behind the political leaks was also contradicted by Andrew Pierce, an assistant editor on *The Times* who had written much of his newspaper's material based on Downing Street documents, on a German TV channel after one of the stories in *The Sunday Times* was nominated for 'scoop of the year' organised by *Press Gazette*. He told ARD's *Weltspiegel* (World Mirror) current affairs programme[xxii]: '*The Sunday Times*, our sister paper, is up for scoop of the year because Pell provided them with leaked documents from a man called Philip Gould.' Pierce later retracted this comment, saying: 'What I should have said was that Benjamin Pell suggests that he was behind it, but I have absolutely no idea where *The Sunday Times* got its scoop from.'

The Downing Street investigation was said to have concluded that a series of private memos had been recovered from refuse sacks. After all this exposure, Pell admitted to one interviewer that some political journalists became wary of dealing with him[xxiii].

The *Sunday Times* distanced itself from Pell and said that he had not helped provide any of the documents or information for its stories about Blair, Gould and Levy. Executives and reporters on the newspaper also privately insist that Pell had no role. They say that they were furious that he had boasted of being responsible, attempting to take the credit, although one source accepted that some 'garbology' might have been involved.

There is some support for the denials by the *Sunday Times* of Pell's involvement in the Levy story. The information commissioner, who regulates the Data Protection Act, investigated a complaint by Levy that his personal data had been obtained illegally. He found that a 'freelance researcher', named by *The Guardian* as Gavin Singfield, obtained Levy's tax details[xxiv]. Describing himself variously as a 'corporate analyst' and a 'business consultant', Singfield is sole director and shareholder of a small company called Corporate Risk Consultants, which offers 'risk assessment' services to clients. He denied any involvement in obtaining Levy's personal tax details.

The *Sunday Times* said that it neither made any telephone calls impersonating Levy nor asked anybody to do so. Richard Thomas warned in 2003, soon after he took over from Elizabeth France as information commissioner, that he would prosecute anyone such as private detectives 'blagging' confidential details from banks and telecoms companies, using impersonation to con institutions into giving out personal data[xxv]. While not commenting on Levy's case, he said: 'That is absolutely clearly a criminal offence: obtaining information without consent. I find it wholly unacceptable that confidential information is coming out through deception. There are a number of prosecutions ongoing and I anticipate in bringing a whole lot more in the future.'

Well-informed political sources later formed an intriguing theory that enemies of Blair in the Labour party were behind the political leaks and used Pell to mask their role.

Pell found several other political stories in the rubbish. He sold to the *Mail on Sunday* documents showing that Janet Anderson, the then culture minister, had accepted 12 tickets to one of London's most exclusive nightclubs, Browns, for her daughter's 18th birthday party, courtesy of Sony Entertainment and the British Phonographic Industry, the record business trade association[xxvi]. Pell tells Jones[xxvii]: 'A perfect example again of how they've ripped me off. *Mail on Sunday*: Janet Anderson, that was a front-page story on 6th June 1999... and they gave me £2,000.... for a front-page story. That is absolutely outrageous... 'Anderson faces quiz' £300 – that will be page-three lead.'

Another target were the Hinduja brothers, the Indian billionaire businessmen given British passports after underwriting the religious section of the Millennium Dome in Greenwich, donating £1m. Peter Mandelson resigned from Cabinet for a second time following reports of his role in the affair. Pell told McVicar about how the Hinduja hired Charles Stuart-Smith, of the public-relations company, Luther Pendragon[xxviii]: 'He's just taken over the, erm, pitch... Hindujas, they're currently in the news. I mean, the biggest news story at the moment is the Hindujas story. And what does Benjamin the binman do? He infiltrates the Hindujas story [by targeting Stuart-Smith].'

Pell says that his political targets have included Frank Dobson, the former health secretary and Labour candidate for mayor of London; Patricia Hewitt, trade and industry secretary; Nelson Mandela, former president of South Africa; the Millennium Dome; and Augusto Pinochet, the former Chilean dictator, all of whom were targeted through one or other of their advisors.

He says that his business targets have included Richard Branson; Camelot, the organiser of the UK's lottery; and tycoon Alan Sugar; that his sport targets have included the Football Association; the Football League; the Grand National; and Royal Ascot; and that his other targets have included the Arts Council and Sadlers Wells.

In discussing his 'lottery story' with McVicar, Pell betrays his attitude towards litigation[xxix:] 'Basically, most litigation finishes on disclosure, cos that's when you start having to tell the truth – to the other side. 'Til then, you can fuck around.'

Pell tells Jones how he doctored a document about Alan Sugar, saying[xxx]: 'It is a bit unethical. I don't actually like doing that, but whatever, who gives a fuck?'

Filmed outside the offices of football's Premier League in London's Connaught Place, Pell says: 'Peter Leaver, ex-chief executive of the football Premier League, the man whose life was ruined by me. He ended up "on the subs bench" because of Benjamin Pell.

'Certainly, I'll be back here about 11 o'clock at night... Up to the end of July, for about a period of nine months, I was systematically going through their rubbish on a daily basis. They lost contracts as a result; they lost the confidence of the clubs as a result; they were losing the confidence of the Press as a result. This man, literally, his life was ruined because of me.'

Pell claims that he cost the Premier League a £2m sponsorship contract. 'Here was their agreement: guaranteed they were going to have the royalties rate, £1 million-worth of timing technology... £2 million of media budget, all because of my story in the *Daily Mirror*... they cancelled the deal. They were going to have all the television negotiations reach the Press. They had every single argument they had within... the organisation reach the Press. They're looking to set up a TV channel called Premier League TV: that reached the Press. Every time they have an argument with a football club, that reached the Press.'

Leaver told *Lawyer*[xxxi]: 'At every single meeting we had, everyone went to speak to journalists afterwards... I often found out what people were nattering about from *The Sunday Telegraph*. You can see, can't you, that there was no such thing as confidentiality. We actually lost a contract as a result of these activities.'

Pell told Jones[xxxii]: 'Not only did Peter Leaver... lose his job, Stephen Pearson lost his job [as commercial director]. In fact, of all the people I used to do in that office, there're only about three or four members of staff left. It was like the end of the Nazi regime when Peter Leaver left. They assumed that everything he done had been completely bogus, and that every contract he was about to sign, because it had ended up in *The Sunday Telegraph*... They thought that he was in league with *The Sunday Telegraph* or something. This poor man just didn't know where to turn. And... the final weekend, Stephen Pearson comes into the office on the Saturday morning, somebody barges in and says, "What the hell are you doing with that shredding machine?" And he gets the sack for shredding.'

'Together, *The Sunday Telegraph* and I brought down Peter Leaver. We had at least, I'd say, probably 25 stories which were absolute gold dust. The trouble is because I had all these legal problems with *The Sun*, I genuinely couldn't ask them for any money because... the football Premier League were injuncting them and everything... Now my problems are over... I'm going to invoice them for about ten grand – at least.'

Pell continued:

And I also do of course- I do Townleys, who are the leading sports lawyers in this country. After my article appeared in the *Sunday Telegraph* in October of last year, regarding Royal Ascot taking sponsorships after 250 years, they [Townleys] went completely mad, and this is one of the funniest letters of an apology that you will ever see in your life... I just hope my counsel reads this out to the jury when my case comes to trial in the year 2006. We've got to hear it in full.

'Mr Douglas Erskine Crumb [chief executive of Ascot Racecourse]', what a name – crazy name, crazy guy. 'Dear Douglas, Re: *Sunday Telegraph*. As you will appreciate, I am extremely disturbed,' yes, you are, mate, you're fucking well disturbed, 'that the *Sunday Telegraph* came into possession of certain documentation, albeit that it appears to have been the least relevant,' that's a load of bollocks, it was the front page of the paper, 'which is likely to have come from my office. I have reported matters to the local CID, who have spoken to the *Sunday Telegraph* and will conduct a thorough investigation... I do not believe there is anyone in my office who has the slightest interest in publicising this matter. The documents must therefore have been stolen either from inside the office or possibly through someone taking a bag of rubbish and those papers being in the bag.' And this bit...this is so funny... 'For your own comfort, on Friday I immediately sacked our cleaners.'

Okay, let's analyse that: *Sunday Telegraph* appears, four days later they sack the cleaners who, as it turns out, I made some enquiries afterwards, have been with the firm for eight years. Never had any trouble with them; never had any thefts, not even Tipp-Ex been stolen, pens being stolen. A story appears in the Sunday newspapers, immediately jump to the conclusion, 'sack the cleaners'.

Another of Pell's heavy-weight targets was the Palestine Liberation Organisation (PLO), headed then by the late Yasser Arafat.

He told the Channel 4 documentary[xxxiii]: 'I was targeting the PLO's rubbish for about a year. We never found out about any Hamas bombs or anything; it was just interesting stuff. You know, just seeing the sort of MP's they were trying to, err, bribe, etc. They had all these horrible Aitken sort of characters in the Conservative Party always being offered speaking opportunities and stuff.'

While watching a preview of the documentary at home, Pell told McVicar[xxxiv]: "Oh my, now that has to go, I mean, especially in the current political climate. Do you want me to be murdered? I've already had my car fire-bombed four times. I've had Hamas phoning up my – I swear to you, Colindale police offered me a safe house last month... You cannot have that bit in. I've had Hamas phoning me up, threatening to kill me... I don't want to be killed by PLO; I don't mind being killed by Jeffrey Archer, but not by Yasser Arafat.'

Pell also tells McVicar[xxxv]: 'In those days, John, I wasn't giving stuff to the papers. This was just for my own benefit, for the synagogue and stuff.'

Pell says that David Leppard and Chris Hastings of the *Sunday Times* even asked him to trawl the rubbish of the Secret Intelligence Service – better known as MI6 – although he says that he refused, thinking it an idea too crazy even for him[xxxvi].

And he makes clear to Jones just how important he thinks he is[xxxvii]. 'I'm already a sort of editor in Fleet Street. I'm the editor of all the papers in Fleet Street, if only they realised it. I'm not saying that in an arrogant way, it's just the case, you know. The fact that they don't pay me what I'm worth, the fact that they mess around... is beside the point.'

Asked which newspaper he would like to edit, Pell says: 'Well, it certainly wouldn't be one of those horrible tabloids I deal with.... I'm mainly interested in politics and music and the media, and I certainly wouldn't want to end up working on *Sunday People* and having to do kiss-and-tells... So, no, I would want to end up on a mid-market tabloid, but not the *Mail on Sunday* cos they're complete bastards. So, I probably- I think there's no paper I could actually edit, I'd have to buy my own newspaper. I'd have to, basically, get my own newspaper to sort it out. Well, maybe some enterprising proprietor will actually think about that. Cos there is certainly- a new paper has to come out which <u>will</u> run the Chris Evans story which I couldn't get in, which <u>will</u> run the stories which are re- quite embarrassing. So, when Elton John is coming to a settlement, and no paper- ... There must be a newspaper, one day, please, which isn't worried about embarrassing Branson, which doesn't put an apology after doing an anti-Evans piece. Maybe one day, I will edit that paper.'

But he also says that he is working on a bin-raiding career away from newspapers. 'I've now started targeting banks and management companies. I'm still doing, obviously, everyone else as well. So with a bigger van, you see, I've got extra capacity.

Asked why he is targeting banks, Pell says: 'Obviously, I've perfected the lawyers, I think I've got that down to a 'T'... But I thought, no, banks, the perfect target cos with a bank you will get secrets about the most famous...I'm not doing the boring life [?] banks and stuff in… the High Street, I am doing the banks in the City, in the West End, the private banks, the banks to the rich and the famous, the Middle Eastern clients, the American clients.

'This is a list of all of the clients of a bank called the Saudi British Bank. "Emad al-Shamari: customer is purchasing a property in Park Street for £5.9 million with a Saudi prince as a partner.... Now, what I think I'm going to do as well is get into the industrial espionage thing. Cos you imagine… how the competitors of MSI would pay me for that sort of information?

'The biggest cellular company, MSI, I think in Europe, if not the world, is absolutely invaluable. Any competing company of MSI would pay private investigators an absolute fortune to find out a scintilla of information about them. Here, I have all of their company forecasts 'til the year 2004.

'I am now, in theory, one of the most valuable people in the world, if only the world would know about it.' And Pell was determined for the world to know about it: he turned from Hendon to Hollywood...

References

[i] "3½-hour rushes," Moving Perspective (filmed 1999).

[ii] Mark Watts, 'Bin raiders that plague MPs,' *Sunday Business* (23.07.00).

[iii] Jason Lewis, 'AS NO 10 AIDE ADMITS HE LEFT LEAKED MEMO IN HIS DUSTBIN, IS THIS THE MAN WHO STOLE THEM?' *Mail on Sunday* (23.07.00).

[iv] Mike Edwards, 'BLAIR CALLS IN SPY CHIEFS TO STOP LEAKS,' *Sunday Mirror* (23.07.00).

[v] David Leppard, Paul Nuki and Gareth Walsh, 'Secret memo shows Labour fear of Hague,' and, 'Blair puts his trust in original spin,' *The Sunday Times* (28.05.00).

[vi] David Leppard, Paul Nuki and Gareth Walsh, 'Secret memo says Blair is out of touch;' Michael Prescott, David Leppard and Paul Nuki, 'The day the magic died,' *The Sunday Times* (11.06.00).

[vii] Paul Nuki, Gareth Walsh, David Leppard and Humfrey Hunter, 'Blair tycoon paid just £5,000 tax,' *The Sunday Times* (25.06.00).

[viii] Andrew Pierce and Philip Webster, 'Blair: Labour looks weak and soft,' *The Times*, Trevor Kavanagh, 'BLAIR: HAVE I LOST PLOT?' and 'Blair's panic memo,' *The Sun* (17.07.00).

[ix] Andrew Pierce and Philip Webster, 'Labour is adrift, Blair warned in new leaked memo,' *The Times*, Trevor Kavanagh, 'Tony, it's serious,' *The Sun* (19.07.00).

[x] Trevor Kavanagh, 'LEAK No. 3,' *The Sun* (27.07.00).

[xi] 'Ministers' bins rifled by snooper,' *The Sun* (24.07.00).

[xii] Kevin Maguire, 'Clifford role in Labour memo leaks,' *The Guardian* (26.07.00).

[xiii] *Today* BBC Radio 4 (26.07.00); John Deane, 'CLIFFORD DENIES DOWNING STREET LEAK CLAIMS,' *Press Association* (26.07.00); Euan Ferguson, 'Euan Ferguson meets Max Clifford,' *The Observer* (30.07.00).

[xiv] Martin Hickman, 'I'M NOT BEHIND MEMO LEAKS, SAYS BENJI THE BINMAN,' *Press Association* (26.07.00).

[xv] McVicar video tape (filmed 24.01.01) DVOR.

[xvi] McVicar audio tape (recorded 30.12.00) MDRI.

[xvii] McVicar video tape (filmed 24.01.01) DVOR.

[xviii] McVicar audio tape (recorded 2000) MDOO.

[xix] McVicar audio tape (recorded 28.11.00) MDRB.

[xx] "3½-hour rushes," Moving Perspective (filmed 1999).

[xxi] Chris Hastings, 'Cherie Booth fights to stop her legal fees being cut,' *The Sunday Times* (11.07.99).

[xxii] Kevin Maguire, 'He roots in rubbish bins. And he's the real contender for scoop of the year: Benji the Binman named as source of story in the running for top press award,' *The Guardian* (21.03.01).

[xxiii] Tom Leonard, 'Benji the Binman cleans up. Tom Leonard learns what happened to the "human dung beetle" with a nose for a good story,' *The Daily Telegraph* (22.03.02).

[xxiv] Kevin Maguire and Stuart Millar, 'Man named in tax hoaxer inquiry: freelance researcher denies involvement as privacy watchdog seeks impersonator of Lord Levy,' *The Guardian* (15.06.02).

[xxv] Robert Verkaik, 'Identity thieves may face prison, warns privacy watchdog,' *The Independent* (08.01.03).

[xxvi] Martin Smith, 'MINISTER TOOK TOP NIGHTCLUB FAVOUR,' *Mail on Sunday* (06.06.99).

[xxvii] "3½-hour rushes," Moving Perspective (filmed 1999).

[xxviii] McVicar video tape (filmed 08.02.01) DVOO.

[xxix] McVicar video tape (filmed 20.12.00) DVRR.

[xxx] "3½-hour rushes," Moving Perspective (filmed 1999).

[xxxi] John-Paul Flintoff, 'On the bench,' *Lawyer* (22.03.99).

[xxxii] "3½-hour rushes," Moving Perspective (filmed 1999).

[xxxiii] 'Scandal in the Bins,' Channel 4 (first shown 11.01.01).

[xxxiv] McVicar audio tape (recorded 12.11.00) MDRG.

[xxxv] McVicar audio tape (recorded 04.10.98) MDRO.

[xxxvi] McVicar video tape (filmed 21.01.01) DVRI.

[xxxvii] "3½-hour rushes," Moving Perspective (filmed 1999).

Chapter 13

Reach for the Stars:
bidding for fame and fortune

When Pell renewed his contact with Aitken's friend, John Mappin, in June 1999, he heard just what he wanted to hear. Pell telephoned Mappin who agreed to try to persuade Aitken's solicitor, Michael Coleman of Harkavys, to have the case against him of stealing documents dropped. Mappin visited Pell at his home in Hendon and said that, unfortunately, Coleman was determined to press on with the case. However, scientologist Mappin had some good news: he could make Pell famous. He would have a film made about Benji the Binman. Mappin, as set out in the judgement of the case that Pell would later bring against Mappin[i], said that he had a friend in Hollywood who would make it happen. This friend, said Mappin, was so influential in Hollywood that he helped John Travolta secure his comeback starring role in *Pulp Fiction*.

Pell and Mappin met again a few days later to discuss the plan. According to Pell's statement for his case against Mappin, as cited in the judgement, his new friend told him that he had worked in Hollywood for several years: 'Your story would make a great movie. Whoever plays you, Benji, whoever plays you...just like Jim Carrey in *The Cable Guy*. This is a 10-million blockbuster movie for the guy who plays you. He will make his fortune like Jim Carrey as a result of playing you. This is a bigger franchise than Seinfeld. This is going to turn into one of the biggest, if not the biggest movie of all time, but the story has to be told right. And there is only one person in this world who can actually tell the story, and this is my best friend.'

Mappin did concede, the judgement noted, that 'he is a salesman and given to use hyperbole'. However, Mappin claimed that he made clear to Pell that there could be no guarantee that any film would be made. Mappin also told Pell that he must pay for the friend in

Hollywood to drop the many different projects on which he was working so that he could explore making a film about Pell. That friend was Iain Jones.

All of this was music to Pell's ears, which not even the penalty clause in the deal could render discordant. Hollywood hotshot Iian Jones would have to be paid to to drop all his other projects to take on Pell's. Pell was so impressed with Mappin and his idea that he agreed to pay him £13,750 from his savings to help the project off the ground. Mappin initially insisted the money be paid in cash, but eventually accepted a cheque.

However, as the judgement recorded: 'Mr Pell said several times during his evidence that he would not have paid anything if he had realised that Mr Mappin's friend was a hairdresser.' It transpired that Jones, contrary to the impression that Mappin gave to Pell, had been to film school but, at the time, was working as a hairdresser, sometimes on film sets, waiting for his big break. He was linked to Travolta and Quentin Tarantino, director of Pulp Fiction – he was their hairdresser.

Jones then flew to London and filmed Pell for a week in July 1999, including footage of Benji the Binman at work. Pell said that he understood the filming was in preparation for a movie about his life story and not for a documentary. Pell signed a contract which assigned all the rights in his life story 'in this or any other universe' to Jones's production company, Moving Perspective.

Mappin then told Pell that he would have to pay £30,000 for Jones to work on the project for another three weeks. Pell protested, but Mappin pressed him for at least another £15,000 so that Jones could film for a further week. According to Pell, Mappin said:

> This is going to be such a big thing for you, Benjamin... This is a small investment. You are earning £10,000 a week. What is £30,000 to someone like you? It's less than a month's money; this is your future we're talking about... This is a small investment when you consider that when the movie comes out you are going to be a worldwide star. The premier will be attended by all the celebrities who you have had stories about. You are going to be world famous; there are going to be Benjamin Pell mugs; there are going to be Benjamin Pell T-shirts.

Mappin later admitted that the figure of £30,000 was 'plucked out of the air'. Pell was persuaded to pay a further £13,750, and Jones continued filming him until mid-July. Mappin continued to press Pell for more money. Over three months, Pell paid a total of £77,500 from his cash reserves. Mappin kept telling Pell that the money was necessary to pay Jones, who returned to London in September 1999 to carry out more filming.

However, there was no evidence in the case that Mappin paid the money to Jones, who denied expecting or receiving any payment. And the judgement recorded: 'As Mappin accepts, Mr Jones had not asked to be paid for coming to London to see Mr Pell.'

Mappin also insisted that Pell sign a new contract giving all the rights in his life story to Jones's production company in return for receiving $500 immediately and a commitment that he would receive 1% of the 'final-approved cost budget'. After signing it, Pell was advised that the contract was unfair. He repeatedly confronted Mappin about it in taped telephone conversations during 2000. In September 2000, Mappin claimed that he did not know who Pell was. Pell made a complaint of fraud to the police, who arrested Mappin and Jones in November 2000.

Pell tells McVicar the following January about how he had seen a detective sergeant about his complaint that day[ii]: 'I shaved this morning cos I had to see DS Ashworth regarding Mappin.' Pell was impressed with the police officer, and hoped that he would be charging Mappin shortly. He continued:

He notices what could be a problem, like the programme which went out last week. 'Scandal in the Bins' has got two huge problems for me when it comes to me giving evidence. And, don't forget, I'll be the main witness for the Crown.

'First of all, on the programme, it said, 'though I didn't say it, that I earned £10 a week from my dad, well, I did at the time of Harkavys and the conviction. Now that conviction was, obviously, at the same time that... this Mappin situation... was happening. Now if I'm there telling a court that I'm earning £10 a week, and yet I'm claiming Mappin stole 80 grand off me, there's a slight problem here. Where did I get the money from? But, I explained, to Ashworth, I never said it. And it's true. Eamonn Sherry, after sentencing, in other words, he says to me, 'You're going to be fined.' And he turns round and says to me, 'How can you pay it off?'

And Sherry says to me, 'Well, how much money are you earning?' And then he turns round to him [the judge] and he says, 'He's earning £10 a week from his father.' So then the judge says, 'Well, he can pay it off, then, over four weeks,' or something. So I never said it; I was never in the witness box. So was never- I never had a chance. So, it's not my lie, or it's not my misunderstanding.

The second, bigger problem, he thinks, is me admitting in the programme that I managed to lie to the court. Well I didn't really actually lie to the court, I made out that I was mad. Anyway, I think these are just trivialities.

Trivialities or not, no charge was ever brought against Mappin or anyone else in connection with Pell's complaint. But Pell did sue Mappin and his company, Story Master Ltd, which was set up to receive Pell's payments. The judge, Justice Gray, began his judgement by saying[iii]:

In this case, I have the unwelcome task of deciding which of the protagonists is telling the truth about the circumstances under which the claimant came to invest what was for him a considerable sum in a project to make a film about his life.

In a comment reminiscent of what Justice Morland said about Harrods' boss Fayed in Hamilton's unsuccessful libel case against him, Justice Gray, noting that Pell was engaged in 'disreputable and dishonest conduct', said:

The question raised by this case does not, of course, relate to Mr Pell's scavenging but rather to the question of whether he was the victim of a deception practised by the defendants. All the same, the matters to which I have referred make it essential for me to approach his evidence with great caution and to look with care to see whether there is other evidence to support his claims.

One of the ironies of this case is that the challenge to the credibility of Mr Pell is made on behalf of a party who has himself admitted that he sought to deceive the court.

The judge decided that Mappin had conned Pell. He ordered the return of the £77,500. Meanwhile, Mappin had fallen out with Jones. Mappin asked Jones to supply him with a copy of the rushes of Pell for the case. Jones refused initially, only letting him have some rushes shortly before the trial. Jones made out of the rushes the documentary that was shown at a film festival in America[iv].

Pell's relationship with the Channel 4 documentary team was also fractious. Victor Lewis-Smith, its executive producer, wrote about it on the day before transmission, saying that within a few weeks of Channel 4 commissioning the documentary, Pell issued the first of many writs over the programme[v]. The first, he says, was sent 'via' Mappin. The programme was twice pulled from the schedules at the last minute. The first time was because Pell had been arrested over Harkavys, and the subject became *sub judice*. The second time it was pulled 'hours before transmission' because Pell's solicitor, Paul Graham, said that a court hearing on a 'minor charge'(a car insurance fraud) had been scheduled, and so the subject was again *sub judice*.

Pell confirmed during his case against Mappin that, following his arrest for theft, he did not want the Channel 4 documentary to be broadcast[vi]. 'I didn't want a documentary to be made about me because of my arrest and I just didn't want it. I didn't want publicity,' adding, 'Having been arrested on 26th February (1999), I wanted to keep an extremely low profile. I thought a documentary at that stage would be commercial suicide for me.'

During the Mappin trial, Pell repeatedly used the excuse that he was 'developing story-lines' for any dishonesty he revealed to Jones[vii]: 'He [Jones] wanted me to enact new situations. These were to develop to pass on to writers in Hollywood. It's not a documentary. Victor Lewis-Smith did a perfectly accurate documentary about me on Channel 4.'

In support of his contention of 'developing story-lines' in the Moving Perspective rushes during his libel action against the *Sunday Express*, he produced a witness statement from a friend saying that Pell never wanted another documentary to be made after the Channel 4 programme. However, Pell repeatedly makes clear to McVicar that wanted further documentaries made about him beyond the Channel 4 programme. While watching a preview of that documentary, Pell asks McVicar why a specific point about the All Saints solicitor had not been included, adding[viii], 'That should be mentioned. Anyway, we can do that for our documentary.'

He complains that McVicar included interviews from people such as his neighbour, 'Linda fucking Cohen'. He says: 'If only we would have co-operated with each other, we could have a 100 times better programme... But this is the CV to open the door to the Benjamin Pell documentary series... This is the CV, cos this is not a proper documentary about what Benjamin Pell does, what his ethos is.'

And later: 'But it's an hour. You can't do the story properly in an hour anyway... So, at the end of the day an hour doesn't do justice to even one of the elements of the story. You can't even tell the Elton John story in an hour.'

After finishing watching the documentary, Pell said: 'We need a hard-hitting eight-part documentary, which takes these fuckers to pieces... we've got to ruin these careers.' Pell told McVicar the following month[ix]: 'It's just a shame that we could never do the programme properly. And if Victor doesn't want to do a "Scandal" number two, we'll get it done somewhere else. I've told you, Richard [Murray] has already spoken to people at Granada who are interested in doing it, so I'm not worried. If Victor doesn't want to be on board, it's up to him. You know, maybe he's the wrong person to have it – to do it. If Victor gives the impression to Channel 4 that he only does frothy, lightweight documentaries, maybe we should be going along to some other documentary maker. Because we don't want this to be frothy or light weight; this is not...this is a hard-hitting expose of Fleet Street and of lawyers.'

And, the month after that, Pell tells McVicar[x]: 'Why can't Victor now go along to Channel 4/the BBC, and say to them, "I can now do you another binman programme, but this time we've got him on board from the beginning; we've got much more evidence; it's a story which is much more exciting than the one you showed last week anyway." Three hundred thousand things have happened in the last two years since we first started the programme, and we should now do a six-parter.'

Interviewed by a journalist from a Jewish newspaper, and filmed by McVicar, Pell says[xii]: 'We're currently working on, hopefully, on another documentary. So, you know, see what the reaction is to that.'

Pell also repeatedly tells McVicar that he should obtain the Moving Perspective rushes because they contain such material that would be useful for a documentary, which makes an absurdity of his claim that he was merely developing story-lines' in them. Pell says[xiii]: We need to get that footage back from Mappin as well... when you see that footage...'

Asked how much Mappin knew about the Fayed saga, Pell says[xiv]: 'Mappin knows everything in my life, literally as much as-more than you, up to the 6th March [2000]... he knows where my hiding-place is; he knows everything. If he wasn't so incompetent, I'd be worried about him, but I don't give a fuck. He's a total arsehole. He knows everything about my life up to and including 6th March, and nothing since... All he knows is up to [my] arrest [over] Fayed... And of course, Mappin has got all of this on film. Me showing him the documents – the Fayed documents... Is that a smoking gun, do you think? ... He's got me in the garage, saying, "Look, and this is the document, this is the cross-examination questions, these are the questions they're going to ask the other witnesses, this is the affidavit from Neil Hamilton..." yeah, he's got all that on film. Yeah, but he's so incompetent.'

In confirmation of the psychiatrist's diagnosis of 'delusions of grandeur', Pell continued:

See, Mappin always used to say to me, 'When you look back in 20 years' time, you will be grateful to me, Benjamin, that you were recording all of this.' Cos you think back to the Beatles. The Beatles now, when you look at them, in the studio doing the White album, or doing 'Let It Be', that is fascinating when you see Paul arguing with George Harrison.

I've always said, 'Of course, I don't mind being followed by a camera.' ...Everyone should have a cam- fucking camera following them. This is why I tape all of my phone calls. This is why I tape people when they're sitting in this room, you know, erm, from fucking newspapers. But that's the limit to what I can do. (Indeed, Pell admitted that he has even taken to recording his parents[xvii].)

There is little doubt that Jones's camera, which Pell had once welcomed, did document his *modus operandi* and did record much incriminating material about Pell, some of which I have set out.

On one of Pell's nocturnal bin raids, Jones asks him what time he will be working until that night. Pell says[xviii]: 'I'll be up 'til 7 o'clock; I'll be home at about, mmm, 2 o'clock; come out again at three; and then work to about, for about three hours, go through the stuff and then go to sleep at seven and get up at nine. Normally it starts with my mother screaming at me. She comes downstairs at seven o'clock in the morning, and the... kitchen stinks, and the whole house smells of my rubbish. I go to bed for two hours, then I get up... So she sees a crazy existence.

'Okay, seven o'clock, I'm willing, I'm just about to go upstairs, my mother comes down saying, "This is it – no more. That is the last time I'll let you work in the kitchen." She's said the same thing for the last seven years. Ten past seven, I normally fall asleep quite quickly. Nine o'clock, the phone rings, waking me up, normally some prat, saying to me why haven't I returned any of their calls or why haven't I paid them [his cleaners] for six months. 9.30 to about 11.30, phone, following up all the journalists who haven't had my story in the day's papers. 11.30, I've got faxing, faxing photocopies, faxing, photocopying, and that basically continues for the whole day.

'Well, I go through a few bags as well. Then about eight o'clock, get ready to load up the van, start going through a bit of stuff, try and get as much room in the van as possible, and then, 8.30, we're off.' Now begins a night of picking up rubbish bags and driving them home.

'Gutter journalism meant, I assume, literally going through people's gutters... It's all been done since the time of Adam and Eve, and the serpent told on them. He was the first Fleet Street journalist. I mean, they're all snakes aren't they?'

And he makes clear his contempt for the law. Jones films Pell on the telephone, saying: 'And I hate the law of *sub judice*; I hate the law of blackmail; I hate the laws of anything. Now, this is my box; I now record all of my 'phone calls. So, I now have on this, er, up to 18 hours of tapes of Fleet Street people pleading with me for stories, bargaining with me over money, asking me to send them stuff, making sure that the fax machine number they've given me is correct; all of these people, who I'm going to bring down if I go down, are all now on tape.' There is not room in this book to name every journalist who has bought material from Pell.

Jones asked Pell to list his newspaper clients. Pell says: '*The News of the World... The Sunday People...* the *Sunday Mirror*, the *Mail on Sunday*, who pay me a retainer, *The Sunday Times*, *The Sunday Telegraph*. The papers I don't deal with, but have had stories in in the past are *The Observer*, which is owned by the same owners as *The Guardian*, so because of David Leigh I managed to get stories in there. *The Independent on Sunday* because of my connection with one or two journalists there, like Steve Boggan [at the time], who had one of the first ever stories about me, I've had one or two stories in there. And then the only paper I've never actually dealt with is the *Sunday Express*, who, literally, have got no money... And now my favourite topic: money, money, money.

'Problem is, I can't be seen... I can't have it both ways... If I go around in a Rolls Royce or a Porsche, it's going to look a bit odd if I'm starting to put bags in it. At least, at the moment, if I'm putting bags in my car, you would just assume that I'm a dustman or something, or I'm a cleaner.

'I have always been obsessive about money.' Asked how much he makes, Pell said: '£5,000 a week, sometimes – some weeks it can be seven, some weeks it can be two. It's a seasonal thing...'

He is also... 'a past master at hiding my own money... I'm the one who actually devised 15 aliases by the time I was 18 years old. I'm the one who's able to hide his money- in fact, I haven't had a single letter from the Inland Revenue for the past nine years. Famous last words, maybe. I could end up like Al Capone in prison for 15 years. But, at the end of the day though, I'm the one who is- genuinely doesn't exist. [I've] seventeen different aliases now.' Pell let Jones film some of his account records: 'Well, I am quite rich actually. Look how much money I've got in my account here. Look, £72,000. Offshore, of course, cos Benjamin Pell is a squirrel. He doesn't want the taxman getting his hands on his money.'

Journalists often prefer not to buy direct from Pell but via a middle man. Pell says that he now uses some hack called Joe Wood to 'sanitise' his stories.

Pell by his own account is an extremely successful professional criminal who traffics in stolen intellectual property. As a criminal, he has with his 'nutter act', for all practical purposes, put himself just beyond the reach of not only the criminal but also the civil law. Indeed, his criminality is all pervasive Take how he describes the way he flouts the law in respect of a crucial tool of his crimes: road vehicles.

Pell revels in describing how he drives around in uninsured and untaxed cars. He told Jones about one car[xix]: 'I've had at least 70 tickets on that car. The car is owned by somebody called Andrew Beckett at 56 Whitcomb Street. Pity is Whitcomb Street is- er, does exist; Andrew Beckett doesn't exist. It is a figment of his parent's imagination, they don't even know about it.'

He read from a police report: '"We then spoke to Pell regarding the Ford Escort. A PNC [Police National Computer] check found that the current keeper was no longer... it was found to have no current keeper." I've never had a car in my life with a current keeper. As you can see with my van, the current keeper is somebody, Andrew Beckett, who doesn't exist. The address is a fictitious address of one of my ex-clients. No car can ever be traced to me.'

On another occasion, Pell shows off his new van, pointing out the crucial feature of its bag-carrying capacity. 'First thing I need to show you is my new van. I got rid of the blue one- well, I haven't got rid of the blue one, I never get rid of my vans. I now have a collection of- of about seven of them, always somewhere in London. So, this is my new van, which has a capacity of 135 bags. It's already full even though the night is yet young.'

In the early hours of one July morning in 1999, he was driving one of his vans when he hit a police car outside the West End central police station[xx]. As his local newspaper reported, he then handed in a fake insurance certificate to magistrates the following February, later claiming to have bought it for £247 from what looked like a genuine insurer in Horn Lane, Acton.

He appeared again at Blackfriars crown court, and was convicted of driving without insurance. Judge Frederick Marr-Johnson said: 'This was a serious offence. You are of good character apart from one previous appearance before this court.' Of Pell's previous conviction, the judge remarked: 'It was clearly not very serious if he was only fined £20.' For the offence of using an insurance document with intent to deceive, he was fined £450 with £400 costs[xxi]

Pell, of course, was raking in a six-figure sum every year, spending hardly anything and not paying tax. And he is always looking to make more. He told Jones about documents he found concerning a rail project by Balfour Beatty[xxii].

This is something which, to be fair to you, won't be able to get me a lot of money from the newspapers, but at least will get me one or two paragraphs in the business section, and will certainly be of a commercially sensitive nature. I would gain more money by selling this to one of the competitors, to one of the competitors of Balfour Beatty than by actually getting it into the newspapers.

Jones asked Pell how much money he could make selling his information in the property industry compared with newspapers. Pell replied:

Oh much more. Much more. Cos you're not dealing with dickhead journalists for a start, and you're dealing there with real money. I mean, for example, I mean the freehold transaction I did about five years ago, we were selling a £4 million building, and I get three per cent of that. So work that out for yourself. That is good money.'

Pell is often angry that clients of his bin-raiding services do not pay him what he thinks they should. And he explains how he takes revenge for that against the cleaners he employs [who know him as Paul Lewis]. Jones filmed Pell playing a telephone answer machine message: 'It's Dora. I just want my money...'

As this message plays, Pell said: 'That's Dora. She always reminds me every week about how many weeks I owe her. So after the eighth week, it's... "Oh, Dora here. You owe me, now, seven weeks..." Pell provided his inimitable running commentary mimicking Dora's voice: 'And then she'll ring me up two weeks later, "It's Dora here, you owe me nine weeks." She's never actually insulted me – very strange woman.'

A second message plays:

Hi, Mr Lewis, this is Sheila. Now I think you're just taking the piss. That woman 'phoned me on Wednesday about my wages, and you still haven't sent them. So I'm telling you now, if I don't get my money by Sunday morning, I'm not doing that job no more, and you're not getting your keys back 'til I get my bloody money. And I'm also going in to see the people today cos I don't know what I've done to you, I've fucking worked for you for three or four years now and never had a complaint, and this is how you repay me. Well that's alright; you're not getting away with it.'

As this message played, Pell commented: 'I've got to pay back my cleaners for what the Fleet Street has done to me on stories. And I sound horrible, and she's white as well. I know, that's the reason I get her. She's not happy with that. Listen. She's not a happy woman.

Why should I pay her on time? I want these people to beg. I mean, I'm begging fucking Fleet Street all the time...'

Sheila leaves another message: 'And, by the way... the money you owe me is £378, and I want every penny of it by Monday, or you will be losing your contracts, okay? Bye bye.' Pell just laughs.

Pell was caught in a dichotomy. Like a magician who reveals how he performs his tricks, Pell's bid for stardom was leaving him exposed. One article, based on rushes shot by Jones, appeared in *Business Age* magazine, revealing how Benji the Binman had access to many company offices because he ran a cleaning business[xxiii]. But Pell, who was growing uncomfortable with the notoriety he had courted, faced the prospect of far greater exposure.

References

[i] Mr Justice Gray, judgement in Benjamin Pell -v- John Mappin and Story Master Ltd (19.03.02).

[ii] McVicar video tape (filmed 17.01.01) DVRB.

[iii] Mr Justice Gray, judgement in Benjamin Pell -v- John Mappin and Story Master Ltd (19.03.02).

[iv] 'Thank You for the Rubbish: It's Worth Millions,' Moving Perspective (first shown 13.01.02).

[v] Victor Lewis-Smith, 'My legal hell with Benji Pell,' *Evening Standard* (10.01.01).

[vi] Transcript of evidence of Benjamin Pell, Benjamin Pell -v- John Mappin and Story Master Ltd, (12.03.02).

[vii] Transcript of evidence of Benjamin Pell, Benjamin Pell -v- John Mappin and Story Master Ltd, (11.03.02).

[viii] McVicar audio tape (recorded 12.11.00) MDRG.

[ix] McVicar audio tape (recorded 30.12.00) MDRI.

[x] McVicar video tape (filmed 06.01.01) DVRY.

[xi] McVicar video tape (filmed 14.01.01) DVRG.

[xii] McVicar video tape (filmed 24.01.01) DVOR.

[xiii] McVicar audio tape (recorded 09.11.00) MDRY.

[xiv] McVicar audio tape (recorded 30.12.00) MDRI.

[xv] McVicar audio tape (recorded 2000) MDOB.

[xvi] McVicar audio tape (recorded 03.01.01) MDOV.

[xvii] McVicar video tape (filmed 06.01.01) DVRY.

[xviii] "3½-hour rushes," Moving Perspective (filmed 1999).

[xix] McVicar video tape (filmed 06.01.01) DVRY.

[xx] "3½-hour rushes," Moving Perspective (filmed 1999).

[xxi] McVicar video tape (filmed 08.02.01) DVOO.

[xxii] "3½-hour rushes," Moving Perspective (filmed 1999).

[xxiii] Yvonne Ridley, 'Dealing in trash,' *Business Age* (August 2001).

Chapter 14

Sunday, Bloody Sunday: the Saville Inquiry

Fleet Street was swept with an extraordinary rumour in January 2002 about an astonishing security breach at Lord Saville's 'Bloody Sunday' inquiry. The inquiry, into the day in 1972 when British paratroopers opened fire on a civil rights march in Northern Ireland and killed 14 people, had been running since 1998. The word in Fleet Street was that confidential documents from this most sensitive of inquiries had leaked. I was working at the *Sunday Express* at the time. Fleet Street is, of course, rife with gossip: journalists love to swap stories about the dodgy activities of MPs, the nocturnal shenanigans of the royals, the sharp practices of everything from the City to law enforcement agencies. Sometimes the gossip goes no further than entering Fleet Street folklore and sometimes, after much journalistic enterprise and endeavour, it finally surfaces in the newspapers, although often in sanitised form. Even those relatively few journalists who like to set the news agenda rather than follow it do not often have the freedom or resolve to chase a Fleet Street rumour. However, I decided to find out whether this particular rumour of a security breach at the Saville inquiry was true.

I had heard that a documentary was being made about Pell by some Americans for cinematic release and that these film-makers had had access to him for a long time, much longer that the Channel 4 team. As a result, I was told, the footage shot by the American film-makers was even more revealing than the Channel 4 documentary shown a year earlier.

The footage, it transpired, was filmed by the Hollywood-based Iain Jones for his American production company, Moving Perspective. He and his colleague, JC Bennett, edited these rushes to produce a documentary lasting just over an hour entitled, 'Thank You for the Rubbish: It's Worth Millions', which was first shown in America earlier that month[i]. Jones had made this documentary as part of an effort to attract a Hollywood movie company to back his planned feature film about Pell. John Mappin, a British businessman, had signed Pell up to co-operate with the project. The documentary, as first shown, in fact contained nothing about the security breach at the 'Bloody Sunday' inquiry.

My understanding was that Pell had been filmed saying that he had obtained the names or identities of paratroopers who were involved in the 'Bloody Sunday' shootings. I decided to chase the rumour because, if true, it had obvious ramifications for the security of these paratroopers, irrespective of whether they were still serving, and it was potentially verifiable by obtaining the relevant footage, which I understood was circulating around feature film executives and others. At the *Sunday Express*, there was much astonishment about the apparent 'Bloody Sunday' inquiry security breach. The editor, Martin Townsend, encouraged me to obtain the tape as quickly as possible. The key to this story was obtaining the footage and, given the rumours swirling about Fleet Street, to do so quickly.

There had been a long-running legal wrangle over the issue of anonymity for soldiers giving evidence to the inquiry. The court of appeal had only the month previous ruled against the inquiry tribunal by finding that the soldiers did not have to go to Northern Ireland to give evidence because of the danger to their lives from dissident Republican terrorist groups. The inquiry's decision not to grant anonymity to the soldiers had also been over-ruled, ultimately again by the appeal court after a legal battle that lasted several years.

Certainly one other journalist was aware of the American documentary and the extraordinary rumours about the 'Bloody Sunday' inquiry security breach, namely Kevin Cahill, a freelance. He told me that, by chance, he had recently met Mappin at a party and asked him about the documentary but Mappin refused to discuss it with him or provide any help.

The American documentary was the subject of much gossip in Fleet Street because some journalists were worried that it would expose their links with Pell. I found out many months later that *Private Eye*, the destination for a lot of Fleet Street gossip, had published an article about the new documentary in January 2002[ii]. It appeared in the magazine's 'Street of Shame' column, which reports on the goings-on in Fleet Street.

Within two days of trying to locate a copy of the 'Bloody Sunday' tape, I obtained it from a confidential source[iii]. The tape consisted of about thirteen minutes of roughly edited footage of Pell telling Jones about what he describes as his '"Bloody Sunday" story'. Readers doubtless remember Pell's claim that he was 'developing story-lines' in the Moving Perspective material. Nonetheless, at least some of his claims on the 'Bloody Sunday' tape are verified by what is actually seen on the footage. Pell is seen on the tape going, at night, to Brick Court chambers, in Essex Street and just over the road from the Royal Courts of Justice. He is seen taking rubbish bags that had been left outside the chambers on the pavement. The head of Brick Court chambers, a leading set of barristers, is Christopher Clarke, 56, who is counsel (or chief lawyer) to the 'Bloody Sunday' inquiry. Pell explains on camera how he took the bags home, and, in his garden, he is seen rummaging through them. He says that he found many 'extremely confidential' documents from the chambers. These included internal chambers documents, such as barristers' work timetables, letters to and from various barristers in Brick Court chambers and numerous documents relating to the inquiry, papers that are visible on the rushes. Anyone watching the tape can see that he did indeed obtain confidential documents relating to the inquiry. Pell talks on camera excitedly about the kind of documents that he had found. And what he found, in the black bags left on the public highway for any passing 'binman' to pick up, is utterly staggering. While it needs to be viewed in order to be comprehended fully, this is the transcript of the 'Bloody Sunday' tape:

> Pell [at home, showing the camera a newspaper article]: This is the 'Bloody Sunday' story. '"Bloody Sunday" inquiry will put our lives on the line, say Paras.' That comes from May 1999.
> Jones: "Is that your story?"
> Pell: No, well, that is the story about 'Bloody Sunday', cos don't forget the story which I've got is too good for the papers.
> [Pell plays telephone answer machine message.]
> Pell: Oh that's Richard Murray... the lawyer from the Telegraph who

wants me to sell the 'Bloody Sunday' story... The question is whether some of the people can be anonymous when they have to give evidence. Cos the whole point, of course, is that you've got a war here, between the IRA and the soldiers of this country, which still isn't over. So they've been fighting for the last two years in court as to whether they have to remain anonymous or not. So imagine how ironic it is when the actual barristers themselves who are involved in the inquiry are throwing away the names of the actual paratroopers when they are being paid by us, the taxpayers, to keep these names confidential. [...]

Pell [outside chambers at night]: Brick Court chambers is one of the leading chambers in the country, and they act for people like the home secretary, for the chancellor of the exchequer, and what is actually more remarkable at the moment is they are the barristers who are currently dealing with what is known as the 'Bloody Sunday' inquiry... Now, one of the questions in this inquiry is the question of anonymity, in which the anonymity of paratroopers is of paramount importance.[...] I am going to Brick Court chambers, the leading barristers chambers in the country. They are known as the 'magic circle' of chambers. But I am telling you this, when this story comes out about their gross negligence, including the 'Bloody Sunday' inquiry, yes, they will be the 'magic circle' of chambers: 'cos they'll disappear.[...]

Pell [in his garden, as he flicks through a pile of documents]: Page after page after page after page... It is all Brick Court chambers. Here, and I love their timetables, 'cos here, you find Christopher Clarke away on holiday in France. And you get a list of all the cases they're dealing with, which, start here, working on Saville inquiry into 'Bloody Sunday'. That's DLJ who is David Lloyd-Jones, so I know what he's doing today. Now this one actually made me laugh. Mark Howard QC who is one of the lawyers there; he lives at [address deleted] in NW3, which is in Hampstead, guess who lives at [address deleted]? Noel Gallagher. So, two of my favourite targets live next door to each other. [...]

Pell: While we are here, we might as well do an older pile of Brick Court chambers because obviously we are going to be showing you a more recent one here... This is 11th June 1999. I mean they always throw this away; this is a list of all the clients they are currently working on. Here you see CC, that's Christopher Clarke, counsel, working on the 'Bloody Sunday' inquiry, and three of them are working on 'Bloody Sunday' inquiry, and the others, some of them are working on the BSE inquiry, which is that thing I was telling you about CJT [he means CJD], which is that mad cows disease. And it's like a 'who's who' of all the big cases, the Department of Culture- don't forget, I've had stories in here regarding the- here's the Saville inquiry... Judicial review... Here, we have [a] perfect example: here, the Queen versus Lord Saville of Newdegate, the Right Honourable Sir Edward Soames, the honourable Mr such and such. Affidavit of Greg McCartney, solicitor of Derry, Northern Ireland. All of this stuff would be highly confidential, would only be passed on to people- as you can see here, the names are used only using initials: B O U and V. That's how confidential this stuff is. But I have all of the exhibits. I shouldn't have any of it. Look, if the Treasury Solicitor knew that I had a letter regarding the Saville inquiry into 'Bloody Sunday'...

Treasury Solicitor, Edwin Glasgow's [a barrister representing some of the soldiers] home address. Here, Kingsley Napley letter regarding the Saville inquiry. Here, 'Whilst doing bits of reading, one matter occurred to me in relation to the report of Christopher Clarke.'

So, here we have Christopher Clarke, the head of chambers at Brick Court chambers, the person who is being paid by the taxpayer... and here we have letters regarding the most confidential matter of this year, and its all been thrown away in his rubbish.

Letters regarding the attorney general. A letter here from the 'Bloody Sunday' inquiry to Right Honourable John Morris...he was the attorney general at the time, and I have a whole copy of it here. Here, this is stuff which I've still got to piece together, but, as you can see from the top here, look, the Republican News... and, can you see there? It's been faxed over from the 'MoD', the Ministry of Defence. '"Bloody Sunday", "Bloody Sunday" investigation.' Can you see that? And this I've still got to piece together, this came from Brick Court chambers last week. [...]

Pell: Okay. And I've got- some of the other stuff is under there. So remind me, I've got to get you two bags which are under there. Okay, here, very important, oh here's some more, look, look, I mean, can I do this here while I've got it here: 'Saville inquiry "Bloody Sunday"', look, 'Confidential and urgent'.

'This is a very important letter dealing with the question of anonymity, and I apologise for the fact that it is impersonal,' and then it goes on a few pages, and it's from P.L. Stockwell, who is 'for and on behalf of members of the Lawton team'. They are the team representing some of the soldiers in the 'Bloody Sunday' inquiry."

Jones: And where did that document come from?

Pell: That came from the rubbish of Brick Court chambers.

Here we have a letter from 'the Treasury Solicitor... draft letter to B, who is party to the new JR [judicial review] application. The Saville inquiry, "Bloody Sunday".' Okay. And then we've got- here's another thing about 'Bloody Sunday': 'I am writing to keep you up to date with regard to the latest ruling made by the tribunal on 5th May dealing with the question of anonymity of witnesses.' [...]

Pell [in his home, as he searches for a specific letter that he found]: In fact, I even have a letter here from one of the barristers. I even remember where it is, I hope (unless my father's moved it; my father has moved it) it was on top of here, where they were admitting that one of the names had been leaked. Where has my father put it? It was on top of here. Anyway, whatever, there was one letter from a barrister admitting that one of the names had been leaked. Ah, here it is, got it...'Dear Christopher', that's Christopher Clarke... 'Following the embarrassment which I caused on Tuesday... I undertook that I would check my sources. In normal circumstances, I would have written directly to the judge. In this situation, I am concerned that it would not be appropriate for me to make any contact directly with the tribunal. I was conscious of the fact that almost anything that I said would add to the publicity and the damage which those around me rightly were telling me I had done. I have to confess that I still have a crystal clear memory of a press cutting which named the individual. I've searched through the mountains of paper in my room and cannot find it,' he sounds a bit like me. Basically, he's saying, 'When one uses a name openly on a daily basis, its use rings no bells of any kind... The irony is that this name-there had been no dispute that it was widely known. Those are the full circumstances of which I made the mistake.' Basically, he had inadvertently given out one of the names. 'I feel apprehensive about writing so fully, if at all, to the members of that tribunal. May I again ask you me to pass on my unreserved apology with such part of my explanation,' etc, etc, etc.

So basically this whole business is terribly embarrassing... As you can see, this poor guy has inadvertently let slip one name, on one occasion: here, we have the actual chambers on several occasions letting these names slip.

Jones: Have you supplied any of this information to any newspapers?

Pell: No, that's too scary. There's no way I want to get shot.

Jones: Who knows that you've got this information?

Pell: Nobody, not even David Leigh. I mean Richard Murray

does...and I only told him [in] a sort of indirect way. He doesn't actually know that I have some of the names. He just thinks that I've got a lot of stuff from those chambers, and he thinks the story is enough that way... But no money would be good enough to pay to compensate me for getting shot. [...]

Pell [in College Green, opposite the Houses of Parliament, in front of a TV crew]: They're discussing what was in Parliament today, regarding the Northern Ireland business. Now I would like to know what their reaction would be if they realised that the judges and the QCs of this country were leaving out confidential documents regarding the 'Bloody Sunday' inquiry on the doorsteps of their offices in Essex Street, just around the corner from the High Court. Maybe that's something which we can ask them...at a future date.[...]

Pell [outside Brick Court chambers]: In many ways, my favourite targets are the barristers because the barristers are at the top of society. Whenever [there is a] public inquiry, it's the barristers who are chosen to chair the inquiry. A QC is chairing the inquiry into the rail crash. A QC is chairing the investigation into competition law. Why? Because they are considered to be paragons of virtue. They can consider the whole picture, etc. And yet these barristers, as I have proven to you: we have been into all four Inns of Court successfully, unquestioned, taking bags out; we have targeted the biggest chambers, the most prestigious chambers in this country, Brick Court chambers, where, on a daily basis, nine or ten bags have been left out, including the names of the 'Bloody Sunday' paratroopers, including stuff about Elton John, Pinochet etc. That is the point I am making to you. How can you expect these judges, who, at the end of the day are just barristers who have gone on a stage further, to have any sort of judgement in this matter, 'cos they are just as biased as these barristers. There but for the grace of God go I.

When I later showed this tape to the chief legal adviser at Express Newspapers, Justin Walford, who was more aware than most of the vulnerability of lawyers to 'dumpster divers', he was absolutely staggered by it, just as I had been. A barrister who is often employed by Express Newspapers happened to be visiting the office just after Walford viewed the tape. Walford immediately told him to go straight back to his chambers to detail to his colleagues just what sort of information the tape reveals can be obtained as a result of documents carelessly discarded by barristers.

The tape emphatically showed that there had been an extraordinary security breach at the 'Bloody Sunday' inquiry. Although Pell repeatedly claimed to have obtained, amongst his haul from Brick Court chambers, documents showing names of soldiers, no such papers were shown on the tape. Nonetheless, several confidential inquiry documents were shown on the tape and had, therefore, indeed leaked. It was evident that such material had leaked, not just because Pell said that it had, but because of the documents seen on camera. The startling fact was that anybody, including dissident Republican terrorists, could have obtained these documents using, or commissioning someone to use, the same method as Pell. Republican terrorists were well known in Britain's security establishment for being accomplished at intelligence gathering. And 'dumpster diving' is the most basic of intelligence-gathering methods.

I contacted Jones, who shot the footage, to find out whether he had seen any documents containing any details of the identities of soldiers. Jones told me that neither he nor his associates had seen any document with the soldiers' names, so none of them was able to verify that Pell had obtained them. He said that, nonetheless, he believed Pell's repeated claim that he had found them. Jones said: 'I hardly wanted to display this list in the film.' If he had done so, he said, the film itself would have been a further breach of the inquiry's security. Jones said his understanding was that Pell had the names of all the soldiers who were in any way relevant to the inquiry, including those who had killed people on 'Bloody Sunday'. He also said that he had recently contacted the MoD to seek comment. He told me that Mappin was an investor in the project, although not involved in actually making the documentary. Jones confirmed that Pell was suing Mappin, adding that the case had led to a rift between him [Jones] and Mappin. He also said that he had filmed at several of what Pell referred to as his 'safe houses', which were various offices in London of clients of his contract-cleaning business where, he said, Pell stored huge quantities of documents retrieved from rubbish bags.

Pell was filmed saying that he would not sell the soldiers' names to a newspaper, but he was somewhat inconsistent on this point because he also said that he had talked about the subject, at least in part, to Murray, a newspaper lawyer, who had wanted him to sell the story. This was the same lawyer who had persuaded Pell to sell the story about Hamilton's documents.

A source at *The Sunday Times* told me that Murray had offered that newspaper the story about the 'Bloody Sunday' inquiry leak. Murray later said[iv]: 'From about July 1999, Benjamin Pell used to phone me from time to time to talk about his antics and to point out the faults of others... I had come to understand that he regularly rummaged through the bins outside barristers' chambers and solicitors' offices, and took it upon myself to persuade him to find something more constructive to do with his talents. I had no wish to encourage his bin rummaging activities and established a rule that he should not tell me about it.

'I do, however, recall that around mid to late summer of 1999 he told me with great excitement that he had started finding documents relating to the 'Bloody Sunday' inquiry in rubbish sacks outside Brick Court chambers. I was frankly horrified that such material, apparently marked as confidential, should be regularly discarded in a public place... Mr Pell was obsessed with the negligence of lawyers who left unshredded documents in their rubbish, but the "Bloody Sunday" material struck us both as a security breach of an entirely different order.'

Murray referred to the irony that members of the chambers had responsibility for protecting the anonymity of soldiers...

> ...whilst at the same time leaving sensitive documents about the inquiry on the pavement in black sacks... Mr Pell was at all times receptive to the idea that something should be done to straighten the matter out, but was afraid that involving any authorities would land him in trouble. We therefore discussed the possibility of turning the negligence of Brick Court chambers into a news story for a national newspaper. My hope was that he would deliver whatever "Bloody Sunday" papers he had into the newspaper's custody, whence they could be disposed of appropriately.
>
> At the same time, the security breach would be closed down by its own public exposure, while he, as the source, would remain anonymous. I suggested to him, provocatively, that a newspaper such as the Mail on Sunday might even be prepared to pay for such a story, but he never overcame his conviction that the safest course was to do nothing.

Pell had been well aware of how newsworthy and lucrative the revelation of the security breach at the inquiry was. In addition, I believe that Pell had been reckless with the confidential inquiry documents, especially given that he freely allowed Jones and Mappin to see them when, by his own account, he did not know very much about them.

I put to Clarke what I had seen on the tape. By doing this, I was also making sure that he knew about the security breach and could take appropriate steps to ensure no repetition. He said that he could not believe that there could have been such a leak. First, he said, he had no correspondence to or from him related to the inquiry at the chambers. When I pointed out that anyone watching the tape could see just such correspondence, he said: 'There's a great wadge of stuff in the public domain.' When I said that some of the documents seen on the tape are not in the public domain, he said: 'There isn't any confidential material of the inquiry at Brick Court chambers, and never has been.' He continued: 'As I say, the inquiry doesn't correspond from or to my chambers. Secondly, if there was any confidential material, it's shredded every evening... It doesn't go out in the bins.'

However, his answers simply did not explain why such material could be seen on the tape. I told Clarke that Pell also claims to have obtained from the rubbish of his chambers names of British soldiers who were due to give evidence to the inquiry, although these are not actually seen on the tape. Clarke denied that Pell could have done, saying: 'The inquiry has not decided which soldiers are to give evidence... I haven't yet made a list to that effect.' I asked whether there were documents identifying soldiers who were the subject of the lengthy legal wrangles over anonymity. He said: 'I know that there are many soldiers who are potential witnesses... And I obviously know that they have names... And there's a list here [at the inquiry's offices], well, there isn't actually a list here, but the details appear at the inquiry's offices on computer... I don't have such a list in chambers.'

He went on to describe the policy of destroying confidential documents at his chambers. 'You put them out in a "confidential" bag and... one of my clerks goes down every evening and shreds them...

I dare say, in due course, somebody takes away the shredded pieces of paper.' He could not explain why Brick Court chambers documents that had not been shredded could be seen on the tape. 'There we are,' he said. 'We shall no doubt see what this film produces.'

Clarke's claims about the practices at his chambers might have been true at the time of our conversation, in February 2002, but they certainly were not true in 1999 when the footage on the 'Bloody Sunday' tape was filmed. And, despite what Clarke said, I remain convinced that the security breaches had happened.

I put the same issue to a spokesman for the 'Bloody Sunday' inquiry, and, again, in so doing, I was making sure that it knew about the security breach and could take appropriate steps. He said that he had 'nothing further to add' to Clarke's comments. He stressed: 'We do shred; we are very careful about our material from the inquiry, certainly... Christopher wouldn't have had anything as sensitive or confidential like that at his chambers... We would be very much at pains to ensure that any confidential material was shredded.' He also raised the possibility that another chambers, acting for one or other party in the inquiry and operating from the same building, might have been responsible for leaving out the documents. 'Our line would be that it's not solely the premises of Christopher Clarke, that other law firms do occupy those chambers,' he said. 'The point would be, it could have come from anywhere,' he continued. 'We would say that it could have come from anywhere, not necessarily, just because it was found outside Brick Court chambers, doesn't necessarily mean it belongs to Christopher Clarke.'

I also sought comment from the MoD, which I had heard was already investigating the security breach after Jones had brought the issue to its attention. I had also learnt that the MoD, as part of its investigation, was preparing to question Pell and raid various locations where he stored documents. Again, I was making sure that the MoD was aware of the matter so that it could take appropriate steps to prevent any repetition of the security breach. When I raised the issue with an MoD spokesman, he immediately said that there was a file on the subject. Having reached for the file, he said, 'The only thing that we can say is that, the claim that a list of names has been found by this "Benji the Binman" character: we can confirm that an investigation is ongoing.' He confirmed that the investigation had been running for about a week, but would not comment on any operational details, such as whether the MoD had tried to speak to Pell or to see what material he had. He did, however, say that the MoD was taking it 'very seriously'.

The MoD had confirmed a crucial piece of information, which had not previously been made public. Having seen the tape, I had come to the view that the evident security breach was a serious issue, but the fact that the MoD was genuinely concerned about it gave the story added credibility. The MoD was taking it very seriously and had concluded that the matter warranted its investigation.

As I made further inquiries, I noticed on the Moving Perspective website a press release dating from the previous December quoting Yvonne Ridley, then the chief reporter on the *Sunday Express*[v]. According to the press release, my then colleague had seen a 'preview of the footage'. She was quoted as describing it as 'one of the most unique pieces of film that I have seen'. The press release reminded me that I had already heard a rumour that she had seen the American documentary. I had seen the 13 minutes or so of rushes in the 'Bloody Sunday' tape (transcribed above), but not the America documentary, and so I did not know what was in that. I had imagined that the 'Bloody Sunday' story had featured in the documentary. If so, I was puzzled why, if my colleague had seen it, she had not written an article along the same lines as I was intending to do. When she arrived back at the *Express* office, having been out at a training course for war reporters (this was after she had been captured – and released – by the Taliban in Afghanistan), she told me that the version of the documentary she saw included nothing about 'Bloody Sunday'. The most striking aspect of what she had seen, she said, was the disclosure that Pell ran an office-cleaning business and used his position as a contract office cleaner to access confidential material at several businesses, including a television production company and a public relations firm.

She said that she had wanted to write an article for the *Sunday Express* about this, but Townsend did not want to run it because, she said he told her, he was not interested in publishing stories about Pell. She put this down to the trouble caused in 1998 when Pell found and sold to *The Sunday People* a copy of the £1m wedding contract between *OK* magazine, which Townsend then edited, and 'Posh & Becks'[vi]. So furious was Richard Desmond, owner of *OK*, that, according to the *People* report, the magazine's lawyers tried, unsuccessfully, for an injunction to stop the newspaper from revealing details of the agreement.

I thought that Townsend's apparent reluctance to publish the story about Pell and his cleaning business was strange, not least because Townsend had shown no reluctance to run my planned article on the 'Bloody Sunday' inquiry security breach. Ridley thought that the contents of the 'Bloody Sunday' tape was a scoop, and felt, as I did, that revealing its contents was clearly in the public interest.

A little later, she gave me a copy of the article that she had written[vii]. She had written a short note to Townsend at the top of the article, in which she said: 'Personally speaking, if we nail this little sod I think that we'll be the champion of celebrities, which wouldn't do our image any harm. He trades on fear, and it would be a pity if we were intimidated.'

The details about Pell's cleaning business chimed with the account I already had from Jones about how he had filmed Pell storing documents at 'safe houses', namely offices around London of clients of his contract-cleaning business. I wondered just how securely Pell was keeping the confidential 'Bloody Sunday' inquiry documents he had taken. The Channel 4 documentary had said that Pell also kept many documents he had taken in his garden shed[viii]. I was worried that this might make the confidential inquiry documents, which, according to Pell's repeated claims on the 'Bloody Sunday' tape, included the identities of British soldiers, vulnerable to being taken by, or behalf of, an Irish dissident terrorist group.

When I asked Townsend about his reluctance to publish the earlier story, he told me that, while it would have been very interesting to journalists, he did not think that it would be of much interest to *Express* readers. He said that, by contrast, an article about the breach of security at the 'Bloody Sunday' inquiry would be of much wider public interest and would clearly be newsworthy and topical. He said that he wanted to publish it the following Sunday.

Before I could write the article, I needed to be especially sure of four points. First, I had to be certain that the 'Bloody Sunday' tape was genuine and actually showed what it appeared to show. I had to be sure that it was indeed Pell who is seen and heard on the tape (and not that someone was impersonating him, or that someone else's voice had been dubbed onto the film) and to check that it could not have been edited in such a way as to distort the meaning of what he was saying.

I watched the tape again, scrutinising it carefully to look for any evidence that the tape had been interfered with in any of these ways. I found none. Second, I wanted to check that the documents shown on the footage were not obviously faked. I examined the tape closely on this point and concluded that the documents were what they appeared to be. Third, I wanted to satisfy myself, especially in light of Clarke's and the inquiry spokesman's comments, that it was evident from the tape that Pell had obtained documents from Brick Court chambers. The tape showed that there was no doubt about that. Fourth, I needed to be certain, again in light of what Clarke had said, that Pell had obtained confidential documents relating to the inquiry. I repeatedly watched the tape carefully and noted three examples where Pell showed to the camera inquiry documents that were clearly not in the public domain.

These three documents were confidential letters that could be seen on the footage: a letter from the inquiry to the then attorney general, John Morris; a letter to the inquiry from P. L. Stockwell, on behalf of members of the Lawton team who was representing some of the soldiers; and a letter to Clarke from another barrister regarding that barrister's inadvertently naming one of the soldiers who was supposed to be anonymous (part of which Pell read out).

I believe that it is a scandal for these documents to have been in the rubbish left out in the street. Lawyers, when questioned about their document-destruction policies, invariably claim to be very strict about shredding documents rather than simply throwing them out in the rubbish. Some, however, do admit that law firms have difficulties in keeping confidential documents properly secure. They point to the problem of the copious amount of paperwork generated by the legal profession, be it for inquiries or court cases. And every document typically goes through several drafts that are discarded. Lawyers with whom I discussed the 'Bloody Sunday' security breach pointed out that many box files of documents were replicated in several law firms acting for various parties. They say that it is the huge deluge of paperwork that makes a leak possible.

Although Pell did not show the camera any names of 'Bloody Sunday' soldiers, I regarded his claim that he had found them as credible in light of the confidential material he had obtained. I also knew before seeing the 'Bloody Sunday' tape that Pell had often been able to find extremely sensitive and confidential information by trawling through rubbish. I thought that this made his claim to have obtained the identities of 'Bloody Sunday' soldiers even more credible. I also knew that Pell was willing to sell documents he retrieved from the rubbish. He did not seem to make any distinction between confidential documents for which there might be a case to bring to public attention and those that should not be published. Rather, he seemed to relish disrupting people's lives by revealing confidential documents – regardless of their public interest.

References

[i] 'Thank You for the Rubbish: It's Worth Millions,' Moving Perspective (first shown 13.01.02).

[ii] *Private Eye* No 1046 (25.01.02).

[iii] "'Bloody Sunday' rushes," Moving Perspective (filmed 1999). Transcript is reproduced later in chapter.

[iv] Richard Murray witness statement, Benjamin Pell -v- Express Newspapers and Mark Watts (22.04.03).

[v] 'Thank You for the Rubbish has screened at Slamdance 2002,' Moving Perspective (16.01.02).

[vi] Amanda Perthen, 'Beckham and Posh sign their lives away in amazing £1m wedding deal,' *Sunday People* (05.07.98).

[vii] Yvonne Ridley, unpublished article about Pell and his cleaning business (written in mid-2001); a version of this article, 'Dealing in Trash,' was published in BusinessAge magazine (August 2001).

[viii] 'Scandal in the Bins,' Channel 4 (first shown 11.01.01).

Chapter 15

Runaround:
the binman plays dumb

One key question over the security breach at the 'Bloody Sunday' inquiry remained. Although the tape provided no evidence that Pell had in any way passed any soldiers' names, or any other details, to dissident Republican terrorists, did the information, nonetheless, found its way to such people? I had heard that a list of names of 'Bloody Sunday' soldiers had already circulated around the Republican community. When I pursued this point with a confidential source, I was told that a list of names of 'Bloody Sunday' soldiers had circulated around dissident terrorist groups, including the Real IRA some months or even years previous. While it was unclear how the names had leaked, I was told that Republican terrorists do not generally use the services of a person such as Pell to obtain information. The suggestion that dissident Republican terrorists had obtained the names of 'Bloody Sunday' soldiers, without any assistance from Pell, was staggering in its own right. As I detail below, this astonishing suggestion later proved correct. The MoD had always said that its great efforts to ensure anonymity for soldiers giving evidence to the inquiry was to help prevent their assassination by Irish terrorists. I thought that dissident Republican terrorists might have obtained the soldiers' names by raiding rubbish bins, or by commissioning someone to do so for them. Pell said on the 'Bloody Sunday' tape that he was too frightened to sell the names even to a newspaper. I do not believe that Pell attempted to supply any information he gathered to any terrorists.

Nonetheless, my findings were clearly deeply alarming, especially as a British Army source had previously told me that, at a confidential security briefing on dissident terrorist groups by MI5 to the MoD and other government agencies, MI5's assessment was that the Real IRA was aiming to kill a serving or former soldier to earn kudos among Republicans. When I told the army source about the contents of the 'Bloody Sunday' tape the reaction was one of utter amazement. The source said simply: 'This is a betrayal of our soldiers. This will cause the most dreadful panic.'

I sought reaction from Jeffrey Donaldson, then the Ulster Unionist MP for Lagan Valley who had long campaigned for anonymity for soldiers who would give evidence at the 'Bloody Sunday' inquiry (and who has since switched to the Democratic Unionists). He told me that he was 'deeply concerned', continuing: 'I think that there is an urgent need for an investigation into how Benjamin Pell came into possession of the documents he claims to have... and also to determine what steps can be taken to prevent this kind of breach of confidentiality in future... My concern is that, whether inadvertently or otherwise, this information may fall into the wrong hands... and could potentially place the lives of these soldiers and their families in serious threat... I also intend to raise this matter in Parliament... If this information falls into the wrong hands, the soldiers [might] not [be] able to give evidence to the Saville inquiry.'

On the Friday before publication, I was in a position to seek comment from Pell. My usual approach, in line with normal Sunday newspaper practice, is first to attempt to put allegations to the person concerned by telephone on the Friday before publication. Journalists want to give people in such circumstances reasonable time to respond to allegations, but do not want to allow so much time that they can 'manage' the story by, for example, leaking it to another newspaper in the hope of more favourable treatment. If an attempt to elicit a response by telephone fails for whatever reason, then a reporter would normally press the questions by doorstepping, with a photographer taking shots from a discreet distance.

The news editor makes such decisions. And I had a feeling that the news editor on the *Sunday Express*, Jim Murray, might prefer an approach that differed from usual practice. Jim was a very peculiar news editor. Known in the industry as 'Mad Dog' since his reporting days, I had first met him when I began working at the *Sunday Express* on September 12, 2001. It was, of course, the day after the most momentous single event of many of our lifetimes. I had good contacts

amongst the dissident Muslim community in London and agreed with
the then City editor, Richard Phillips, that I would concentrate on
trying to find out the identities of London-based people linked to the
al-Qaeda terrorist network that was behind the September 11 attacks
in America. We agreed that this would be of obvious interest to the
news section. Later, Phillips introduced me to Murray, telling him that
I was an 'investigative journalist'. I will never forget how Murray said
that he had a great idea for an investigation and began wittering on
about some non-story that would probably have been a non-story
before September 11, let alone immediately after it. He recalled seeing
what he said was an interesting article about how people in the travel
industry typically earn low wages. Wouldn't it be interesting, he said,
to find out how much the people at board level earn in the travel
industry to compare with these low wages.

Phillips and I exchanged bemused glances as we tried to shift the
conversation to the article that I was researching about Osama bin
Laden's London network. Needless to say, Murray's 'great idea for an
investigation' never had a sniff of newsprint, while my article about
al-Qaeda's London contacts, which I wrote with Ridley, made a
decent spread. Somehow, someone else's by-line appeared instead of
ours. By any measure, it was not a great re-introduction to the
Sunday Express, which had been my first national newspaper some
ten years' previous.

The security breach at the 'Bloody Sunday' inquiry was the first
time I would write about such a potentially contentious subject for
Jim, and, given his peculiarities, I thought I should check with him
my approach to Pell before telephoning him to seek comment as I had
intended. Murray insisted that I should doorstep Pell at his home, and
that I should leave doing so until the morning before publication – a
Saturday. He stressed that I should not first try to telephone Pell; he
was concerned about losing exclusivity of the story.

I told Jim that this would not give us much leeway if it proved
difficult to contact Pell on the day before publication. Although it was
not my preferred approach, I did not protest too much partly because
of my experience (and that of other reporters) of trying to elicit a
response from Pell by telephone previously (note his then solicitor's
advice about not talking to the Press in chapter 6). I would have

protested more, however, had it dawned on me that I would be making my first approach to Pell on the Jewish Sabbath. Journalists, in general, do approach people for comment on their Sabbath or other religious holidays. However, most would prefer to avoid that if it is a realistic possibility.

Meanwhile, I had already emailed to Townsend a draft of the article, which focussed on the security breach at the inquiry and the resulting, still-secret MoD investigation. In a note at the top of the article, I warned: 'Please be careful about printing it off – in case it goes astray!'

A few minutes later, Townsend emailed back to say: 'This is really good. I think you can afford to bring the name of Benji the Binman up a bit higher because it will give the whole thing a human face – albeit a pretty seedy one. Otherwise the beginning reads rather dryly.' He was right, and I altered the piece accordingly, although I still focussed the intro on the security breach rather than Pell. Newspapers, in my view, tend to personalise stories too much and I felt that this article should not be about Pell so much as the extraordinary security breach at the inquiry and its potential consequences.

I still needed to give Pell a chance to comment on the disclosures in the 'Bloody Sunday' tape. I wanted to ask him whether he accepted that he was filmed with material from Brick Court Chambers (I could not see how he could deny this because the footage had clearly been shot with his knowledge and co-operation), whether he accepted that he had said he had found a list of names of 'Bloody Sunday' soldiers, and whether he had in fact obtained such a list. If so, I wanted to know to whether he had shown or given the names to anyone and if so to whom, where the relevant papers were and whether they were secure. I expected Pell would be defensive, given the contents of the tape, but I thought he would realise that he needed to explain his position. I could not imagine, however, what he could say.

I arranged to meet a photographer near Pell's home in Hendon, north London, at about 8.30am on the Saturday before publication. I told no one else about the doorstep, as is usual practice, to ensure that the person concerned is not tipped off. Photographers invariably accompany reporters on such jobs.

The plan was to wait until 9am before knocking on Pell's front door; the reason for arriving earlier was in case he left the house before 9am. I arrived at 8.30am and waited at a discreet distance, but the photographer called to say that he was lost and would be late. The photographer arrived some 20 minutes later and I walked up the road to meet him about 30 metres from the house. As we chatted about where the photographer should position himself, I noticed that Pell emerged from his house. I said something like: 'That's him. I'm going to talk to him, you'll have to do the best you can.'

Pell was alone and walked down the road away from us. I walked fast to try to catch up with Pell and, at least, see where he was going. I did not run, to avoid attracting attention. Pell showed no sign that he had noticed us. At the bottom of his road, Pell turned left. I hurried to the junction so that he did not go into a building without my seeing him. After a short distance, Pell crossed the road and walked into a building on Finchley Lane. The number of the building was 48-50, but there appeared to be no sign outside the building to say what it was. I initially thought that it might be a community centre. In a sense, I was right. As I waited and watched the building, several small groups of people, some of them wearing skull-caps, went into the building. It was a synagogue. The photographer drove up, and I asked him to park his car outside the building so that he could take pictures when Pell emerged. I asked him to keep watch and alert me if he emerged while I went back round to Pell's road to collect my car. I was of course cursing the photographer whose late arrival had made it necessary for us to wait when the job should by this stage have been finished.

I was in no doubt that, in the circumstances, I had to wait for Pell to come out of the synagogue and would put my questions to him then. We had to give Pell a chance to comment, even though the circumstances were far from ideal. We could not risk trying to contact him at home later because we could not be certain that he would return there that day. If Pell told me that he would comment later away from the synagogue, I would have agreed to this because there was plenty of time for us to speak later that morning or that afternoon enabling him to comment before the first edition deadline. Jim agreed that we should wait outside the synagogue, although our conversation was cut short by my mobile because my battery had gone flat. And, for the next hour or so, the photographer and I waited in our respective cars. No one showed any sign of noticing us. Several people finally started to leave the synagogue. I thought that Pell could emerge at any moment. I wanted to telephone the photographer to check that he was ready. As my mobile telephone was down, I called him from a telephone call box that was on the pavement outside the synagogue. While I was in the call box, Pell emerged. He stopped at the entrance to the building, where he was chatting for some time with a group of about three other people. There was a large huddle of people around the synagogue entrance by now. I wanted to wait until Pell walked to the pavement before approaching him. I telephoned the photographer to check that he had seen Pell. He asked for a description to confirm who Pell was. From his car parked not far from the synagogue, he took several shots of Pell, without anyone showing any sign of noticing.

By the time I left the telephone box, the large huddle of people at the entrance to the synagogue had diminished to about 20 people. Pell was chatting in a small group of about four. As I waited on the pavement beyond the lawn to the front of the synagogue, I reached inside my jacket to switch on my tape recorder. I waited for Pell to walk to the pavement before introducing myself. The conversation began like this:

> Watts: Benji, I need to have a- need to have a word with you.
> Pell: Oh, really. What is it?
> Watts: I'm Mark Watts, from the *Sunday Express*.
> Pell: Oh sorry, I don't talk to you.
> Watts: We're doing a story...
> Pell: No...
> Watts: I need to tell you. Do you know about this film that's being made?
> Pell: Oh really, oh very exciting. No idea, no idea, sorry, bye bye.
> Watts: The 'Bloody Sunday' documents?
> Pell: Oh no. What?
> Watts: You are recorded on the film saying that you've got hold of –
> Pell: Oh really, oh really.
> Watts: ...documents from Brick Court chambers.
> Pell: No, really. Well, I didn't know that, sorry.

Watts: You're filmed with- it's definitely you...
Pell: Oh really, no. Well you'll have to ask these things for me 'cos
I haven't seen any [he began walking away...].

Journalists often experience obfuscation, but this was obfuscation on speed. I believe that Pell, unable to come up on the spot with a well-thought-through lie to explain away the footage, resorted to a plainly untenable position. As I attempted to draw Pell away from his fellow congregants, so that we could have a private conversation, he ignored me and tried to re-immerse himself in conversation with two or three fellow congregants. Those who overheard the first part of this conversation must have been utterly bemused by it: they could not have had a clue to what I was referring. One congregant asked me why I wanted to speak to Pell.

After a minute or so, Pell walked away from the synagogue with a couple of congregants, in the direction of his home. I followed him. By the time I caught up with him, he was only with one congregant, who I later learnt was Joseph Abraham. I tried again to put my questions to Pell, as the three of us walked along Finchley Lane. Pell involved Abraham in the conversation as much as he could, constantly making asides to him, some of which I could not hear. My exchange with Pell continued like this:

Watts: I've seen you on this film.
Pell: Oh really, have you? [Speaking to Abraham] Wow, somebody else has seen this film! Wow. Okay.
Watts: Is it true?
Pell [to Abraham]: Mark Watts, one of the most inefficient journalists in Britain. You know, three years ago he tried following me for about two days.
Abraham: Who's this, this one?
Pell: Yeah, this guy. Complete prat. He's worked for about four different newspapers in the past.
Watts: I think you've confused me for somebody else. [I had not previously 'followed him'.]
Pell: Well no, I don't think I have.
Abraham: Wasn't he the 'human rights' one? [Unintelligible discussion between Pell and Abraham.]
Pell: Why don't you speak to Yvonne Ridley, your girlfriend? Yvonne Ridley will help you. And if invade my privacy darling, I'll

use the human rights act against you. [I was bemused by my *Sunday Express* colleague being referred to as my 'girlfriend', although that caused some amusement back at the office.]

[Unintelligible discussion between Pell and Abraham.]

Pell: And considering this guy is too stupid even to know what the human rights act is.

Watts: Benji, have you sold this list to anybody?

Pell: Oh really. Wow.

Watts: Have you sold it to anybody?"

Pell [to Abraham]: He won't get a single answer out of me, which means he can't write the story. But he'll still write a story. Don't forget the *Mail on Sunday* managed to put me on the front page – three times when I didn't even give them a comment, so. When you want to learn how to do journalism properly, why don't you read my book in three years' time, okay. 'Til then, piss off. [The reference to a book must have been the one that McVicar was planning to write.]

Watts: Did you–

Pell: If you've got any photographers outside my house, I'll get the police to remove them. I can assure you.

Pell had clearly not realised that the photographer had already taken several pictures of him outside the synagogue. Nor did he appreciate the irony of Benji the Binman, who made his living and his name trawling rubbish for confidential documents, seeing a photographer outside his house as an invasion of his privacy. And, despite my continuing to press him on what he had done with the Paras' names, he carried on treating it as a joke.

Watts: Well the thing is, Benji, you say you know nothing about it, but I've seen the film in which you say all this.

Pell: [Unintelligible mumbles to Abraham.]

Watts: You know the film we're talking about.

Pell: [Unintelligible mumbles to Abraham.]

Watts: It's your friend Iain Jones and John Mappin. I think you're suing one or other of them, or both of them.

Pell [to Abraham]: You're right. It's sad though, I mean to think that, the way people have to make a living, and they really don't know what they're doing. I know, you're right.

Watts: So, do you think the way you make your living is a good one? Stealing rubbish? What about the human rights of the people you steal from? What about their human rights? Don't they have human rights too?

Pell: [Speaking to Abraham] Isn't it sad, it's a sad profession, isn't it? ... Mark Watts has worked for about four newspapers in the past, one of the most inefficient journalists in Britain, not as stupid as Yvonne Ridley of course, who used to be a colleague of his. Speak to Yvonne Ridley, Watts, okay. She'll tell you everything. Unless she's been captured again by the Taliban [laughs with Abraham].
Watts: Well, I'm giving you your opportunity to say something about this list, about the 'Bloody Sunday' inquiry documents. Of course we're going to write a piece about it, you don't have to say anything if you don't want to, but-
Pell: Anything you do will be given in evidence against you [laughs with Abraham]. He can't even speak English properly... Watts you're pathetic.
Watts: It was very nice to meet you.
Pell: Fuck off.

And with that, after an exchange lasting just under seven minutes, Pell walked off with Abraham. Pell, it turned out, was not going home, but to a friend's house for lunch. This showed that we were right to talk to Pell when he came out of the synagogue rather than risking an attempt to approach him at his home later. I had given Pell every opportunity to respond to the key points, and it was obvious that he was never going to give a meaningful response to any allegation. I also made it absolutely clear to him that he should not think that refusing to make a meaningful response would prevent us from running an article.

I returned along the road to chat to the photographer and check that he had been able to take some pictures. He showed me on his digital camera that he had taken some pictures of Pell. I filed the essence of Pell's response, nonsensical as it was, and returned to the office.

Jones, who had flown from the States to London with Bennett to film more footage for their documentary, called me that afternoon. In a bizarre coincidence, he told me that they were outside Pell's house and they were doorstepping him. While Pell had been doorstepped on other stories in the past, he managed the distinction of being doorstepped separately twice in one day. Jones explained that he was with Bennett and that Pell was hiding in his home and was refusing to speak to him. I told Jones that it was a remarkable coincidence because I had doorstepped Pell only that morning. Jones had not been aware of that and said that he would have liked to come along to film it. However, as I told him, I would not have wanted that; I did not want to do anything that would turn the approach into a 'circus'.

In the office, Jim, the news editor, called out to me. He wanted to alter the copy, in particular, the beginning of the article. I objected to some of his changes, especially those at the beginning of the article. He said that he wanted to make the article punchier, saying that I was 'too broadsheet'. Some of Jim's changes did make the article easier to understand. But some caused the newspaper trouble. One problem with Jim's alterations was that the article no longer raised the possibility that terrorists might have exploited the security breach themselves, and this was a crucial point to make.

As the article went through the editing process, crucial quotes were cut. These included Pell's comment on the 'Bloody Sunday' tape that he was too scared to sell the names to a newspaper, Jones's explanation as to why the names were not shown in the documentary, a direct quote from the MoD spokesman, a quote from Clarke, and even a quote from Pell. A potentially misleading headline was added, causing the newspaper even more trouble. The first I saw of the final form of the article was when I bought a copy of the newspaper the following day[i]. I was horrified by the headline, although I was relieved to see that, while important elements had been cut, the final article still stated that there was no evidence that Pell had attempted to supply any documents to terrorists.

Some insight into Pell's reaction that day was given by his barrister friend, Richard Murray. He said[ii]:

> I was woken by Pell telephoning me. He had seen the Sunday Express article, and was already so upset that I began to have serious concern for his health. I could hear that he was hysterical and in tears, and his attempts to explain what it said were interspersed with shouted conversations with his parents in the background. He was terrified that he would receive visits from the IRA, the police, the secret services, and the rest of Fleet Street. He was urgently thinking about where he could most safely go into hiding. It was clear that the Pell household was in utter pandemonium.

Another friend of Pell's, cabbie Tahir Shafi, said that they spoke on the telephone the evening before the publication of the first article[iii]: 'As soon as he started talking, I knew that he was very upset as he was screaming down the 'phone at me much more than normal.'

And Pell's mother, Rita, said[iv]: 'Since the two *Sunday Express* articles appeared, he has been a different person. He has been depressed and difficult to live with.'

On the day after publication, a confidential source made urgent efforts to contact me at the office. I did not, in general, work at the office on Mondays, and I had several calls from a *Daily Express* colleague relaying increasingly desperate messages from this confidential source. The source wanted to speak to me immediately about the 'Bloody Sunday' article. I met this and other confidential sources, and they told me that the Security Service, MI5, together with the Metropolitan Police Special Branch, had launched an 'urgent' investigation into matters raised by the article. This was an incredible development because it is very rare for a newspaper article to trigger an MI5 investigation.

Of course, for Pell, it was not the first time that he had attracted MI5's attention. The sources identified the surname of the principal MI5 investigating officer, although I do not know whether the name was real or, as is more likely, a 'cover' name, and gave me a telephone number where messages could be relayed to that officer. I was told that the MI5 investigating officer was working on the investigation with two Special Branch officers. I was able to verify my sources' information. This was obviously going to make a good follow-up to the original expose. They said that the MI5 investigation was separate to the MoD investigation, which was making slow progress. They said that MI5 was responsible for security in general and considered that it was responsible, in particular, for the security of the soldiers who were due to give evidence to the inquiry. They said that MI5 wanted to find out, as a matter of great urgency, whether any Irish terrorists – in particular dissident groups such as the Real IRA – had any details about the identities of any of the 'Bloody Sunday' soldiers. In particular, they said that MI5 wanted to find out whether Pell had the names of 'Bloody Sunday' soldiers and, if so, what he had done with them.

I took the view that, while I could not do anything that would help identify a confidential source, I was happy to provide assistance with information that was now in the public domain. I said that my article was essentially based on a video-tape of footage of Pell. While it was clear from the tape that he had obtained confidential inquiry documents and that he claimed to have the soldiers' names, no names were shown. The confidential sources said that the MI5 investigating officer wanted a copy of this tape and to meet the documentary's producer. I promised to try to help.

I told Jones, who was still in London at that time, about the MI5-Special Branch investigation and asked whether he was willing to meet the investigating officers. He said that he would help with the investigation, and I understand that he met them and did co-operate. Jones and Bennett kept me informed about developments in the investigation, and their role in it, so far as they were aware.

At a later meeting, the confidential sources who had told me about the MI5-Special Branch investigation updated me on its progress. They said that the MI5 investigating officer had discovered that *Sunday Life* had published an article in January – before mine – about the leak of a list naming former Paras set to give evidence to the 'Bloody Sunday' inquiry that had been found in rubbish by Pell[v]. The article, which cited the 'Thank You for the Rubbish' documentary, covered similar ground to mine. However, I had not been aware of it.

The confidential sources said that the investigating officers were gathering as much information as possible before they decided whether to approach Pell. I learnt that the investigating officers had formed the same judgement as me, namely that it appeared Pell had obtained the names of soldiers. I also learnt that they had discussed at some length whether the Metropolitan Police should arrest Pell and raid addresses where he keeps documents. However, they were mindful that Pell had previously been convicted of taking rubbish, but had only been given a small fine. The investigating officers had concluded that the security issue was far more serious than the 'technical' issue of whether taking Pell's tàking rubbish was a crime. The focus of the investigation was in establishing whether soldiers' names had leaked and, if so, who had them. I learnt that their concern was not only to find out whether the material was in the hands of terrorists but also, if it was not, whether it could reach them in the future. In particular, I was told that they were concerned about how secure the documents were at this time.

Back at the office, I told Townsend about the developments and he agreed that we should run a follow-up, which also gave us an opportunity to include points that had been cut from the first article. Meanwhile, we had no reaction from Pell following the first article.

The second article reported the fact that MI5 had launched an investigation after the previous week's revelations. In repeating the previous week's disclosures, I wrote it as I had originally expressed it in my version of the first article rather than the clumsy form that Jim had written.

Reporters writing potentially contentious articles usually stick to the formulations that their newspapers have already published if there has been no complaint because they regard this as the 'safest' option. This is partly because the published article has already been passed by the newspaper's lawyer. However, I did not think that Jim's version was the safest option and much preferred my formulation to the one that was published, and so I stuck to my words. I repeated that we were making no suggestion that Pell had tried to supply terrorists with any documents. The changes made to the second article during the editing process were much more sensible than those made to the first, including the headline[vi].

Donaldson put down a written Parliamentary question, as he had told me he would. This is his question and the answer he had from Adam Ingram (defence minister responsible for the armed forces)[vii]:

Donaldson: To ask the secretary of state for defence when he expects to receive a report on the circumstances leading to the loss of confidential information regarding the identity of the soldiers who are due to give evidence to the Saville inquiry; what steps have been taken to (a) recover the lost documents and (b) offer protection to the soldiers and their families; and if he will make a statement.

Ingram: Inquiries by the police have revealed that a number of documents relating to the 'Bloody Sunday' inquiry were left outside barristers' chambers in London. There is no indication that any of these documents contained information regarding the identity of the soldiers, nor anything else that would affect the safety of them or their families. The police inquiries continue, and I am being kept apprised of their progress.

The issue was later taken up by Quentin Davies, the backbench Conservative MP. These are his two questions and answers[viii]:

Davies: To ask the secretary of state for defence what information he has received on instances of information on the identities of British soldiers or former soldiers who may be called upon to testify to the Saville inquiry falling into unauthorised hands; and if he will make a statement.

Ingram: I understand that the names of 76 soldiers (some of whom are deceased) have been disclosed inadvertently by the 'Bloody Sunday' inquiry, mainly in historical documents passed by the inquiry to the interested parties. Two names have been disclosed inadvertently by the team of lawyers representing the majority of soldiers. The name of one soldier has been compromised as a result of a security breach in the Treasury Solicitor's department; this is the subject of a continuing investigation.

Many soldiers' names have become publicly associated with 'Bloody Sunday'. Senior officers were not granted anonymity in 1972, while other soldiers have made statements or given interviews in which they name themselves or colleagues.

The soldiers whose names have been compromised have been, or will be, provided with security advice and additional protective measures where appropriate.

Davies: To ask the secretary of state for defence whether he has recently reviewed the security arrangements for the handling of information relating to British soldiers and former soldiers by Treasury counsel and others concerned with the Saville inquiry; and if he will make a statement.

Ingram: Security arrangements in Government departments, and for those acting on their behalf, are reviewed regularly.

The 'Bloody Sunday' inquiry is independent of government and its security arrangements are a matter for the inquiry itself. My understanding is that, in safeguarding sensitive or personal information, the inquiry aims to follow normal public-sector procedures and standards. [The disclosures triggered a lot of Press coverage[ix.]]

Jones subsequently told me that he provided much of the footage he had taken of Pell to Special Branch for its investigation, along with copies of audio tapes of telephone conversations recorded by Pell.

Two months after the publication of my articles, Bennett sent an email saying: 'We continue to help with the Special Branch investigation despite threats not to.' However, despite the 'Bloody Sunday' tape that I had supplied and the tapes Jones had supplied, the MI5-Special Branch investigation was subsequently dropped.

Around a year after Ingram's answers, Sandra Woodley, a solicitor at the Metropolitan police directorate of legal services, told me: 'There was an investigation, and it didn't get to the stage of Mr Pell being interviewed. It was looked into and, on the advice of the CPS, the matter was not proceeded with any further.'

The Home Office, in line with its usual policy, could 'neither confirm nor deny the involvement of the Security Service in any investigations or comment on their activities'.

And there was no sign of any further action by the MoD.

All this suggested that the British authorities recognised that, as I had revealed in the *Sunday Express* in February 2002, dissident Irish terrorists almost certainly knew the identities of 'Bloody Sunday' soldiers. Their knowledge of these identities probably resulted from several instances of lax security that pre-dated Pell's obtaining confidential 'Bloody Sunday' inquiry documents. As I had made clear in my *Sunday Express* articles, there was no evidence that Pell had supplied material to terrorists, but his obtaining confidential inquiry documents starkly illustrated the shortcomings in the security surrounding the soldiers. And the only useful action the British authorities felt they could take was to alert those soldiers whose lives, and whose families' lives, had been put in increased danger as a result of such shortcomings.

References

i Mark Watts, 'This grubby snooper found the names of "Bloody Sunday" Paras in a lawyer's dustbin…' [potentially misleading second clause of headline not repeated here] *Sunday Express* (17.02.02).

ii Richard Murray witness statement, Benjamin Pell -v- Express Newspapers and Mark Watts (22.04.03).

iii Tahir Shafi witness statement, Benjamin Pell -v- Express Newspapers and Mark Watts (25.04.03).

iv Rita Pell witness statement, Benjamin Pell -v- Express Newspapers and Mark Watts (25.04.03).

v Sinead McCavana, 'Sunday Para files discovered in bin,' *Sunday Life* (20.01.02).

vi Mark Watts, 'Dustbin snooper with the names of "Bloody Sunday" Paras is facing MI5 probe,' *Sunday Express* (24.02.02).

vii Written questions, 'Saville inquiry,' *Hansard* col 33W (04.03.02).

viii Written questions, 'Saville inquiry,' *Hansard* col 709W (15.04.02).

ix See, for example: Matthew Hickley, 'Blunder over "Bloody Sunday" soldiers,' *Daily Mail*; Andrew Sparrow, '"Bloody Sunday" soldiers named,' *The Daily Telegraph*; '76 named in blunder,' *Daily Express* (all 16.04.02).

Chapter 16

Getting Away with It: perjury in the High Court

Pell finally broke his silence over the *Sunday Express* articles about the 'Bloody Sunday' inquiry security breach. Having made no reaction to the first article, Pell instructed a solicitor, David Price, to write a letter of complaint after the publication of the second. Pell began as he meant to carry on: he was disingenuous in the extreme. Price wrote to Townsend, the newspaper's editor, complaining that both articles were defamatory and that his client had never been filmed saying he had a list identifying the names of the British paratroopers. At this point, I showed the 'Bloody Sunday' tape[ii] to Justin Walford, the chief legal advisor at Express Newspapers, who pointed out that the leaked document about the apparent conflict of interests of Elton John's solicitors that had landed the *Daily Express* in legal trouble had emanated from the same chambers as the 'Bloody Sunday' papers. It was clear to us that Pell had failed to tell his solicitor the whole truth – and not the first time. This only became clear to Pell's solicitors when a *Sunday Express* lawyer played the 'Bloody Sunday' tape to one of them. Pell later claimed to have 'forgotten' making those comments that were captured on the 'Bloody Sunday' tape. He changed the story he had given in his complaint, saying that his comments on the 'Bloody Sunday' tape were untrue, and that it was a show reel to stimulate fictional story-lines. He claimed the tape was 'part fact and part fiction'.

Pell's claims to have been developing story-lines' in the 'Bloody Sunday' tape are as risible as his claim to be a journalist. Pell never mentioned this claim to me during my conversation with him on the day before publication of the first article. Nor did anyone familiar with the footage make any such suggestion to me. The 'Bloody Sunday' tape appeared to me to be akin to the Channel 4 documentary[iii] on Mr Pell, although covering some different matters: it showed Pell at work and talking about his activities. Of course, he ran his old 'developing story-lines' defence. I first became aware of this nonsense in March 2002 during his action against Mappin. At the trial, Pell was asked by Mappin's barrister about the accuracy of a transcript of the 3½-hour rushes tape[iv], which comprised footage shot by Jones. Pell replied[v]: 'Well, my Lord, it is an accurate transcript, but one has to remember, this was not a documentary being shot. I was developing story-lines, so what I say doesn't have to be accurate or factual. I never intended it to be seen by a court, by a newspaper, by the Ministry of Defence, by anyone....We were developing story-lines. I don't know whether you've ever worked on a set, Mr Wolanski, but that is the way people work.' Wolanski then put to him that he'd been telling lies to Jones.

'They aren't lies, Mr Wolanski. Are you telling me when you go to the Old Vic that an actor is lying?'

Pell was not asked in the trial about his comments on the 'Bloody Sunday' tape but during the "discovery" process in his subsequent litigation against the *Sunday Express*, when parties must disclose to each other copies of relevant documents under their control, Pell failed to produce the leaked inquiry documents, even those that can be seen on the tape. We specifically asked for copies of them, but Pell still failed to produce them. By his own admission, Pell had not searched for documents pre-dating July 1999 or those located anywhere other than his home. Through his solicitors, he said that he only searched for documents dating from July 1999 because that was when Jones starting filming him. He also claimed: 'The only place that our client keeps documents is at his home address.' When questioned about this, he claimed that he had disclosed any disclosable document 'previously at another location'. Pell was insisting that the inquiry documents he had taken did not include the 'Bloody Sunday' soldiers' names. When pressed for these documents, he claimed that they were not relevant papers that should be disclosed. When pressed again, he claimed that he could not find them. Therefore, it is impossible to know for certain whether Pell did obtain soldiers' names as he says on the tape.

In the only reference in the McVicar tapes to 'Bloody Sunday' is in respect of Michael Mansfield whom he was targeting over another matter[vii]: 'He's also working at the moment on the "Bloody Sunday" inquiry. So, I've been doing Michael Mansfield for the last six weeks or so... I'm getting stuff about Mansfield; I'm getting letters about Mansfield; I'm getting letters to Mansfield; I'm getting his itinerary.' He later says that he found some documents from Mansfield's rubbish about a colleague who was contesting a charge of running a red traffic light and about a former employee of the Labour party bringing a disability discrimination case against the employer, although there is no evidence that he succeeded in obtaining 'Bloody Sunday' material from that source.

Price claimed on behalf of Pell, in his complaint to the *Sunday Express*, that the newspaper had obtained the 'Bloody Sunday' tape from Mappin and Jones. During the discovery process, Pell asked us to disclose the source of, first, the tape and, second, of the information that I received about the MI5-Special Branch investigation. We pointed out that these were confidential sources, and we could therefore not identify them.

Price also said in his complaint that his client was working on several television projects, which, he suggested, we had damaged because commissioning editors at the BBC and Channel 4 had sought urgent assurances about the articles. This was later contradicted by the relevant people at the BBC and Channel 4. Pell was unable to produce any documents confirming that he had any such commissions.

In addition, Price told the *Sunday Express* that Pell had been excluded from his synagogue as a result of the articles. Pell later claimed in a witness statement that he had prayed at this synagogue daily for the previous nine years[viii]. Pell had seemingly forgotten that he had previously been suspended for two weeks after threatening a little girl there with a knife[ix]. Filmed at the synagogue, Pell admits this on the 3½-hour rushes tape...

> There's a family I enjoy terrorising here, the Abraham family. Every time the children see me, they start crying. A few months ago, I brought this huge knife with me, and so this girl, one of the three children comes out here, I thought this time it'd be the coup de grâce,

literally. So as she came out, I said: 'Aaagh.' And she screamed, you could have heard her screaming from here to Hollywood.

Anyway, so, she goes back running into the synagogue, she brings her father out, and her father says, 'Did you threaten to knife my daughter?'

I said: 'Are you crazy? I mean, I wouldn't do something like that.' Anyway, I hide the knife in the synagogue; about half an hour later somebody finds it and takes it straight up to the Rabbi.

And the Rabbi immediately throws me out, and says- gives me a message via someone that, 'I don't think young Mr Pell is in a sane position to come back here for a few days. Can you find out what's wrong with him.'

Anyway, everyone else who's heard this story, I was trying to defend myself, I said, 'I mean this is ridiculous. Do you really think I was going to kill this girl?'

And so the person who runs the place, Benny Guy... said to the Rabbi: 'If that madman is mad enough to bring a knife, he'd be mad enough to use it.'

And I can't understand it, all I know is that every time I come into the building, I have to be physically now removed because they start crying otherwise.

Lovely to have power over people."

After this was pointed out to his solicitor, Pell invoked his 'developing story-lines' defence. It seems that 'the knife was made of plastic'. We approached Rabbi Abraham David of the Od Yosef Hai Synagogue for an account of the reasons for Pell's exclusion and whether he had been previously excluded. He declined, so our lawyers served him with a witness summons, meaning he would have to attend the trial to testify.

In addition, we asked Pell to produce documentation confirming the ban and the reasons for it. His lawyers told us there was no such material. However, an article in the *Jewish Chronicle* later suggested otherwise[xi]. It quoted Rabbi David as saying: 'We wrote him a letter asking to find somewhere else.' His lawyers still insisted that there was no such letter, saying that Pell was mystified by the quote.

Despite the misleading nature of Pell's complaint to the *Sunday Express*, Townsend recognised that the headline for the first article gave a potentially misleading impression, one that contradicted what

I had written. As a result, the *Sunday Express* offered to pay Pell £5,000 and his legal costs to settle his complaint. However, the newspaper's lawyers had problems eliciting any proper response from Pell. A confidential source suggested that Pell and Price had fallen out. I believed that Pell's misleading instructions would cause tension between any solicitor and client. Pell was said to have written an 'impenetrable' note to Price, and the solicitor was trying to work out whether he was still acting for him.

According to McVicar, Price once told him that Pell 'plays dirty' in litigation. I subsequently learnt from a confidential source that Price recommended to Pell that he should accept the £5,000 as a reasonable sum to settle his complaint. Price's advice was that a jury was unlikely to award him a higher figure because he had such an appalling reputation. Pell was angered by Price's advice and it led to a rift between them.

The difficulties the *Sunday Express* had in eliciting answers from Pell unnerved the newspaper at a time when I believe it should have shown resolve. The newspaper was trying to settle the complaint before proceedings were issued for a defamation action in the High Court, and with good reason.

The libel laws in the UK have long, in effect, prevented the country from enjoying a truly free Press. In the past, this was the result of ridiculously high libel awards that looked especially perverse when compared with levels of compensation that people typically win for serious physical injuries such as losing limbs or an eye. This phase was, ironically enough, heralded in 1987 by the award of £500,000 to Jeffrey Archer against the *Daily Star*, another Express Newspapers title. In recent years, such high libel awards have been much more rare. The courts seem to regard £200,000 as the maximum libel award for the most serious possible case, as illustrated by the two nursery nurses who were falsely accused of child abuse at work in a Newcastle city council inquiry report, the contents of which were subsequently splashed across the newspapers. I know of no example of defamation that is worse than this case, and a harrowing account of it in *The Guardian* is particularly worth reading[xiii], and in 2002 each was awarded £200,000. That is quite some contrast with Archer. However, the sting of a defamation action against a newspaper is increasingly not so much the damages awarded, as the legal costs to which it is exposed. The losing side is liable for all the legal costs, which have spiralled over the past few years and will typically top £1m for a case that goes to trial. Dan Tench, a media partner at the solicitors' firm, Olswang, set out the problem in the media section of *The Guardian*[xiv]:

> The swingeing costs awards now arising are forcing newspapers to think carefully about defending any libel action. There is a strong imperative now to settle actions early, not only paying the claimant damages but also undertaking not to repeat the words complained of. In time, important investigative journalism may be silenced by the threat of spiralling costs. After rolling back the size of damages awards in libel actions by arguing that enormous costs had a chilling effect on the freedom of the Press, the media now face more than losing all the ground gained. But this time, it is the lawyers and not the defamed parties who stand to gain.

Worse still, in practice, a newspaper that wins a libel case may find it impossible to recover its own legal costs from the claimant. So even a winning newspaper could easily be left with a costs bill of half a million pounds. For example, Associated Newspapers found itself in exactly this position in 2003 after winning a libel case brought against two of its newspapers, the *Daily Mail* and the *Evening Standard*, by two soldiers, Sarah Pedder, a former Army captain, and Sergeant Al Dummer[xv]. The newspapers reported in February 2002 that the pair had an affair while on active duty in Oman. The two were ordered to pay Associated's costs, but announced that they could not pay and would go bankrupt instead. Associated had known that the pair would probably not pay its costs if it won because their lawyer was working on a contingency-fee arrangement (better known as 'no-win, no-fee basis'), which has made it possible for non-wealthy people to bring libel actions. Associated's legal director, Harvey Kass, was quoted by *Press Gazette*, the magazine that covers the newspaper industry, as saying:

> We took a decision not to bow to the pressure newspapers often feel when faced by claimants operating on no-win, no-fee.
>
> We fought this case because we believed in our articles. We are often faced with claimants and their lawyers who think that their inability

to pay court costs if they lose will deter us from fighting.

Associated is known in the newspaper industry for investing in its journalism, and this includes taking such a principled – and correct – stand over defending libel actions. The same cannot be said for Express Newspapers, despite the reputation of its parent company, Northern & Shell, publishers of *OK* and an array of porn magazines, for a tough approach to litigation. In its nervous attempt to avoid a libel action, Express Newspapers, which doubted whether it would recover costs from Pell even if it successfully defended his prospective claim, doubled its offer to him – to £10,000 plus his costs. It paid the £10,000 into court, without making any admission of liability. Richards Butler, the solicitors' firm acting for Express Newspapers and its employees, including Townsend and me, (and itself a former target of Pell's bin raids) also made an offer of amends, a then relatively untried procedure introduced in the Defamation Act of 1996.

By making a formal offer of amends, a newspaper admits it published defamatory material about the complainant and offers to publish a 'suitable correction' and 'sufficient apology', and possibly to pay compensation, to be agreed by the two sides. If there is no agreement, any level of compensation is determined by the court, taking into account any correction or apology published. If the offer is rejected, then it becomes a complete defence provided the newspaper or its journalists did not publish the defamatory material knowing it to be false. A defamatory statement is not, of course, necessarily false (think of all those defamatory statements that Fayed made on television about Hamilton, but the jury found that they were justified: see chapter 1), but a newspaper that relies on an offer-of-amends defence at trial cannot defend itself in any other way, including proving its defamatory statements were true.

Given the difficulties the *Sunday Express* faced with the headline that it published for the first article, I agreed that making an offer of amends was a sensible approach having been assured that we were merely admitting to having published defamatory – but not false – material. I felt, by contrast, that making separate offers of payment was unnecessary although newspapers are under enormous commercial pressure to do so. If a newspaper loses a libel action, but the jury awards damages that are lower than any payment offer it had made to the claimant, then the claimant is liable for the costs of both sides since the date of the offer. This will inevitably mean that the claimant loses financially, while the newspaper's losses can be massively reduced. (The real winners in this scenario, as with just about every legal scenario, are the lawyers.)

If a newspaper loses a libel action and had made no payment offer, or one that is lower than the damages awarded, then it is liable for the costs of both sides. A newspaper therefore considers what damages might be awarded by a jury if it loses a libel action, and often offers a figure comfortably above that level. In this case, the *Sunday Express* initially offered £5,000, but then upped it to £10,000. We eventually retained Geoffrey Shaw QC, whose advice to us throughout the course of the action was consistent: a jury would be unlikely to award more than £10,000 to 'a man of Pell's ilk' even if we lost. This was courageous advice because if a jury awarded more than £10,000, his assessment would have proved a costly misjudgement. Barristers in this kind of situation are under pressure to urge a newspaper to make an overly high offer safe in the knowledge that if it is accepted no one will ever know for certain whether they had misjudged the case because a jury will never decide on the award; and if it is rejected and the offer proves far higher than the damages awarded, it is a mistake with no costly consequence for the newspaper.

Pell rejected both the offer of £10,000 and the 'offer of amends'. He claimed to have had an opinion from Geoffrey Robertson QC, a leading media barrister, to say that £75,000 was the appropriate level of compensation, which was greeted with derision at the *Express*. In time, however, the ever-nervous *Express* would offer even more.

Pell told McVicar that he actually targeted Doughty Street chambers[xvi]... where one Geoffrey Robertson QC works.

Meanwhile, Pell falsely claimed that, despite quoting Jeffrey Donaldson in my first article, I had never spoken to him about the subject. Fortunately, I had taped my telephone conversation with him. My recordings proved crucial later when the Ministry of Defence press office initially claimed that no one there had spoken to me about the Bloody Sunday inquiry security breach. I could prove otherwise with my tape recording of the conversation, illustrating the vital importance of journalists' taping such exchanges. Pell also falsely claimed that I had 'ambushed' him outside his synagogue with Jones and Mappin, a lie he repeated in a witness statement[xvii]. Pell pursued his theory that Mappin was the source of the tape for the *Sunday Express*. Pell threatened to sue Mappin on the grounds that he was the source of the articles. In reply, Mappin's solicitor told Price: 'Our client is not the source of the two articles.'

Pell gave an interview at his home to the *Sunday Telegraph*, which reported[xviii], 'One room has been given over to his current fixation: a libel action against a Sunday newspaper... Papers are strewn in piles around the floor, and a desk is laden with computer equipment.'

Price ceased to act for Pell. Pell's new solicitor who had already acted for him against Mappin, told the *Sunday Express* that his client wanted additional damages because the articles had been followed up in, at least, one newspaper in Northern Ireland[xix], the *Aldershot News and Mail* (which covers the area where the Paras are based)[xx], and on Google's website, and indicated that he was prepared to issue proceedings and to seek aggravated, or exemplary damages, or both.

By June, Pell had instructed another firm of solicitors to act for him. This time, it was because his solicitor had moved firms. Having won his case against Mappin, Pell recovered £77,500 plus costs and he was preparing to use it to sue again: this time over the *Sunday Express* articles. Before issuing proceedings, Pell's solicitor raised additional complaints on behalf of his client.

In particular, Pell falsely claimed that I had said to him in front of a large number of fellow congregants: 'I have information that you have obtained a secret list of the names of soldiers in the "Bloody Sunday" inquiry and you have passed them onto the IRA.' I neither never said these words nor was the substantive part of our conversation in front of a large number of fellow congregants. Indeed, I have already set out a meticulously accurate transcript of this *taped* conversation (see pp224-227) .

When we asked for more detail, via his solicitor Pell elaborated further fictitious exchanges and even claimed that I had been accompanied by Jones and Mappin. At this stage, he did not know that I taped the conversation. When he told him that he had been taped, he claimed that his memory, which is renowned for being especially retentive, was faulty and that, for example, he remembered 'go away' when he said 'Fuck off.'

Nonetheless, proceedings were issued in July against Express Newspapers and me. He sued for libel in the two articles and slander spoken by me outside his synagogue. In his particulars of claim, which sets out his case, Pell began[xxi]: 'The Claimant currently works in the media as a writer and television presenter. In the past, he was well known as a supplier to national newspapers of documents about celebrities obtained from outside the offices of their legal or other professional advisers. He had ceased obtaining and supplying such material by February 2001.' Evidence would emerge, however, that he had not stopped raiding the bins.

In any event, this was a claim that Pell often made, but the timing of when he 'ceased' such activities varied. After launching his libel action, he told one interviewer that he 'decided to retire' when Brian Dowling, the Big Brother winner, signed up to one of the biggest celebrity agencies[xxii]. However, that was later than February 2001, as Dowling did not win Big Brother until July 2001. When Pell was arrested by police in connection with taking Hamilton's legal documents, he told them that he had not been taking rubbish since his conviction for the theft. Speaking in December 2000 to McVicar about his statement to police, Pell said[xxiii]: 'I said, "The stuff you got out of the garage, I would like to explain to you that that stuff all comes from last year before I was convicted for theft. Now that I realise, of course, that it's an offence to go through rubbish, I no longer take rubbish."' He was convicted on November 22nd, 1999, well before his claim in the libel action to have ceased raiding the bins in February 2001.

Pell also had a track record of avoiding admitting to his bin-raiding activities. When John Reid, Elton John's manager, took legal action against him, Pell claimed that he was a freelance journalist and played down his bin-raiding activities. He did so in order to claim falsely that he had a confidential source, whom he should be allowed to protect.

He gave yet another reason for his supposed retirement to another interviewer just before launching his libel action, saying that he stopped raiding bins in February 2001 when he went to the chambers of Michael Mansfield, hoping to find documents relating to the defence of Barry George who was later convicted of Jill Dando's murder. The interviewer reported[xxiv]: 'Mansfield, though, had been forewarned and the rubbish bags removed. Aware that his targets were wise to his game, Pell decided to quit at the top, as it were, of his profession.'

Pell claimed in his pleadings that he was entitled to aggravated damages (which are awarded because of factors that increase the damage caused to the claimant) for several reasons[xxv], including that the defamatory material had left him with 'a wholly undeserved fear of reprisal, including the possibility of assassination'. Pell, as we know, often claims to be fearful of being killed for one reason or another.

He continued in his particulars of claim by making a series of false assertions, many of which he knew to be lies. For example, he said: 'The claimant also had to deal with the concerns over the articles of those had had commissioned projects from the BBC and Channel 4 and Channel 5 and publishers Methuen involving the Claimant. All of these entirely foreseeable consequences ensued.'

Pell claimed that when I spoke to him I was accompanied by Jones and Mappin, and that I had 'shouted hostile questions' despite his 'making it clear that he wished the second defendant to leave him alone and complaining to the second defendant that he was disturbing him on his day of rest,' although he later changed his story to claim that other congregants complained that I was disturbing on his day or rest (in fact, nothing of the sort can be heard on the tape from anyone). He complained that I 'caused him to be photographed as he left the synagogue', adding: 'As the second defendant ought to have checked (if he did not know already), it is against the Orthodox Jewish religion to be photographed on the Sabbath.'

We took advice from Jewish friends about this, but no one to whom we spoke had heard of such a restriction. Pell further falsely alleged that I never spoke to Donaldson about the issue, that Donaldson never said that he would raise questions about the issue in Parliament, and that I relied on quotes from him supplied by Kevin

Cahill, the freelance journalist, who had acted 'on the instructions of Mappin'. I had spoken to Donaldson, and I had quoted what he had said to me; Cahill had also spoken to Donaldson about the issue, not on the instructions of Mappin, or of anyone else, but because of a genuine concern on his part about the security breach; and Donaldson did raise a question in Parliament. And, Pell claimed, I did not ask Christopher Clarke, the head of Brick Court chambers, whether the names could have been taken from outside his chambers. Of course, I had done exactly that. Pell told several untruths and outright lies in his particulars of claim, which amounts to committing perjury. There were to be more examples of Pell's perjury. And as this book has documented, Pell has a long history of lying on oath.

Pell also said in his particulars of claim: 'The Claimant had never obtained a list of the names of the "Bloody Sunday" paratroopers let alone passed them on to any terrorists.' In fact, in both articles, I wrote: 'There is no suggestion that Pell sought to supply them [terrorists] with any documents,' and this point survived the editing process and appeared in the published versions.

And, in something of a change from his initial position, Pell said in his claim: 'It is accepted that the Claimant did give the impression that he had a list of some of the paratroopers' names in a film shot by Mr Jones.'

Although Pell sought aggravated damages, he had evidently dropped the idea of seeking exemplary damages (which are awarded specifically to punish defendants).

In answer to a request from us, Pell named the two projects that he claimed had been commissioned by the BBC over which concerns about the *Sunday Express* articles were raised: *The Pellicam Brief* and *Liquid Assets*. He said that Celia Taylor had commissioned the former, and Sarah Hey the latter, and that they had raised their concerns with Victor Lewis-Smith, who was making the programmes.

Taylor, a senior BBC commissioning executive for documentaries, told us that the BBC had commissioned a pilot one-hour documentary, *The Pellican Brief*, in which Pell would give his 'personal view' on everyday topics such as rail travel[xxvi]. However, said Taylor: 'I became aware in about November 2002, that Mr Pell had fallen out with the independent producers of the programme.' She did not know why they had fallen out. She said that she had not seen the two *Sunday Express* articles about the 'Bloody Sunday' inquiry security breach, until they were drawn to her attention for her statement for the libel case. Referring to Pell's claims in the action that she had raised concerns over the articles with Lewis-Smith, she said: 'This is incorrect. I did not at any stage raise any concerns with Victor Lewis-Smith as I was not even aware of the articles... The articles published in the *Sunday Express* in February 2002 had absolutely no impact on the discussions between the BBC and Mr Pell relating to *The Pellican Brief*.'

Hey, a BBC assistant producer, also contradicted Pell's claims[xxvii]. She told us that she helped with the production of one edition of *Liquid Assets*, which is a BBC3 series about the finances of famous people. While researching the edition about Elton John, she read that Pell had been responsible for finding various documents about the singer's spending, and so asked him for an interview. He was duly interviewed for the *Liquid Assets* programme on Elton John[xxviii]. Pell had given the impression in the action that his role in this programme was rather more than simply being one of several interviewees in one programme of the series.

Like Taylor, Hey had not even aware at the time of the articles and, therefore, hadn't raised with Lewis-Smith. She added for good measure: 'I can categorically state that the articles had no impact whatsoever on my dealings with Mr Pell.'

Pell also claimed that he had been in discussion with Max Eilenberg, an editor at the book publishers, Methuen, over the possible publication of his biography, and that he also had concerns over the *Sunday Express* articles. Pell said that he assumed this because, following the articles, Eilenberg cut off all contact with him and did not return his calls.

Eilenberg, the publishing director at Methuen Publishing predictably told a different story[xxix]. He said that Pell approached him in late 2001 to discuss a book about the murder of Jill Dando, the television presenter. Eilenberg recalled that Pell claimed he was either a contributor or co-writer of the book. He said that Pell told him he had initially discussed it with another publisher, but it had withdrawn from publishing the book. The book was in fact written by McVicar and published by Blake[xxx].

Pell also discussed with Eilenberg, in December 2001, his plan for an autobiography. Eilenberg said that he asked Pell to give him some suggestions for the autobiography and some draft sample prose. He continued: 'I did not at any stage give any indication of a firm interest on Methuen's behalf to take on the project. Any encouragement that was given was given only in the most general terms, as I would give encouragement to any aspiring writer. I do not recall receiving further material in respect of the autobiography, for example the outline proposal or the sample prose, subsequent to this conversation.'

He said that Pell subsequently sent him several emails and telephoned the office and left messages for him. 'I cannot recall whether I returned any of these calls.' He also was unaware of the articles. Thus, as with the two BBC producers the articles had no impact on his decision to ignore Pell.

And Pell's claim in the case to have ceased raiding the bins was also undermined. David Barnes, the senior clerk at the barristers' chambers at 1 Atkin Building, which is an extension to 5 Raymond Buildings – one of "Benji the Binman's" favourite targets – told us that at around 6.30pm on January 16th, 2003 he went to his car, which was parked near the rubbish bins for 1 Atkin Building and 5 Raymond Buildings[xxxi].

> I saw a man I firmly believed to be Mr Pell leaning over the bins... They are large, round commercial bins about five feet high and, to see into them, it is necessary to lean over the top and peer in. This is what I saw Mr Pell doing. As I came out of the door of the chambers, it appeared that Mr Pell had heard me, and he almost immediately moved away from the bins. Mr Pell looked directly at me and then walked off. [After being shown a picture of Pell] I can confirm that this is the man I saw looking into the bins outside chambers on 16th January 2003. I believed it to be Mr Pell at the time as I had previously seen a television documentary about Mr Pell. I had recognised him from this. I had also seen photographs of Mr Pell in various newspapers... After I had seen Mr Pell, I went back into chambers and I immediately sent an internal message to all members of chambers warning them of what I had seen.

Pell later claimed he was at home when Barnes said he saw Benji the Binman at work, producing telephone records showing calls made at the relevant time from his mother's telephone number to his solicitor.

Pell also offered an explanation for why he did not answer my questions[xxxii]: 'I did not respond to his questioning as, being an orthodox Jew, my faith does not allow me to discuss matters such as these on the Sabbath.' Not for the first time was Pell seeking to exploit his faith to excuse his conduct. His explanation, however, is contradicted by his comments to McVicar about meeting Hollingsworth, the freelance journalist, for the first time on a Sabbath to discuss new targets for Pell; he was also willing to talk at another time on a Sabbath to a reporter from the *Mail on Sunday* about its planned story on Fayed.

Meanwhile, Pell's solicitor pursued *The News Letter* in Belfast and the *Aldershot News and Mail* seeking apologies for their articles that followed-up the *Sunday Express*. He told the editors of each that Pell would take no further action provided they publish a correction and apology.

Geoff Martin, editor of *The News Letter*, agreed and 'corrected' something its article had never said; the editor of the *Aldershot News and Mail*, James Taylor, showed rather more resolve. He said: 'In both our articles, we were very careful not to suggest that Mr Pell had passed on information to terrorists or profited financially. However, we felt the contention in the *Sunday Express* that names of soldiers involved in the "Bloody Sunday" incident had been left in a dustbin which was publicly accessible was of great public interest and raised serious questions about the security surrounding the whole of the "Bloody Sunday" inquiry.'

He said that this was borne out by comments to his newspaper from the MP for Aldershot, Gerald Howarth. 'The article also referred to other incidents, completely unrelated to Mr Pell, which could have led to the identification of the paratroopers. The second article was about the government admitting security blunders which led to the soldiers' identities being publicly leaked. It naturally referred back to the earlier article when the issue of security was last in the public arena.

'For these reasons, I am not prepared to publish an apology since I believe our articles were justified.'

He offered a right of reply instead. While this was a reasonable offer, Pell declined it. The *Aldershot News and Mail* handled the matter in a manner from which some national newspapers could learn.

References

[i] David Price witness statement, Benjamin Pell -v- Express Newspapers and Mark Watts (23.04.03).

[ii] "'Bloody Sunday' rushes," Moving Perspective (filmed 1999). Transcript is reproduced in chapter 13.

[iii] 'Scandal in the Bins,' Channel 4 (first shown 11.01.01).

[iv] "3½-hour rushes," Moving Perspective (filmed 1999).

[v] Transcript of evidence of Benjamin Pell, Benjamin Pell -v- John Mappin and Story Master Ltd, (11.03.02).

[vi] Transcript of evidence of Benjamin Pell, Benjamin Pell -v- John Mappin and Story Master Ltd, (12.03.02).

[vii] McVicar video tape (filmed 08.02.01) DVOO.

[viii] Benjamin Pell witness statement, Benjamin Pell -v- Express Newspapers and Mark Watts (08.04.03).

[ix] "3½-hour rushes," Moving Perspective (filmed 1999).

[x] McVicar video tape (filmed January 2001) DVRV.

[xi] Nathan Jeffay, '"Binman" collects £125,000 from the *Express*,' *Jewish Chronicle* (11.07.03).

[xii] 'Scandal in the Bins,' Channel 4 (first shown 11.01.01).

[xiii] Bob Woffinden and Richard Webster, 'Cleared,' *The Guardian* (31.07.02).

[xiv] Dan Tench, 'Defame and be damned,' *The Guardian* (19.05.03).

[xv] Dominic Ponsford, 'Associated win soldiers libel case,' *Press Gazette* (01.08.03); '£500,000 bill for soldiers accused of desert affair,' *Daily Mail* (26.07.03).

[xvi] McVicar video tape (filmed 08.02.01) DVOO.

[xvii] Benjamin Pell witness statement, Benjamin Pell -v- Express Newspapers and Mark Watts (08.04.03).

[xviii] David Thomas, 'The binman lifts his lid. For years, he made a living raiding famous people's rubbish bins for confidential documents. But Benjamin Pell, who begins a new career on television this week, is unrepentant: "There's no excuse for not shredding,"' *Sunday Telegraph* (21.04.02).

[xix] Ian Starrett, 'Secret list of names "in dustbin",' *The News Letter* (18.02.02).

[xx] Mark Farnham, 'Paras' names "could be in the hands of the IRA,"' *Aldershot News and Mail* (21.02.02); Mark Farnham, 'Paras' Ids are leaked,' *Aldershot News and Mail* (18.04.02).

[xxi] Particulars of claim, Benjamin Pell -v- Express Newspapers and Mark Watts (18.07.02).

[xxii] '60 second interview: Benjamin "the Binman" Pell,' *The Metro* (30.10.02).

xxiii McVicar audio tape (recorded 30.12.00) MDRI.

xxiv David Thomas, 'The binman lifts his lid. For years, he made a living raiding famous people's rubbish bins for confidential documents. But Benjamin Pell, who begins a new career on television this week, is unrepentant: "There's no excuse for not shredding,"' *Sunday Telegraph* (21.04.02).

xxv Particulars of claim, Benjamin Pell -v- Express Newspapers and Mark Watts (18.07.02).

xxvi Celia Taylor witness statement, Benjamin Pell -v- Express Newspapers and Mark Watts (23.04.03).

xxvii Karen Sarah Hey witness statement, Benjamin Pell -v- Express Newspapers and Mark Watts (23.04.03).

xxviii *Liquid Assets*, BBC3 (first shown 16.02.03).

xxix Max Eilenberg witness statement, Benjamin Pell -v- Express Newspapers and Mark Watts (16.04.03).

xxx John McVicar, 'Why Barry Bulsara Executed Jill Dando,' Artnik (2003).

xxxi David Barnes witness statement, Benjamin Pell -v- Express Newspapers and Mark Watts (08.04.03).

xxxii Benjamin Pell first witness statement, Benjamin Pell -v- Express Newspapers and Mark Watts (28.10.02).

Chapter 17

Sunday Express Crusader's sword turns to jelly

At the *Sunday Express*, we were closing in on Pell as we exposed his lies. And I had a significant break through when I obtained a large volume of video and audio tapes that had been recorded by McVicar. That alarmed Pell enormously. He instructed his solicitor to complain about the fact that I had obtained these further tapes, saying that it would aggravate the damage to his client. No wonder he complained: the McVicar tapes showed Pell confessing to an attempt to pervert the course of justice in one case (chapter 1), committing perjury in another (see chapters 4 to 6), and much else.

But the extent of the panic at the *Sunday Express* to prevent the libel action progressing any further was so great that it was considering defying the advice of our QC and increasing its payment offer from £10,000 to £25,000. I made sure that the owner of Express Newspapers, Richard Desmond, in addition to Townsend and the lawyers, were aware of the gravity of the material that I had gathered about Pell. My view was, and remains, that the evidence I had found was enough to put Pell in jail. Nonetheless, the higher offer was duly made – and rejected.

Pell duly served his main statement for the libel case[i]; he again committed perjury, both repeating lies he had already told in pleadings in the case and telling new ones.

Pell said in his statement: 'I must emphasise that the material I collected was left outside the office buildings and I have never taken documents from inside any office.'

However, in 1999, he told McVicar[ii]:

I'm starting to do the cleaning of a company called Absolutely Productions, who do the Jack Docherty programme on Channel 5. So, I- we get their cleaning contract, which is great because they are a television pr- I'd never done a TV company before. And they had acts on every week and stuff. And from that office, I was getting home addresses, phone numbers of all of these stars. So, at that stage, I had got, I think, a week or two before Christmas the home number of Andy Coulson from The Sun. I remember I went to dinner-Saturday night dinner in, I think, just about Christmas time, I was showing people all of these telephone numbers. 'Look, I've got Ben Elton's home number. I've got Griff Rhys Jones's home number. I've just found it-' you know, wanking off on the fact that I had all of these people's home numbers.

And on another occasion two years later, he says[iii]:

Absolutely Productions was the company I was cleaning; they actually made the Dom Joly programme. But we were doing their cleaning; literally, we were doing their cleaning. Now, they also did… the Jack Docherty programme… on Channel 5… On 11th March, I give Ally Ross a story, which I get- I don't- see normally- of course, all my clients- 99 per cent of my clients were just complete non-entities: who's interested in architects in the Borough or chartered surveyors in Islington? But, of course, I had an internal memo from Jack Docherty from Channel 5, saying your programme is boring, nobody's watching it, you know, we're going to scrap you. And I gave that- and I thought, 'This is nasty of me,' cos there I am doing their cleaning, taking their shilling, but I thought, 'No, this is too good to waste.' So I gave that to Ally Ross, of course not- you know, cos Ally Ross never knew where I was getting my information from, he just thought I was a hacker or something. So, I gave him that. 'Oh, brilliant, we're going to lead on that next Monday.'

In addition, Pell admits on tape to McVicar that he lied by telling the High Court that he took John Reid's rubbish from the pavement, when in fact they were on the premises of his office in a storage space accessible from the pavement.

Pell referred in his statement for his libel case to the fact that he was convicted of the theft of documentary waste from outside the solicitors then acting for Jonathan Aitken, and added: 'That is the only time I have ever been convicted for any criminal offence.' Another lie.

The McVicar tapes contained clues that Pell in fact had another conviction. Pell does not specify what it was in the tapes, but he refers to the fact that he routinely drove in untaxed, uninsured vehicles, which had no MoT certificate, and that he was due in court after the police had caught him. For example, he told McVicar in 1999[iv]: 'About two weeks before, or a week before, I had been in court on a- just on a small driving thing: no insurance, no MoT.' No reference was ever made to it any such conviction in the many articles published about Pell in the national newspapers. However, he did tell one interviewer[v]: 'At the height of my powers, I was driving around in London in an untaxed, uninsured car with three bald tyres and nine points on my licence, so getting in hot water over a few rubbish bags [the Harkavys documents] was the least of my worries.' I decided to search through the local newspapers covering Hendon in north London, where Pell lives, and I found a report about how he had been convicted at Blackfriars crown court for driving without insurance.

To confirm Pell's perjury in claiming only to have one conviction relating to the theft of Aitken's legal documents, we obtained from Blackfriars crown court the certificate of his conviction for driving without insurance[vi]. The certificate shows that Pell was indeed tried and convicted on November 7th, 2000 of 'using insurance document with intent to deceive,' and was fined £450 and ordered to pay £400 costs. Pell was livid that we had obtained this document, and telephoned the court in a furious rant. A court clerk pointed out to him that we were entitled to it.

Pell claimed in his statement to have had nothing to do with articles based on leaks either from 10 Downing Street or about Lord Levy. However, he keeps changing his story about that. His statement continued: 'I have never been interested in political stories as my interest has been almost entirely in the show-business world.' He was presumably not interested in political stories, apart from those about Hamilton and Fayed, Aitken, Cherie Booth, as well as Janet Anderson, Lord Bell, Frank Dobson, Patricia Hewitt, the Hinduja brothers, Nelson Mandela, the Millennium Dome, Pinochet, the PLO, and, of course, the 'Bloody Sunday' inquiry. And while he had found documents relating to show business, he also trawled and sold material about the Football Association, Barry George, the lottery, Royal Ascot, and Sadlers Wells and the Arts Council.

Turning to the footage that included the 'Bloody Sunday' tape, Pell claimed in his statement: 'What Mappin and Jones told me was that Jones would film me, both collecting documents, talking about my life and my dealings with Fleet Street and developing story-lines based on these details. This filming was not to make a documentary, but was solely for Jones's research. There was never any intention that this footage should be shown publicly, although it was the intention that some of the material would be used as a show reel to be shown to Hollywood studios.' Pell's claims that the footage was not intended to be truthful or for a documentary are contradicted by what he tells McVicar.

He produced a witness statement from one friend, saying that Pell never wanted another documentary to be made after the Channel 4 programme. This appeared to support Pell's contention that he would never have agreed to Jones making a documentary about him. But his taped interviews with McVicar show that Pell did want another documentary made.

Pell turned in his statement to my seeking comment from him on the Sabbath before the publication of the first article in the *Sunday Express*. Again he invoked his orthodoxy: 'The Sabbath is the most important day of the week. We do not work, write letters, use the computer or make telephone calls on the Sabbath.'

Pell, in his statement, developed his fictional story-line that Mappin and Jones were present when I doorstepped him. He said: 'Jones was holding what seemed to be a tripod. One of the female congregants told me that she had seen him carry it across the road at one point. "Could it be a gun?" she asked me.' This was fantasy on top of fiction. However, Pell made no further mention of what Mappin and Jones were supposed to have been doing while I questioned him.

The statement contained a series of lies about the events that led up to my questioning him, for example exaggerating the number of congregants who overheard our conversation. Other claims were evidently false from my tape recording of the encounter. Pell falsely claimed that he walked back into the synagogue after I introduced myself to him, that I walked away from the synagogue down the road, and that a young boy from the congregation ran down the road to see whether I was waiting for Pell.

According to his statement, Jones doorstepped him with a camera at his home in the afternoon. Pell said that Jones seemed to disappear, so he went to the synagogue. According to Pell, one member of the board of his synagogue said to him: 'Who are these people? You have brought this upon yourself.' This person added: 'You do realise that one of them is still here.'

Pell continued: 'I could not believe it. I looked outside and Jones was back again. He was filming the synagogue and was obviously waiting for me to leave.' He also resurrected his claim to be a journalist... we were back in Benji-land again.

And he made the following claim in his statement: 'At the beginning of 2000... I decided to break the story about the Hamilton case to the *Mail on Sunday*. It was MY story and it appeared in the newspaper because of information that I gave them. Once again, this is an example of how a myth is built up about me in the Press and, because I do not generally give interviews or react in any way, people assume that the things written about me are true. Nearly every cutting about me makes reference to the Hamilton story, yet they all get it completely wrong. I was not exposed by the *Mail on Sunday* for passing on documents. The accurate description is that I passed the story to the newspaper. I did the exposing, not their reporter.'

This, of course, is disingenuous given Pell's account to McVicar of how the *Mail on Sunday* was 'disgusting' for turning on him in revealing the story, how Hollingsworth's admissions to the newspaper were the crucial factor in enabling it to run its article, and given that he told Max Clifford that not he but Hollingsworth supplied the story to the newspaper. Pell also complained during my conversation with him about how it had 'managed to put me on the front page... when I didn't even give them a comment'.

Pell claimed: 'There is nothing in the past that justifies an allegation that I would pass on a document to a third party who is not a journalist.' Of course, he had admitted to McVicar and Jones on tape to a long history of supplying documents to surveyors and others in the property industry, providing material to help Fayed fight his libel action against Hamilton, and giving papers from the PLO to his synagogue and about Camelot to Branson. Indeed, anyone he knew who had a fax machine was bombarded with the fruits of his labours.

Pell continued: 'I was a hard working and inoffensive character going through the refuse sacks left outside the offices of professional advisors. No more than that. A grit in the oyster, doing what journalists have done over the years. An unblemished private life and someone who, until recently, was a very popular member of his local synagogue. It may not be an activity that many others would undertake. That does not make me "unwholesome", "sinister" or "sleazy".' And so it went on...

The statement of his mother, Rita Pell, struck me as supremely ironic. Referring to the *Sunday Express* articles, she said[viii]: 'Lies about Benjamin are particularly hurtful to him and to all his family as the Jewish faith places much importance on *lashon hara*, which is a Hebrew phrase, which means that it is forbidden to tell lies about people.' What, then, does she make of a son who, thinking that his Jewish faith justifies his lying, lied to his own family over failing his law degree, the re-takes of which he only passed after cheating, and who lied to his family over his bin-raiding activities. Pell lies to his associates, as he did with Hollingsworth, Clifford and Fayed's lawyers (see chapters 1 and 2); he sold to newspapers stories he knew to be false (see chapters 8 and 9); and he committed perjury by lying in court cases, even initially lying to police when he was arrested him for theft (see, for example, chapters 4 to 6, and 10)? And, as set out in this and the previous chapter, he lied in his libel action over the *Sunday Express* articles. So, the question many of us wondered was: will he go the same way as Archer and Aitken, who had lied in their libel actions and ended up in jail for committing perjury?

As Benji the Binman's libel case neared the trial, I went through the evidence we had of Pell's perjury with our QC, Geoffrey Shaw. And Shaw, who always believed we would succeed in having the case dismissed at the outset of the trial, became increasingly confident. He thought that the evidence we had of Pell's perjury would be fatal to Pell's case. However, we had a problem.

The *Sunday Express* had become extremely concerned about the embarrassment it feared would result from evidence of editing mistakes, which are at least in part attributable to the newspaper's infamous lack of resources. The newspaper, which relied overwhelmingly on part-time casual sub-editors, could not even identify who had subbed the article. In nervous attempts to settle the case, it increased its payment offer step by step, upping its offer of £25,000 to £30,000, then £60,000. My understanding is that the proprietor, Richard Desmond, insists on approving any payment at Express Newspapers over £30,000, so I believe that he sanctioned the higher offers.

The newspaper's objective to avoid a trial was also motivated by its fear that it would be saddled with a costs bill approaching £500,000 even if the jury found in our favour. I opposed the increases, but told the newspaper that since it faced the far more serious financial consequences, even if we won, I felt that it should have the final decision (after, of course, consulting with me) on the offers it made.

Pell rejected each. He was showing extreme nerve, and it is hard to say whether his reaction was brave or stupid. His solicitor indicated that he would no longer even accept £75,000, which Express Newspapers had dismissed when that figure was first floated. He wanted £125,000. This was again regarded by the Express as absurd. However, Pell had in the *Sunday Express* an opponent with astonishingly weak resolve. Three weeks before the trial was due to start, the newspaper increased its offer to a ridiculous £125,000 plus costs, without making any admission of liability. I protested, but I was told that the *Express* had already made the offer by the time I knew about it. Again, I believe Desmond decided that this offer would be made. Again, Pell rejected it. However, he had the option of taking the offer on the eve of trial, and our solicitors at Richards Butler and I believed that Pell would do this. Meanwhile, confidential sources at Pell's former synagogue said that he was saying he would win at least £200,000 damages from the *Sunday Express*, although other sources said that he was under intense pressure from his own solicitors to accept what they regarded as a high offer.

Pell repeatedly demanded to know the identities of my confidential sources for the *Sunday Express* articles. He ultimately made an application to the High Court to order me to disclose them. This was extraordinary given that Pell had in the past expected to be treated as a confidential source, and have his identity concealed, by newspapers to which he sold stories and given his attempt to avoid revealing how he obtained Elton John's documents, pretending to be a journalist protecting a confidential source. I wondered whether his barrister, Geoffrey Robertson, could show such hypocrisy as his client by advocating such an application. Robertson, as mentioned in chapter 4, had represented the journalist, Bill Goodwin, who refused to identify a confidential source, and had made an impassioned speech on his behalf before the European Court of Human Rights. Goodwin told me that it would be impossible for Robertson to advocate Pell's application. Our solicitors, commenting on barristers in general, said that they thought it 'touching' that I had such faith in the sincerity of barristers. Whether Goodwin's and my assessment was correct or not, it soon emerged that Robertson was not acting for Pell. Instead, Pell instructed a barrister called Ronald Thwaites QC, who is best known for criminal defence work such as representing the London crime underworld figure, Terry Perkins, who was convicted for his role in the £6m Security Express robbery carried out in 1983. Police sources like to tell the anecdote about how the abrasive style of Thwaites once caught him by surprise when it led a female usher at the Old Bailey to pour a glass of water over his head.

After Pell retained Thwaites, he changed his mind about the issue of exemplary damages and decided to mount a claim for them in his libel action. Pell advanced a fantastic theory that the *Sunday Express* articles were published to help Mappin in Pell's legal action against him. This was supposedly achieved by, for example, putting pressure on Pell to withdraw the Mappin case. This amounted to a false allegation against me and others at the *Sunday Express* of a criminal conspiracy to attempt to pervert the course of justice in the Mappin case, ironic given Pell's taped admissions on his participating in such conduct in relation to the Hamilton-Fayed case and his repeated perjury in this and other cases. Pell asked us whether he we would agree to his amending his claim accordingly. We refused, so he sought the court's permission.

The pre-trial hearing, on the issue of confidential sources and exemplary damages, was before Mr Justice Eady, starting just over a week before the trial was due to begin. Express Newspapers was in an especially strong position on the sources issue because it had shown such firm resolve to uphold an important journalistic (and legal) principle three years earlier when faced with an order to disclose the confidential source of a leaked Elton John document; Pell, in his taped interviews with McVicar, has identified himself, ironically enough, as that source. On the other issue in the pre-trial hearing, Shaw, on our behalf, told the court that in all the material in the case there was no evidence to support the notion that the *Sunday Express* articles were published to help Mappin in Pell's legal action against him.

Pell's solicitor had signed a witness statement stating they he believed that such evidence was contained in our witness statements[ix].

The hearing lasted three days. Mr Justice Eady roundly rejected the application to order me to identify my confidential sources. Turning in his judgement to Pell's application to amend his claim to add exemplary damages, the judge said that some explanation was required for such a late amendment[x]. 'The account that has been given is to be found in the witness statement of the claimant's solicitor, [Peter] Jennings, but it is one that Mr Shaw submits lacks credibility. Mr Jennings pinpoints the content of the defendants' witness statements… as confirming "what we had always believed, namely, that the publications were designed to assist John Mappin in his defence of a fraudulent misrepresentation claim brought by the claimant and down for trial a few weeks later." … Mr Shaw says there is nothing to support the conspiracy theory in those statements and the explanation for the delay cannot, therefore, be valid.'

Referring to my witness statement, in which I stated that I was not responsible for the headline of the first article and certain other passages, the judge said: 'That may technically be in issue, but it is hardly likely to be rejected and, certainly at the moment, there is nothing to set against that evidence.'

'The meaning relied on by Mr Pell depends to a large extent, although not exclusively, on the impression created by the headline.' However, the judge suggested, 'He [Watts] cannot be fixed with responsibility, still less quasi-criminal responsibility, for something he did not write.'

The judge dismissed Pell's application. Costs for both sides for the hearing, totalling in excess of £60,000, were, accordingly, awarded against Pell.

Shaw had long held the view that he would succeed in having the case dismissed at the outset. At the pre-trial hearing, he announced that he would be making the dismissal application at the start of the trial. While confident of winning at trial, I had not been so certain that we would win a dismissal application. However, one Sunday just over a week before trial was due to begin, I became confident that his assessment would prove right as I finished going through the evidence with Shaw at his chambers. Shaw, his junior, a Richards Butler solicitor and I headed for a nearby restaurant for a much-deserved break at lunch-time, buoyed by the evidence I had found of Pell's past perjury.

'This case is really rather fascinating,' Shaw said to me en route. 'The only trouble with these cases', he continued, as we walked past the Royal Courts of Justice on the Strand, 'is you so rarely actually get to fight them.' This sentiment was exactly what the solicitor and I already feared, having predicted that Pell would simply take the latest Part 36 offer on the eve of trial, before we could even make our planned dismissal application. In fact, the vast majority of libel actions are settled before they reach trial.

However, the concern at the *Express* about the potential for embarrassment was demonstrated on the last working day before trial. One of our witnesses was Jim 'Mad Dog' Murray, the news editor, (see chapter 15) who had made some crucial changes to the first article. An email sent by Murray to *Sunday Express* staff exactly a week before the Pell trial was due to start, was leaked to *The Guardian*, and it illustrates why he has earned his nickname. One of the Express team stated the view, with which I agreed, that Murray stood to be ripped apart in the witness box over the memo and what it reveals about his approach to journalism. Here are some extracts[xi]:

> Previously, we have deliberately chosen to be neutral in our reporting of stories, presenting both sides without taking a strong opinion.
>
> We'll still present both sides, but we now have to take a very strong attitude or angle on the story...
>
> We need to be aggressivley [sic] on the attack while not making the stories libellous...
>
> We should always be looking for someone to blame...
>
> Unlike most papers, we do not have many sex stories or scandals, but that will change. We are aiming to have six sex stories a week.

In an ideal world, we should have a 'cabinet minister affair' story... sex and scandal at the highest level of society always sells well, but these stories are notoriously difficult to get.

We should be looking out for vicars having flings, Oxford don having flings, Royals having flings, showbiz stars having flings... all the usual suspects...

A lot of our stories are what could be termed as dry... they don't make the reader laugh or cry.

The same, of course, could not be said of Murray's writing.

On the Friday before trial, I was on the telephone to Emma Lenthall of Richards Butler discussing some last-minute work that I still needed to complete, when suddenly she said: 'Oh. It's all over.' A fax had landed on her desk: Pell had accepted the £125,000 paid into court. The sense of disappointment was palpable. It was what we had feared. Well, certainly it is what I feared, although the *Sunday Express* had proved willing to go to extraordinary lengths to prevent the trial going ahead. It had limited its potential financial exposure, and it prevented the spectacle of having Murray explain under cross-examination his memo that had just been leaked. Pell had taken an enormous gamble as he played the libel lottery, and, because he was up against a weak-willed *Sunday Express*, it paid off for him – to an extent. He would have to pay £62,719 costs of both sides for his unsuccessful pre-trial application and would have to meet a further £56,617 of his own costs (with the Express picking up £182,300 of his costs), leaving Pell with just £5,664 of his damages.

References

i Benjamin Pell second witness statement, Benjamin Pell -v- Express Newspapers and Mark Watts (08.04.03).

ii McVicar audio tape (recorded 1999) MDRV.

iii McVicar audio tape (recorded 03.01.01) MDOV.

iv McVicar audio tape (recorded 1999) MDOR.

v '60 second interview: Benjamin "the Binman" Pell,' *The Metro* (30.10.02).

vi Certificate of conviction, Benjamin Gerald Pell, The Crown Court at Blackfriars (07.11.00).

vii McVicar video tape (filmed 20.12.00) DVRR.

viii Rita Pell witness statement, Benjamin Pell -v- Express Newspapers and Mark Watts (25.04.03).

ix Peter Jennings witness statement, Benjamin Pell -v- Express Newspapers and Mark Watts (20.06.03).

x Mr Justice Eady, judgement in Benjamin Pell -v- Express Newspapers and Mark Watts (01.07.03).

xi Ciar Byrne, '*Express* looks to "sex up" Sunday,' *The Guardian* (04.07.03).

Epilogue: Trash-Can Dream

Exposure of Pell's activities, his lies and his boasts were catching up with Benji the Binman. And, as he feared, it was putting him out of business. He claimed that he had retired from selling to newspapers the fruits of his bin-raiding activities. We already had evidence that this was untrue, and his claims about the timing of his 'retirement' varied. And then word reached me about one last hurrah from Pell.

An extraordinary story about Robbie Williams and gambling splashed and ran across two pages in *The News of the World*[i]. It was picked up by other newspapers, including two Express Newspapers titles, the *Sunday Daily Star* and *Daily Express*, as well as the *Daily Mail*[ii]. Two confidential sources revealed that it was another Benji the Binman story. The problem was: the story about Robbie was untrue. No doubt, Pell's mother would disapprove about the telling of such lies. The singer started suing. The *Daily Mail* and *Daily Express* soon ran similar retractions and apologies. The *Daily Mail* said[iii]: 'In an article headlined "Robbie's £2m habit" on February 10 we said Robbie Williams was addicted to gambling and had lost that sum at cards. We are happy to put the record straight and make it clear that Robbie is not addicted to gambling and has not lost substantial amounts of money. He gambles only for small stakes and his losses total no more than £2,000 over the last 18 months.

'We apologise for any distress our article caused Robbie.'

A diary story ran in the media business page of *The Observer*, which recorded[iv]:

> Interesting apology to Robbie Williams in Friday's Mail retracting a diary item which suggested – falsely – Williams was addicted to gambling. The story, supplied by a fantasist who had never met the singer, first appeared as a splash in The News of the World and m'learned friends are still thrashing out a settlement. The original piece was written by hack Lee Harpin who now spends much of his time writing obituaries, summarising the lives of celebrity Christian and stairlift promoter Dame Thora Hird, and singer turned entrepreneur turned bankrupt Adam Faith. 'Let's see if you can f***ing libel the f***ing dead, you f***ing prat,' was deputy editor Neil Wallis's witty imperative to the poor Harpin when allocating him his new role.

And who supplied to *The Observer* this insight into the troubles of Benji the Binman's client, Lee Harpin? It was, of course, Pell. This is despite the fact that, according to Pell, Harpin, like him, is Jewish.

And who was the 'fantasist' who supplied the untrue story about Robbie Williams and his gambling addiction to *The News of the World*? Again, it was Pell, who also had sold stories about Robbie in the past. *The News of the World* duly published an apology to Robbie Williams and made a 'substantial donation' – reportedly £50,000 – to a charity at the singer's request.

When I sought an interview with Pell for this book, I specifically raised with his solicitor the issue of Pell's role in the false Robbie Williams gambling story, and how it showed that he was once again selling rubbish to the Press, but there was no comment.

Since July 2003, Pell continued to fight the *Express* over legal costs. In April 2004, he failed in an attempt to suspend an assessment for the *Express* costs for successfully resisting Pell's pre-trial application. Nearly all of Pell's 'winnings' was eaten up in legal costs.

Pell's reputation so perturbed Murray, the *Sunday Express* news editor, that after the libel case ended he confessed to colleagues that he was no longer throwing away his rubbish at home for fear of visits by Benji the Binman. He was storing all his rubbish, he said, in his garage.

And Pell's solicitor, it seems, became a little over excited when talking about the case to his local newspaper. He repeated his false claim, made in court with the protection of privilege, that the articles were published to put pressure on Pell to settle the Mappin case. I pointed out to the solicitor that this was false and defamatory, that an attempt to introduce this very claim in the libel case had been rejected by the judge, and that he had better correct it. He had also issued a press release on behalf of his firm stating wrongly that the *Sunday Express* and I had accepted that our articles about Pell were false and defamatory (we had merely accepted that they were defamatory).

Pell's solicitor and his firm had to retain another solicitors' firm, Reynolds Porter Chamberlain, to deal with this prospective new libel case. The solicitor played down his claim by saying that it was merely a 'theory'. He agreed to write a letter for publication in the local newspaper making clear 'that my theory, which I had expressed to your newspaper, has not been tested in any Court.' His firm corrected the press release, which remained on its website, removing the claim that we had accepted that the two articles about Pell were false. They also paid my costs.

But what of Benji the Binman? In 2003, word circulated around Fleet Street that Pell was behind the false Robbie Williams 'gambling' story. It confirmed what journalists already widely believed: the Pell roller-coaster had come off the rails. Having developed a highly effective method of obtaining newsworthy documents, Pell, who had always been rejected by his contemporaries at school, at university and throughout his life, and who, by his own account, has always been friendless, had failed to match his parent's expectations and had failed in his attempt to become a solicitor, simply could not refrain from boasting about his 'achievements'. Partly as a result of that, he has featured in many newspaper articles, two documentaries and this book. While busily exposing stories about other people that they would rather remain hidden, Benji the Binman has himself become the story. Worse, he has saddled himself with a reputation amongst journalists for being unreliable and untrustworthy. This, in part, is because he has doctored documents he has found to make them seem more interesting, in part, because he has 'done the dirty', or threatened to 'do the dirty', on associates too many times. Journalists too, in general, are rejecting Pell. Even when Pell has worked with other people and even developed friendships with them, he has ultimately fallen out with them. Hollingsworth, Jones, McVicar: the pattern is the same. He tells Jones[v]: 'Every good friend I've ever had, I've always fallen out with. I've never kept- I've got not friends, basically.'

People say to me, 'Do you have a girlfriend?'
I say to them, 'I don't have a boyfriend; I don't have a girlfriend; I don't have any friends.'

He told another interviewer[vi]:
What can I do in my life? How can I relate to other people? Can I trust anyone? I've been betrayed so many times by friends of mine. Friends, people you've confided in, then turn against you, which may be my fault, who knows? I probably am an evil character.

Some people may be inclined to feel sorry for Pell. However, I believe that Pell, in the same way as he manipulates people by exploiting his tendency for madness, exploits the pity that others feel for him. In many ways, Pell has been on a life-long trawl for approval. He has been desperate for approval from his parents; from his associates; from the rich and famous, and their advisors; from journalists; and from the public at large. The failed would-be lawyer has even sought approval from lawyers, who became his prime target and nemesis, saying[vii]: 'I cannot see how anybody cannot realise that rather than being this loner, eccentric, I've actually been, here, a victim of these people for three or four years and I'm now deserving of praise.'

And his dream of stardom as a television celebrity presenter, which in the end relied on one of his latest friends, Lewis-Smith, was shattered when that relationship went the same way as the others. He continuously seeks to place the blame for his predicament on everyone except the person with whom it truly lies: himself. And in an attempt to mask his marked inadequacies as a human being – from others and, perhaps, from himself – he behaves highly vindictively towards others, even sometimes to those to whom he was once close. All these factors have conspired to leave Pell cornered, rather like the rat that turned up in McVicar's kitchen. McVicar used a broom handle to whack that peculiarly docile rat over the head, striking it stone dead. The Sewer Rat, meanwhile, has become the skewered rat.

References

[i] Lee Harpin, 'ROBBIE'S £2M GAMBLING ADDICTION,' *The News of the World* (09.02.03).
[ii] Carol Jenkins, 'GAMBLING IS NEW ADDICTION; ROBBIE LOSES £2M ON CARDS,' *Sunday Daily Star* (09.02.03); Ruth Hilton, 'STAR WHO BEAT DRINK AND DRUGS TURNS TO GAMBLING FOR HIS KICKS – ROBBIE'S NEW VICE,' *Daily Express* (10.02.03); Mark Reynolds, 'Robbie's £2m habit. After drink, drugs and sex, singer gets hooked on playing poker,' *Daily Mail* (10.02.03).
[iii] *Daily Mail* (04.04.03).
[iv] *The Observer* (06.04.03).
[v] "3½-hour rushes," Moving Perspective (filmed 1999).
[vi] David Thomas, 'The binman lifts his lid. For years, he made a living raiding famous people's rubbish bins for confidential documents. But Benjamin Pell, who begins a new career on television this week, is unrepentant: "There's no excuse for not shredding,"' *Sunday Telegraph* (21.04.02).
[vii] McVicar video tape (filmed 08.02.01) DVOO.

INDEX